SCIENCE FICTION
THE 100 BEST NOVELS

An English-Language Selection, 1949-1984

by

David Pringle

CARROLL & GRAF

FOR MY MOTHER
AND IN MEMORY OF MY FATHER,
MAURICE JOHNSTONE PRINGLE
(4th February 1924 - 29th October 1984)

Library of Congress Cataloging-in-Publication Data
Pringle, David.
  Science fiction.
  Includes index.
    1. Science fiction, American—Stories, plots, etc.
2. Science fiction, English—Stories, plots, etc.
3. Bibliography—Best books—Science fiction.
4. Science fiction—Bibliography.   I. Title.
PS374.S35P74   1985   823'.0876'09   85–32532
ISBN 0–88184–259–1

First published in 1985 by
Xanadu Publications Ltd., 5 Uplands Road, London N8 9NN England

First published in the United States by
Carroll & Graf Publishers, Inc.
260 Fifth Avenue
New York, NY 10001

Typeset by John Button
Myrtle Cottage, Laurieston DG7 2NL, England

Printed and bound in Great Britain by
Redwood Burn Ltd., Trowbridge, Wiltshire

Foreword

It seems to me that there are few modern commentators on science fiction better qualified to make a selection of this sort than David Pringle, and I am happy to agree with most of his choices. I can't claim to have read every book included here but I was surprised, when I came to study the list, at how many I did know! During my main period of enthusiasm I found unreadable many of the 'Golden Age classics' so praised in the fifties, and although I'm sure the inclusion of the likes of Robert Heinlein is necessary to give the book balance, I must say I remain blind to their virtues. But many of David Pringle's choices are actually readable! Not a few are very well written, and a handful come from some of our best modern writers.

There's no question that the earlier books mentioned here (and some of the later ones) were seminal to the development of sf subject-matter and, to some extent, its treatment. We find the political satire of *Nineteen Eighty-Four*, the post-disaster story of *Earth Abides*, the romantic and ironic metaphors of *The Martian Chronicles*, the paranoid conspiracy theme of *The Puppet Masters* and the unplanned-for disaster of *The Day of The Triffids* all in the first three years. In the early fifties there were certain attempts to break narrative conventions (in Bester, for instance, with his brilliantly imagined use of telepathy and teleportation), but in the main sf story-telling was extremely conventional—William Burroughs excepted. Because this is a selection of novel-length stories, examples of experimentalism only begin to appear in the late sixties; many of the fresh narrative techniques were being explored in the mid-sixties in shorter forms, however, and it is a shame that some of the best writers to bring attack and adventurous techniques to sf (e.g. Langdon Jones and Harlan Ellison) are excluded for this reason, while some who *are* included such as Robert Sheckley, M. John Harrison and J.G. Ballard are not necessarily represented by their best work. Short-story collections by Ellison and Sheckley are readily available, and I would recommend Harrison's *The Ice Monkey* and *The Machine in Shaft Ten*; Langdon Jones' *The Eye of the Lens* remains a remarkable collection of short, mainly experimental fictions, and I should also mention Barry Bayley's *The Knights of the Limits*, as well as his novel *Soul of the Robot*.

Again, very few women were writing full-length stories until relatively recently. I'm glad to see Leigh Brackett represented, disappointed not to find C.L. Moore, Katherine MacLean or Judith Merril. I am glad, however, to endorse David Pringle's choice of Joanna Russ's *The Female Man*, which I believe is an outstanding piece of fiction on every level. By the time the list gets into the seventies there are a few more women novelists appearing and of these the best, in my opinion, are those who have used sf to express their own righteous anger, producing feminist fiction in a form which best suits what they have to say. Too few people, it seems to me, have chosen the sf form as a means of harnessing and directing their impatience, sense of injustice, political frustrations and general indignation at the greed, folly, violence and unconscious (or conscious) misuse of power displayed everywhere today. Brian Aldiss once said that sf could never claim to be a mature form until as many women as men read it. I would agree, and add that the form overall (as opposed to many individual exceptions) will have come into its own when as many good women writers find it suitable for their needs.

It would be a good sign, I think, if the next list of 100 Best SF Novels (from 1985) contained a predominance of books by women, and by black people—only two black writers (Delaney and Butler) are included here—as the present list contains (for understandable reasons) a majority by white middle-class men. The potential is there. I continue to believe that it has a good chance of being realized.

How can you know if this selection is actually the best hundred sf novels published since 1949? I'm sure any individual would quarrel with some of the choices. I'm also pretty certain that most readers would agree on at least fifty of the books mentioned here. And that, I think, is an excellent percentage.

MICHAEL MOORCOCK

Contents

Author's
Introduction

What is science fiction?

For many people nowadays, science fiction—'sci-fi' as the media folk miscall it—means movies. It means *Star Wars*, *E.T.* and *2010*. For others it signifies television shows such as *Doctor Who* and *Star Trek*, or radio series like *The Hitch-hiker's Guide to the Galaxy*. For some, it may denote the comics, from 'Superman' to 'Judge Dredd'. Yet again, it may mean computer games such as 'Space Invaders' or 'Trader'. Clearly, science fiction has many faces. It could even be defined as a type of advertising, used to sell instant mashed potato or the services of British Airways.

However, the present work is not a study of such pop-cult phenomena. It is strictly about the written word, about science fiction in book form. Let us call the subject matter of this volume 'sf'. All the rest is sci-fi. Written sf is at least as old as the *voyages extraordinaires* of Jules Verne, which began to be published in English translation in the 1870s. It is older than the 'scientific romances' of H.G. Wells and his imitators, which appeared in abundance after 1895. For several decades it was kept alive principally by popular magazines—magazines which were founded in the 1920s, 30s and 40s, and bore titles such as *Amazing*, *Astounding* and *New Worlds*. These periodicals encouraged the writing of sf short stories and novelettes—and, in due course, they gave birth to the modern sf novel.

Yes, but what *is* science fiction?

There is no short answer to this vexed question. In the present context, the best reply is simply to point at the pile of one hundred novels which are listed in this book, and to say 'there—those are science fiction!'—but I cannot duck the issue quite so easily. After all, I chose those hundred titles, and I must have done so according to *some* definitional criteria, however murky and instinctive. Here, for better or worse, is my own working definition of sf. It is neither elegant nor watertight, and I do not make great claims for it. *Science fiction is a form of fantastic fiction which exploits the imaginative perspectives of modern science.*

As with any definition, one has to explain the constituent parts. By 'modern science' I mean the scientific world-view of the 19th and 20th centuries, especially that world-view as it has come to be accepted by the intelligent layperson ('SF is no more written for scientists than ghost stories are written for ghosts' as Brian Aldiss once put it). It can be argued that the scientific world-view first became common property in the mid to late 19th century. By that time, the Newtonian understanding of the physical universe had filtered down to the lowest intellectual levels. Perhaps even more important, Lyell's geology and Darwin's evolutionary biology had begun to make a strong impression. These scientific advances opened up new imaginative perspectives for the common man and woman—perspectives of space (distant stars and galaxies), perspectives of time past (dinosaurs and 'cave men'), and perspectives of time future (the end of the human race and of the earth). Above all, they established the idea of *change*, the realization that we have evolved from ape-like ancestors and that we may continue to evolve in the future. The impact of 19th century socialist theories, including Marxism, was also very important. They showed that society too was subject to drastic change. Utopia ceased to be a vague location on a fanciful map, and became a future possibility. People became aware of how much their society *had* changed as a result of technological innovation (the steam train, the electric telegraph, and so on), and they began to realize how much more it was going to change in the foreseeable future. It was against this background that Verne began to write his *voyages extra-ordinaire* and Wells began to produce his scientific romances. Science fiction had become a necessity.

For a long time sf had no sharply-defined identity. In Britain, occasional novelists wrote stories in the Wellsian tradition. Aldous Huxley is perhaps the best known, although Olaf Stapledon, author of *Last and First Men* (1930) and *Star Maker* (1937), has a claim to being the greatest. Stapledon did not call his books 'science fiction'—the term is supposed to have been invented in America in 1929—but he was certainly aware that his self-

9

imposed task was to illuminate, in fictional form, the perspectives of modern science. 'To romance of the far future,' he wrote in the Preface to his first novel:

> . . . is to attempt to see the human race in its cosmic setting, and to mould our hearts to entertain new values.
>
> But if such imaginative construction of possible futures is to be at all potent, our imagination must be strictly disciplined. We must endeavour not to go beyond the bounds of possibility set by the particular state of culture within which we live. The merely fantastic has only minor power. Not that we should seek actually to prophesy . . . We can only select a certain thread out of the tangle of many equally valid possibilities. But we must select with a purpose. The activity that we are undertaking is not science, but art . . .
>
> Yet our aim is not merely to create aesthetically admirable fiction. We must achieve neither mere history, nor mere fiction, but myth. A true myth is one which, within the universe of a certain culture (living or dead), expresses richly, and often perhaps tragically, the highest admirations possible within that culture.

Stapledon's own essays in myth creation have their failings, yet they are tremendously impressive. Their primary purpose was to help the reader attain a new sense of humanity's place within the grand sweeps of space and time. Stapledon chose the largest subject possible, the Meaning of the Universe, and he tackled it courageously.

Since the deaths of H.G. Wells in 1946 and Olaf Stapledon in 1950, the imaginative endeavour which they helped begin has become ever more urgently relevant. Scientific knowledge has doubled, trebled, quadrupled—and more. At the same time the technological fruits of science have become increasingly available to us (and to our political masters). From plastics and antibiotics to microprocessors and gene-splicing, from jet aircraft and atom bombs to the space shuttle and laser weapons in orbit, from television and transistor radios to interactive videodiscs and computer networks, the *new things* which have entered our lives are baffling in their profusion and often frightening in their implications. There is no need to rehearse them all here. If science fiction was in some sense a necessity to the Europeans of the late 19th century, then it is ten times as necessary now, in the late 20th century, and it is of growing importance not only to Europe and North America but to the entire world. Science fiction has become very popular in Japan, the Soviet Union, Latin America,

China—and its spread is continuing apace, part of the immense cultural fallout of the West.

At its best, sf provides our urbanized, technologized society with its most valid *myths* (to use that word as Stapledon used it in 1930)—literary myths which do not necessarily compel faith but which help us to understand the devastating changes that sweep our world. This is the most incredible, overwhelming period of development and disruption through which the human race has ever passed; and sf, whatever its shortcomings, is the characteristic literature of the age. It is a body of stories which we tell ourselves in order to overcome our fear and puzzlement. At root, sf is an attempt to comprehend all that is happening to us.

So sf is a form of fantastic fiction which exploits the imaginative perspectives of modern science. While bearing in mind that it is difficult to draw sharp boundaries between literary *genres*, I would argue that there are two other forms of contemporary fantastic fiction. These are the Supernatural Horror Story and the Heroic Fantasy. By the supernatural horror story I mean such works as Bram Stoker's *Dracula*, the stories of H.P. Lovecraft and his imitators, and most of the books of Stephen King. Characteristicaly, these describe the irruption of some supernatural force into the everyday world, and they are horrific precisely because the forces and phenomena described are irrational—which is to say they are inexplicable in terms of the modern scientific world-view. By heroic fantasy I mean such works as J.R.R. Tolkein's *The Lord of the Rings*, the whole sword and sorcery *sub-genre*, and all those books which carry titles like *The Elfstones of Shannara*. Usually, these are set in completely imaginary worlds, never-never lands where the modern scientific world-view is suspended and 'magic' rules. The emotional tenor of these works is not so much horrific as pleasurably escapist.

Science fiction, as distinct from the other types of fantastic fiction, always attempts to locate itself in the real universe, and to present the reader with fantastic developments which are explicable in terms of the scientific world-view. Of course, many sf writers cheat: they use sleight-of-hand rather than genuine scientific knowledge, but that does not matter as long as the reader is more or less convinced that the marvellous things described could conceivably come within the bounds of scientific rationality. Thus such dubious propositions as the likelihood of

11

time travel, telepathy, faster-than-light space flight, and alternative universes have long been accepted in legitimate sf. If the authors, through the skilful use of pseudo-science and gobbledygook, can make things sound plausible in terms of their scientific world-view, then they have achieved their aim. Even so, some readers make a distinction between 'hard' sf, the sort of thing which is written by physics graduates, and 'soft' sf, in which the writer tends to be more concerned with the *feel* of a technological world than with its workings.

Categorization can be invidious, and many writers are drawn to sf because it seems to offer them more freedom than any other 'category'. There are many eccentric individualists among those who are commonly labelled sf writers, and to construct a definition which neatly covers all of their works is utterly impossible. My definition is offered as a working tool, no more. It describes a subject matter and an approach which is common to most of the books covered in this volume. I say 'most' rather than 'all' because rules are made to be broken, and some of the best writers will delight in confounding our expectations.

This book contains brief essays on one hundred English-language sf novels which were first published between 1949 and 1984. Some appeared as magazine serials before they achieved book form (in all cases, the dates I have given are those of first book publication); others were published initially in hard covers. In my opinion, these hundred titles are 'the best' that contemporary science fiction has to offer. Admittedly the reasons for selection are personal, but I have endeavoured to make my choice as balanced as possible, without pretending that it is anything other than an individual's choice. There are in existence various awards and prizes for The Best Science Fiction Novel of the Year (the Hugo Award, the Nebula, the British SF Award, the John W. Campbell Memorial prize, and so on), but for my present purposes I decided to ignore them entirely. Many of the hundred novels listed herein did win awards; on the other hand, many did not. You will find no further mention of the awards in this book, and if you are eager to know which novels were winners I recommend that you consult Peter Nicholls' excellent *Encyclopedia of Science Fiction*, and similar reference works.

As I say, this is a personal choice, although I would not be so foolish as to claim that I have been wholly uninfluenced by the critical consensus on modern sf. Yes, there is such a consensus, and I have indeed been influenced by it. I could hardly have escaped the influence, since I have been editor of *Foundation: The Review of Science Fiction* for the past five and a half years. That journal, which is published three times a year by North East London Polytechnic, was founded in 1972, and has become one of the two or three leading periodicals in its field (the Canadian sf *Studies*, begun in 1973, is another). Inevitably the past editors and the regular critics who write for *Foundation* have affected my judgement of contemporary sf. I salute them, and in particular I should like to name John Clute, Malcolm Edwards, Peter Nicholls, Brian Stableford and Ian Watson, but I must stress that the choice of novels presented here is my own, not theirs.

Why have I chosen 1949 as my starting point? There are several reasons. I could have begun my listing in the 1890s or even earlier, with the scientific romances of Wells and his contemporaries, but that early ground has already been covered in several histories of sf and in numerous reference books. Surely no-one needs to be told again that *The Time Machine*, *The War of the Worlds* and *The First Men in the Moon* are among the enduring masterpieces of science fiction. I wanted the present volume to be usefully up-to-date, so I decided to concentrate on the sf of the post-World War II period.

As it happens, relatively few sf novels were published in the immediate post-war years; the flood did not commence until 1949-1950. I wanted to begin with a strong title, a novel which is generally recognized as major: George Orwell's book suggested itself as the obvious choice. So I settled on 1949 because it was the year of *Nineteen Eighty-Four* (it was also the year of that other fine work, George R. Stewart's *Earth Abides*). Moreover, it was in 1948-49 that major publishers began to issue science fiction novels which were labelled as such.

The term 'sf' did not appear on the covers of novels published before and during World War II. A.E. van Vogt's *The World of Null-A*, issued by Simon and Schuster in 1948, is credited with being the first sf category novel to appear from a mainstream American publisher. In the following year Doubleday began their celebrated sf line, with Max Ehrlich's *The Big Eye* as their premier title, soon to be followed by works from Asimov, Heinlein, Bradbury, and other sf writers who had built a reputation in the magazines. In Britain, it took a little longer for the public to become aware of sf as a book-publishing category; nevertheless, 'science fiction' seems to have become a widely-used term in the early 1950s. The success of John Wyndham's *The Day of The Triffids* encouraged the London publisher Michael Joseph to experiment with an sf line, and others such as Hart-Davis, Sidgwick and Jackson, Weidenfeld and Nicolson, Dobson, and Heinemann also dabbled. Surprisingly, it was as late as 1960 before Victor Gollancz began a regular sf list.

The present selection concentrates on science fiction novels published *as books*; hence it is highly appropriate that I should begin my survey in 1949, which is, roughly speaking, when sf book publishing began. It also happens that I was born around that time (in March 1950, to be exact) and so this volume covers the years of my life. I have grown up with sf, as has the majority of my readers. (For what it is worth, 1950 was also the year of the first Hollywood sci-fi movie, *Destination Moon*.) It is hard for us to imagine what it was like for readers of sf in the pre-1949 period, when a belief in the likelihood of rocket flights to the moon was almost enough to have one certified, and when sf books were so scarce that one could read an entire year's output in next to no time and be left hungering for more.

Of course, there were the sf-specialty magazines, those pulp repositories of dreams. The sf periodicals did not die in 1949; far from it. That year saw the founding of *The Magazine of Fantasy and Science Fiction*, a title which is still going strong in the 1980s. In 1950 there came *Galaxy*, a monthly which had a great initial impact, and which endured for more than two decades. In Britain the chief sf magazine, *New Worlds*, did not really hit its stride until the middle 1950s, though it had been founded in 1946. Science fiction magazines remain important to this day, for they are manufactories of new talent. Countless hardcover and paperback anthologies have been culled from the pages of the magazines, and many of the sf novels mentioned herein would not have been written were it not for those publications. In 1982 I became co-publisher and co-editor of a new British quarterly, *Interzone*, which is dedicated to sf short stories and has now published over a dozen issues. I have credited the magazines wherever possible throughout this book.

Nevertheless, I am writing here about novels, not magazines, and not short stories. I have given full entries to two or three books which are collections of short stories rather than novels proper—an example is Ray Bradbury's *The Martian Chronicles* —but in each case it can be claimed that the collection forms a unified work, a novel as near as dammit. Collections of unrelated short stories are mentioned only in passing, and only in those cases where I feel that a particular author has achieved some of his or her most notable work in shorter forms.

I have a great fondness for science fiction, and I have a continuing faith in the form's literary value and potential. But it is time to make a confession. In writing this book, a task which has necessitated a good deal of intensive reading and re-reading over a nine-month period, I have discovered that there are fewer than a hundred masterworks in modern English-language sf. No more than ten or a dozen of these novels can be described as literary masterpieces. If one is in a generous mood, perhaps another dozen or so can be called masterpieces *of their sort*, but that still leaves over seventy which are decidedly less than masterpieces. Some of them are old favourites of my own, books which gave me great pleasure at fourteen or eighteen or twenty-two. Some are other people's favourites, novels which have been outstandingly popular or influential, or which seem to be especially good representatives of their type. A small minority, perhaps as many as ten, are books for which I have little or no personal enthusiasm: they have been included for the sake of balance and variety.

I am aware that the title of the book is a misnomer. There cannot be a hundred 'best' of anything, but to call it *A Hundred Better SF Novels* or *A Hundred Good-to-Brilliant SF Novels* would be silly, an all-too-public hedging of bets. Like Anthony Burgess in his *Ninety-Nine Novels: The Best in English Since 1939*, I find myself working to an arbitrary number and a faintly untruthful title. Perhaps I should borrow the statement with which he ended his introduction: 'If you disagree violently with some of my choices I shall be pleased. We arrive at values only through dialectic.'

Talk of literary values may strike some readers as odd. Surely, they will say, sf is a form of paraliterature, or pop lit. It is inherently vulgar, at best crudely vigorous and naïvely inventive—and open to fruitful sociological analysis. What bearing do the values of literary criticism have here? On the other hand, some of the more aggressive sf fans make the claim that science fiction is its own universe of discourse, a unique form which is not susceptible to evaluation by traditional literary standards. It requires wholly new means of evaluation, means which may turn black into white and make the frivolous seem profound. While I must admit to occasional sneaking sympathies with these points of view, I am obliged to reject them in the end.

In the long term, each of the novels described here will stand or fall on its own merits: the *genre* props will decay, the tides of fashion ebb away. Then we shall be forced to judge these books on their individual qualities. Structure and style, characterization and wit will become the salient points, points which we look for in any novel. Above all, we shall judge each author's vision, and when we do so we shall be looking for a quality of truthfulness. Great novels 'tell it like it is': they are true to reality, to human nature, to the spirit of their age. Science fiction novels cannot escape these demands. However fanciful the plots and ideas, however ornate the décor, they must, in the end, have authenticity if they are to live.

Darko Suvin, sf's most formidable critic, defines science fiction as 'the literature of cognitive estrangement'. I have no love for his terminology, but his definition does point to two necessities. The 'estrangement' is what makes sf different from most other fiction, it is what strikes us immediately as colourful and intriguing: the changed worlds, the far planets, the bizarre alien beings (or bizarre *human* beings). But we must not forget the cognitive element: the knowledge, the perception, the vision, which makes the gaudily or wondrously estranged relevant to the here and now. Without that relevance, that authenticity, sf is mere diversion, good for a few hours' entertainment and then fit only to be thrown away and forgotten.

I believe that a fair number of the novels listed here will not be forgotten in the coming decades, for they have truthfulness.

Having made this large claim, I should say a few words about omissions from my list. Obviously, I have omitted all works of modern fantastic fiction, which I do not regard as sf. I have ignored novels which may be placed in the aforementioned classes of supernatural horror and heroic fantasy. I have also left out fabulations, unless they have a significant scientific or technological content. The term 'fabulation' may be taken as descriptive of such hard-to-define books as Brian Aldiss's *The Malacia Tapestry* (1976) and John Crowley's *Little, Big* (1981).

These titles are missing from my list not because I regard them as less than fine works (they are very fine indeed), but because I do not see them as science fiction.

At this point, undoubtedly, there will be objections to my procedure, just as there may be a measure of disagreement with my earlier off-the-cuff definition of sf. We have often been warned against definitions—for instance, by the critic Mark Rose, who writes in his book, *Alien Encounters*: 'A literary *genre* is not a pigeonhole but a context for writing and reading . . . Instead of thinking of science fiction as a thing, a kind of object to be described, it is perhaps more useful to think of it as a tradition, a developing complex of themes, attitudes and formal strategies that, taken together, constitute a general set of expectations.' In terms of an ever-changing context of generic expectations, perhaps there is a sense in which novels such as the Aldiss and the Crowley *are* sf. For the purposes of this book, however, I am obliged to stick to a less permissive use of the term. I know that science fiction is not a 'thing', but I must assert that sf is these hundred books, and these hundred books are sf.

Nevertheless, there are many indubitable works of science fiction that do not appear in my list, and there may be several recognized sf writers who will feel slighted because they are not represented at all while others are included three or four times over. By now we are no longer talking about definitions: we are down to the irreducible matter of taste. My taste in sf may be a poor thing, but it is my own. I admit to blind spots—for example, I have little affection for the type of sf story which has been called 'planetary romance' (the Prisoner of Zenda meets Ayesha on Barsoom) whose leading practitioners nowadays include Marion Zimmer Bradley and Anne McCaffrey, two authors who are entirely missing from my list. I also admit to ignorance, for after all I have not read everything. English-language sf has become a very large field in the last thirty-five years, from *Nineteen Eighty-Four* to 1984, and I did not have room to mention everybody who can claim a share of the patch.

There are certain writers, from Barrington J. Bayley and Richard Cowper to James Tiptree and Jack Vance, whom I particularly regret omitting, and of course there are new (and relatively new) people who keep coming to one's attention. If I had been permitted a hundred-and-first entry I might well have included a 1985 novel by Bruce Sterling called *Schismatrix*, an exciting, imaginative work, of a type that strongly appeals to me.

Enough. Let the list stand, for all its imperfections and partiality. The purpose is not to arrive at an irreproachable final judgement, but to provoke people into reading more good science fiction. Perhaps the list will also help to correct a few of the false generalizations about sf which seem to be common—for instance, the generalization that sf consists almost entirely of stories about space travel. In fact, fewer than half of the hundred novels described here touch on the subject of space travel, and many of those that do—for example, Walter Miller's *A Canticle for Leibowitz*—deal with it only glancingly. Another false assertion about sf is that it is inherently childish, an escapist fantasy fiction for kids, and I can only make the counter-claim that the best science fiction addresses itself to adult concerns. These hundred novels (with a few obvious exceptions such as Heinlein's *Have Space-Suit—Will Travel*, written specifically for early-teenage readers, and possibly Clarke's *The City and the Stars* glowing with a somewhat naive and child-like sense of wonder) are intended for adult minds.

But then one runs straight into another, contradictory, generalization: that sf consists for the most part of doom-laden horror stories about disaster and dissolution. Modern sf has imagined good places and bad, utopias and dystopias, just as it has pictured wonderful expansive futures and bitter, terminal cataclysms. You should not damn the whole by describing a part. Horror fiction has its own virtues, but the point is that sf is much *larger* than horror: it encompasses many modes. It can be horrific, yes, but it can also be romantic, ironic, elegaic, comic, cerebral. It can partake of the pastoral, or of the Menippean satire. It can be a multitude of things, a protean form indeed.

I believe that the flexibility of the form is brilliantly demonstrated in the hundred titles I have selected for discussion. Many of them are superbly entertaining books; a number are deeply moving, and a few will disturb you profoundly. Some of the finest English-language fiction of the past thirty-five years is touched on here. This book invites you to enjoy it.

DAVID PRINGLE
Brighton, 1985

Brief Bibliography

The best one-volume reference work on sf is *The Encyclopedia of Science Fiction*, edited by Peter Nicholls with associate editor John Clute (London, Granada, and New York, Doubleday, 1979). A second edition is now overdue. Runner-up to the Nicholls book is *Anatomy of Wonder: A Critical Guide to Science Fiction*, edited by Neil Barron (New York and London, R.R. Bowker, second edition 1981). The best history of the *genre* remains *Billion Year Spree* by Brian Aldiss (London, Weidenfeld and Nicholson, and New York, Doubleday, 1973). I am told that a new edition of this is in preparation.

Scholarly works on sf are now surprisingly numerous, and worthy recent examples include *Metamorphoses of Science Fiction* by Darko Suvin (New Haven, Conn., Yale University Press, 1979); *Science Fiction: Its Criticism and Teaching* by Patrick Parrinder (London, Methuen, 1980); *Alien Encounters: Anatomy of Science Fiction* by Mark Rose (Cambridge, Mass., Harvard University Press, 1981); and *The Entropy Exhibition: Michael Moorcock and the 'New Wave' in British Science Fiction* by Colin Greenland (London, Routledge and Kegan Paul, 1983).

Studies of individual authors abound, and I should like to mention in particular the (American) Oxford University Press series 'Science Fiction Writers' under the general editorship of Robert Scholes. This includes such volumes as *Robert A. Heinlein: America as Science Fiction* by H. Bruce Franklin (1980) and *Olaf Stapledon: A Man Divided* by Leslie A. Fiedler (1983).

Similarly, there are many bibliographies of individual writers, and I single out for mention the 'Masters of Science Fiction and Fantasy' series edited by L.W. Currey and published by G.K. Hall and Co. of Boston, Mass. This series includes my own *J.G. Ballard: A Primary and Secondary Bibliography* (1984).

The best books of interviews with sf writers are *Dream Makers: The Uncommon People Who Write Science Fiction* by Charles Platt (New York, Berkley, 1980), and its sequel, *Dream Makers II* (Berkley, 1983).

Foundation: The Review of Science Fiction is published three times a year by the SF Foundation, N.E. London Polytechnic, Longbridge Road, Dagenham RM8 2AS, United Kingdom. *SF Studies*, also thrice-yearly, comes from Robert M. Philmus, English Dept., Concordia University, 7141 Sherbrooke Street W., Montreal, Quebec H4B 1R6, Canada.

1
GEORGE ORWELL
Nineteen Eighty-Four

My first choice is one of the best-known novels of our time, so I shall not attempt to describe it in very much detail here. This harrowing story about the tribulations of a minor official in a future totalitarian state has provided us with much of the political argot of the age—words and phrases such as 'Thought Police', 'Newspeak', 'Ministry of Truth', 'doublethink', and 'Big Brother is watching you' were all invented by George Orwell for this book. It is quite simply a novel which has changed the world. It is written in a good plain style which has made it accessible to millions of readers, and by affecting the minds of those millions Orwell ensured that his dark predictions did not come true. Of course, it has been pointed out many times that he was not really concerned with prediction at all—he was writing, in an exaggerated form, about how things actually *were* in the 1940s.

The book did not have 'Science Fiction' printed on its cover. By what right, then, do we claim it as sf? The story is set thirty-six years into the future from the time of writing; more importantly, it depicts certain technological devices which are used to control the population of Airstrip One in the state of Oceania—chief among these is the *telescreen*, a wall-mounted television set which watches you even as you watch it. That is a pure sf image, and perhaps a predictive one (with fibre-optic cables such as we have in the 1980s a device like that could become a reality). But the novel's links with sf are deeper and more fundamental than these details would suggest.

Like so many of his generation, Orwell (whose real name was Eric Blair, 1903-1950) was profoundly influenced by Wells. In his essay 'Wells, Hitler, and the World State', Orwell wrote: 'It was a wonderful thing to discover H.G. Wells. There you were, in a world of pedants, clergymen and golfers . . . and here was this wonderful man who could tell you about the inhabitants of the planets and the bottom of the sea, and who *knew* that the future was not going to be what respectable people imagined.' Although he went on to criticize some of Wells' political ideas, it is clear that Orwell regarded the earlier writer's work as a great liberating force. Many other imaginations were stimulated in a similar way—to such an extent that a whole tradition of 'post-Wellsian' fiction came into being in Britain and further afield. Now-forgotten authors such as J.D. Beresford, S. Fowler Wright and John Gloag contributed novels and stories to that tradition, as did more enduring writers like Olaf Stapledon, Aldous Huxley and C.S. Lewis. None of their books was published as science fiction, for the term did not come into general use on this side of the Atlantic until the early 1950s. If a generic label had to be pinned on these exercises in 'the Wellsian kind of thing', then they were usually known as scientific romances.

E.M. Forster's novella 'The Machine Stops' (1909) was a scientific romance which set out to rebut the notion that one could perfect the human race through the application of modern technology. Huxley's *Brave New World* (1932) was another such cautionary tale. Both are examples of the anti-utopia, or 'dystopia'. Orwell's *Nineteen Eighty-Four* is a successor work, the bleakest dystopia of them all. It was the example of Wells, both in terms of the forms he invented and the subject matter he used, and moreover it was the debate that Wells began and which continued throughout the work of at least a dozen other writers, that made Orwell's masterpiece possible. I see *Nineteen Eighty-Four* as a Janus of a book, facing two ways: it is both a culmination of the British scientific romance, and a source book for much of the science fiction which has followed. It sums up the terrible experiences of the 20th century's first half, and it casts a long shadow of foreboding over its second half, our half.

First edition: London, Secker, 1949 (hardcover)
First American edition: New York, Harcourt Brace Jovanovich, 1949 (hardcover)
Most recent editions: London, Penguin and New York, NAL (paperbacks)

2
GEORGE R. STEWART
Earth Abides

Like Orwell's *Nineteen Eighty-Four*, this book was not published under the 'science fiction' label—yet it has come to be accepted as one of the great American sf novels. There is no doubt that it *is* sf: the science which so effectively underpins the narrative is ecology (far from being a buzz-word in 1949). George Rippey Stewart (1895-1980) taught English at the University of California and wrote over thirty books, ranging from historical novels to scholarly studies of place-names. He had an abiding interest in the history and landscape of America, and a deep understanding of the ways in which the environment has shaped human activity. His novels *Storm* (1941) and *Fire* (1948) are about the efforts of Americans to cope with natural catastrophes. In his finest work, *Earth Abides*, he describes in meticulous detail the aftermath of a more unusual disaster —a mysterious plague which kills the vast majority of the human race.

Isherwood Williams, a graduate student of geography, returns from a sojourn in the mountains to discover that everybody is dead. At the beginning of the novel he is like a Robinson Crusoe who has an entire continent to sustain him. He ranges through empty towns and cities, watching the devolution of the landscape with a disinterested scientist's eye. He befriends a dog; he observes plagues of insects and rodents; he watches the fields go to seed and the highways crack up. All this is described with a superb naturalism which draws on a rich fund of knowledge. At length Ish returns to San Francisco, where he meets a female survivor who becomes his wife. They have children and a small community forms around them. Years go by as they live the life of their pioneer ancestors, an existence made slightly more comfortable by their foraging in the detritus of civilization.

Ish tries to teach his children to read books and to understand all the achievements of humanity's past, but young Joey, the brightest of his kids, dies. The others go their own way, learning the physical skills necessary to cope with their environment but

23

showing no interest in the past. As the decades pass the few survivors of the pre-plague era die off, until only Ish is left as a witness to the greatness that has been. His grandchildren and great-grandchildren regard him almost as a tribal deity, an incomprehensible old man who babbles of impossible things. They have become a band of hunter-gatherers, in harmony with their surroundings, roaming the West Coast like the Amerindians of old. History has gone full circle, and Ish realizes in his dying moments that 'men go and come, but earth abides'.

The novel is written with great conviction and emotional intensity. It moved me to tears when I first read it. The poet Carl Sandburg wrote in the 1950s: 'If I should be naming five novels out of the last ten years most worthwhile, most worth reading, I would certainly include a book titled *Earth Abides*. It reads as a good story and has profound meanings. I thank Brother Stewart for writing it.' Just so. In this beautiful meditation on ecology, old age, and the implacability of change, George R. Stewart wrought, albeit unknowingly, one of the masterworks of science fiction.

First edition: New York, Random House, 1949 (hardcover)
First British edition: London, Gollancz, 1950 (hardcover)
Most recent edition: London, Corgi Books (paperback)

3

RAY BRADBURY
The Martian Chronicles

Ray Bradbury (born 1920) has long been acclaimed as one of America's finest short-story writers. This was the book which established his reputation. It is a collection of closely-linked stories about the exploration and colonization of the planet Mars. Given that theme, and the fact that most of the stories had appeared in the (lesser) sf magazines of the late 1940s, it is natural to assume that the book is unequivocally science fiction. In fact, that definition has often been disputed, since Bradbury shows no interest in science as such. His space rockets are like firecrackers; his Mars people are Halloween ghosts; while his Martian land-scape is an arid version of the American mid-west. Moreover, Bradbury was known as a frequent contributor to *Weird Tales* (a magazine of the fantastic and horrific) and he has since published books such as *Dandelion Wine* (1957) and *Something Wicked This Way Comes* (1962), which are fantasies of childhood magic far removed from the concerns of sf. None of Bradbury's Martian stories appeared in *Astounding S-F*, the leading magazine of 'hard'—which is to say rationalistic—science fiction. That magazine's purist editor, John W. Campbell, would have rejected Bradbury's stories out of hand. The stories may have had 'religion', but they had no physics; they were almost blasphemous in their disregard for the facts of time and space.

Or so it once seemed. Modern science fiction has become much more diverse since 1950, and Bradbury's radicalism now looks rather tame. I would certainly contend that *The Martian Chronicles* falls within the definition of sf, since it uses all the trappings of interplanetary fiction, as well as such familiar motifs as telepathy, invisibility, and the threatening nuclear armageddon. The innovative thing about Bradbury's work was that he used all these elements to achieve personal, private ends, ignoring the consensus views on how a good sf story *should* be written. He put far more emphasis on style and mood than he did on technical detail or scientific plausibility, thus offending the already hardening sensibilities of editors and writers who had grown up with the American sf magazines during the 1930s and 40s. His reward was a stunning popular and critical success: he was taken up by the literary world at large and invited to write for the highest-paying general magazines, as well as for Hollywood. In all the subsequent clamour, his effect on the sf *genre* has been overlooked: despite opposition from certain quarters, his work became an example to many younger writers, and even if they didn't emulate him they felt that he had helped free them to be themselves.

So *The Martian Chronicles* is an historically important work. It now seems dated, its poetry at times rather precious, its wistfulness more than a little sentimental, but the best passages still have a magical quality. My favourite of the *Chronicles* is the one entitled '—And The Moon Be Still As Bright', in which a band of roughnecks from Earth begins to despoil the empty cities of Mars. One of these men is moved to rebel, and takes to the hills as a lone defender of the dead Martian culture. He is eventually hunted down and shot, but not before his actions have made most of the others aware of their own wrongdoing. The twilit atmosphere of this story pervades much of the rest of the book. I also like the chapter called 'The Off Season', with its evocation of the Martian sand ships: 'The wind hurled the sand ship keening over the dead sea bottom, over long-buried crystals, past upended pillars, past deserted docks of marble and brass, past dead white chess cities, past purple foothills, into distance . . .'.

First edition: Garden City, Doubleday, 1950 (hardcover)
First British edition: London, Hart-Davis, 1951 (hardcover; retitled *The Silver Locusts*)
Most recent editions: New York, Bantam Books, and London, Granada (paperbacks)
(Recent British editions have restored the American title)

4
ROBERT A. HEINLEIN
The Puppet Masters

Throughout the 1940s the most influential science fiction magazine was John W. Campbell's *Astounding S-F*, and that magazine's chief contributor and leading light was Robert Anson
Heinlein (born 1907). He was a tough-minded ex-Navy man
with engineering training, who on occasion liked to compare
himself with Stevenson, Kipling and Wells, in that he was 'really'
a man of action and affairs, forced to take up the slightly effete
profession of writing because of ill-health. He did not begin to
write until he was 32, by which time he had variegated experience
in business and politics as well as in military service. This stood
him in good stead when he started to produce hard-edged, realistic near-future stories for sf magazines. Many of his stories
were about the politics, law and industrial relations of the coming space age, and they formed a continuous so-called 'Future
History'. These works of the 1940s are collected in such books as
The Man Who Sold The Moon (1950), *The Green Hills of Earth*
(1951) and *Revolt in 2100* (1953). At the same time Heinlein
wrote a number of more fanciful stories, including the excellent
tale of time travel 'By His Bootstraps', but these were published
initially under pseudonyms. After World War II he began a long
series of sf novels for teenagers, notable for their verve,
conviction and technical accuracy. His first new post-war novel
for adults was *The Puppet Masters*.

But this one did not receive serial publication in *Astounding*.
In 1950 a new monthly magazine called *Galaxy Science Fiction*
appeared, which promptly became the leading periodical in the
field, and one of the first serials it ran was Heinlein's *The Puppet
Masters*. A surprising number of the 1950s novels I have chosen
for this volume first appeared in *Galaxy*, and its importance as
a stimulus to American sf should not be underestimated.
The first-person narrative of *The Puppet Masters* opens in the
year 2007. The hero is a secret agent who works for a CIA-type
organization. Together with his boss—known throughout as the

'Old Man'—and a beautiful female colleague he refers to as 'Sis', he investigates the reported landing of a flying saucer in Iowa. At first assumed to be a hoax, it turns out to be terrifyingly genuine—and the first of many. The alien vessels carry intelligent slug-like organisms which attach themselves to the backs of human beings, tapping into their hosts' nervous systems and taking control of their minds and actions. The human puppets and their hideous masters intend to take over the whole world: they must be fought without mercy.

The story moves along vigorously, full of violence, paranoia and a subliminal nastiness. When one bears in mind that it was written in the USA of the early 1950s, it is easy to see the puppet masters as stand-ins for the Communist Menace. Whether or not one agrees with Heinlein's implied political views, one has to admit that the novel delineates a certain state of mind with great energy and skill. Much of the 'charm' of the book lies in the method of narration, a mixture of wisecracks and laconic senti-mentality which leaves no doubt that Heinlein had learned a thing or two from Hammett, Chandler and the 'hard-boiled' school of crime fiction writers. There is also a curious sub-plot which revolves around an intensely emotional Family Romance (I use this phrase with Freud in mind). It turns out that the 'Old Man' is indeed the hero's father; there is even a hint that the heroine might genuinely be his sister. At a couple of high points in the narrative the hero breaks down in tears. He is a strong man who is only too ready to weep and be comforted by his 'Sis'. It is all rather strange. Perhaps Heinlein can best be described as an unconscious artist: without quite realizing what he is doing, he reveals, very honestly, that all our manly aggressions are rooted in extremely boggy emotional ground, well watered by the tears of longing and frustration.

First edition: Garden City, Doubleday, 1951 (hardcover)
First British edition: London, Museum Press, 1953 (hardcover)
Most recent editions: New York, NAL, and London, Pan (paperbacks)

5

JOHN WYNDHAM
The Day of The Triffids

I well remember the thrill that Wyndham's book gave me when I first read it at the age of thirteen. The hero awakes in hospital, his eyes bandaged after a minor operation. He knows it is Wednesday, but there is an odd lack of weekday noises; he hears no motor traffic, just a strange shuffling sound and an occasional human cry. Finally he tears off his bandages to find that almost everyone in the world apart from himself has gone *blind*. It is a brilliant opening, one of the best hooks in popular fiction. The style is unpretentious, very English, very middle class, a trifle cosy, a bit stiff-upper-lip. But the narrative is tremendously involving. Bill roams the streets of London, dodging the panic-stricken people. He soon meets up with an attractive young woman who also retains the ability to see. They are the chosen ones indeed. Then the triffids arrive, large ambulatory plants, possibly of extraterrestrial origin, which have been bred for their valuable oil. In a suddenly blinded world they have come into their own, lurching through the city streets and lashing out with their fatal stings. In summary it sounds absurd, but Wyndham makes it all surprisingly convincing. He plays on collective post-war fears by suggesting that the universal blindness has been caused by the premature activation of a secret military device in Earth orbit. He hints that the triffids are nature's revenge on an overweening human race. But it would be a mistake to stress the 'moral' in what is first and foremost an exciting escapist romp.

The author, whose full name was John Wyndham Parkes Lucas Beynon Harris (1903-1969), had served a long apprenticeship in the British and American pulp magazines—though he did not let that show. To most readers 'John Wyndham' was a new writer in 1951 (most of his previous work had appeared under the bylines 'John Beynon Harris' or 'John Beynon'). He became a bestseller in Britain, and reviewers frequently compared him with H.G. Wells. In fact he had considerably less depth and originality than Wells. His subsequent novels, *The Kraken Wakes*

1953) and *The Chrysalids* (1955), also did extremely well and inspired many imitators. They are the quintessential British 'disaster novels', now a recognized sub-category of modern science fiction. In each of them some cataclysm overwhelms the Earth, and a few plucky individuals struggle to survive, usually without too much difficulty. In truth they are rather genteel books, tales of apocalypse tamed.

The Day of the Triffids portrays a very *enjoyable* catastrophe. Millions die, but the reader feels no pain. Bill and his handful of well-disciplined friends are given plenty of opportunity to prove their manliness. There is much sexual opportunity too. At one point the hero is exhorted to take on several 'wives'; there just aren't enough fit men to go round. In the event he sticks to monogamy, but what a pleasant predicament. There is no overt sex in the book, though the reader is free to let his fantasies spin off from the page . . .

The story ends with the hero and heroine living happily on the Isle of Wight, and there is no doubt that their children will grow up to be stalwart English types. Contrast this with the aching sense of loss that one feels in the closing chapters of George Stewart's *Earth Abides*. Wyndham's novel lacks the profundity of the earlier book, but for all that it is an effective piece of modern myth-making. In a sense it is full of nostalgia for the Home Front of World War II, projecting as it does a rather jolly, Dunkirk-spirit, keep-the-home-fires-burning view of things.

First edition: London, Michael Joseph, 1951 (hardcover)
First American edition: Garden City, Doubleday, 1951 (hardcover)
Most recent editions: London, Penguin, and New York, Fawcett (paperbacks)

6

BERNARD WOLFE
Limbo

If *Brave New World* and *Nineteen Eighty-Four* are the two great dystopian visions in modern British fiction, then Bernard Wolfe's *Limbo* has some claim to being their closest American equivalent. Yet, curiously, it has failed to exercise that claim, either in the popular imagination or in the literary-critical consensus. I think it is a masterpiece, although I must admit that it has been a sadly neglected one. Perhaps its central image—of a near-future society in which men cut off their own limbs to prevent themselves from waging war—is too disturbing, too crazed, to make for ready acceptance. It is easier to imagine us succumbing to the 'feelies' and *soma*, or indeed to the everlasting boot in the face, than it is to project ourselves into Wolfe's limbless, lobotomized world of 1990.

But what a grand cornucopia of a book *Limbo* is! It is big (413 pages in the Ace paperback edition), blackly humorous, and full of a passionate concern for the problems of its day—particularly the problems of war, institutionalized violence, and humanity's potential for self-destruction. It is a novel which goes gloriously over the top, replete with puns, philosophical asides, satire on the American way of life, comments on drugs and sex and nuclear war, doodles and typographical jokes, medical and psycho-analytical jargon—a veritable *Tristram Shandy* of the atombomb age. In an afterword the author pays tribute to Norbert Wiener, Max Weber, Dostoevsky, Freud and, surprisingly, the sf writer A.E. van Vogt. 'I am writing,' he continues, 'about the overtone and undertow of *now*—in the guise of 1990 because it would take decades for a year like 1950 to be milked of its implications.'

Bernard Wolfe (born 1915) earned a B.A. in psychology from Yale University, and for a short time he worked as a bodyguard to Leon Trotsky in Mexico, though he was not present when Trotsky was eventually assassinated. His first book, *Really The Blues*, was about jazz music, and he went on to write a variety

31

of novels and non-fiction works. Evidently a man of parts. Except for a few short stories, *Limbo* remains his only venture into science fiction, yet it gives ample proof that he understood the form better than most. 'The overtone and undertow of *now*' is precisely the subject matter of all the most serious sf.

The plot concerns the travels and travails of Dr Martine, a neurosurgeon who in the year 1972 fled from a limited nuclear war to the haven of a forgotten island in the Indian Ocean. He has spent eighteen years there, performing lobotomies on the more antisocial of the simple natives (this is a humane continuation of the natives' ancient practice of *mandunga*, or crude brain surgery). In 1990 Martine sets out to rediscover the world. He finds a partially destroyed North America in which the ideology of 'Immob' holds sway. In this grotesque post-bomb society men have their arms and legs removed and replaced with computerized prosthetics, in the belief that self-mutilation will prevent the recurrence of world war. It is a faulty equivalent of the islanders' *mandunga*, the lobotomy which cuts away aggressive urges. Martine is horrified to discover that much of the inspiration for 'Immob' comes from a diary which he himself wrote and lost in that fateful year of 1972. He is the unwitting prophet of this nightmarish state; his jokes of eighteen years ago have been taken all too seriously. In any case it has all been in vain, for things are falling apart and a new war is about to begin. The story ends with Martine fleeing to his peaceful island as the bombs fall once more on the cities of America. It sounds grim and fatalistic, but in fact the novel is enormously funny and invigorating, and in the end holds out a kind of hope. Rich with ideas, all-embracing in its references, it is a book which uses the science and psychology of 1950 to grapple with the largest issues of our century. It is time that *Limbo* was recognized for what it is: the most ambitious work of science fiction, and one of the most successful, ever to come out of America.

First edition: New York, Random House, 1952 (hardcover)
First British edition: London, Secker and Warburg, 1953 (hardcover; retitled *Limbo '90*)
Most recent editions: London, Penguin (paperback, abridged), and New York, Ace (paperback, unabridged)

7

ALFRED BESTER
The Demolished Man

This is a novel which features ESP—extra-sensory perception—a commonly-accepted scientific term for telepathy and kindred powers of the mind. Despite the experiments of Dr J.B. Rhine and his successors in the USA, the scientific status of ESP remains dubious: most scientists would deny that mind-reading, precognition and the like are even remotely possible. This has not deterred science fiction writers from using ESP as a recurring motif in their novels. Like time-travel and faster-than-light spaceflight, it is one of those 'impossibilities' that sf takes in its stride. And ESP does make for good stories, as Alfred Bester demonstrates in this sparkling thriller.

It is set in the world of the 24th century. Space travel has become commonplace, and there are human colonies on Mars, Venus and the major satellites of the outer planets. One of the novelties of Bester's fast-moving narrative is that it leaps from scene to scene, sometimes from planet to planet, within the space of a paragraph; he makes the entire solar system seem like the suburbs of New York. A minority of the population has ESP powers. These people are organized into the 'Esper Guild', one of the purposes of which is to train normal folk in telepathic skills. The protagonist, Ben Reich, is a non-telepath. The fabulously wealthy head of a huge business empire, he is an obsessed and driven man, mistrustful of all those who are gifted with ESP. He sets out to commit a murder, and elicits the aid of a corrupt member of the Esper Guild. The latter's assistance is essential, since in this society murderers can be detected telepathically before they carry out their crimes. Reich wishes to kill a business rival, using an antique weapon known as a *gun* . . .

The murder is duly committed, and the bulk of the story is taken up with a protracted duel of wits beween Reich and his nemesis, a charming telepathic police chief called Lincoln Powell. The penalty for Reich's crime is demolition—total destruction of the personality—and he and Powell move in an ever-tightening spiral until that shattering climax is reached. It is a very ingenious story, and it all takes place against a swiftly-changing backdrop which is sometimes quite literally riotous with colour. Consider, for example, Number 99 Bastion West Side, the Rainbow House of Chooka Frood, madam and clairvoyant: 'Number 99 was an eviscerated ceramics plant. During the war a succession of blazing explosions had burst among the stock of thousands of chemical glazes, fused them, and splashed them into a wild rainbow reproduction of a lunar crater. Great splotches of magenta, violet, bice green, burnt umber and chrome yellow were burned into the stone walls. Long streams of orange, crimson and imperial purple had erupted through windows and doors to streak the streets and surrounding ruins with slashing brush strokes.' It reminds one of some psychedelic hippy pad, described fifteen years before its time.

Alfred Bester (born 1913) has written comparatively little science fiction, and yet he is second only to Robert Heinlein as an influence on the sf field in America. Such later writers as Philip K. Dick, Samuel R. Delany and William Gibson reveal that influence in differing ways. Moreover, unlike Heinlein he has had a major impact on certain younger British writers, notably Michael Moorcock and M. John Harrison. What impressed all these people is Bester's style, his dash, his New York-bred 'street wisdom'. He brought to sf a certain profanity and iconoclasm allied to a species of idealism (usually expressed as 'sympathy for the common man') and a willingness to experiment while never deviating from a strong narrative line. *The Demolished Man*, his first novel, still seems fresh after more than three decades.

First edition: Chicago, Shasta, 1953 (hardcover)
First British edition: London, Sidgwick and Jackson, 1953 (hardcover)
Most recent editions: New York, Pocket, and London, Penguin
(paperbacks)

8

RAY BRADBURY
Fahrenheit 451

The burning of books is a subject which holds a horrid fascina-
tion for Ray Bradbury. He has touched on it in several of his
short stories as well as in this, his nearest approach to a full-
length sf novel. The title refers to the temperature at which paper
is supposed to catch fire, which itself may be an immodest metaphor for the 'ignition' of Bradbury's prose style. Unlike other sf
writers of his day he has an intensely self-conscious style:

'Without turning on the light he imagined how this room
would look. His wife stretched on the bed, uncovered and cold,
like a body displayed on the lid of a tomb, her eyes fixed to the
ceiling by invisible threads of steel, immovable. And in her ears
the little Seashells, the thimble radios tamped tight, and an
electronic ocean of sound, of music and talking and music coming in, coming in on the shore of her unsleeping mind. The room
was indeed empty. Every night the waves came in and bore her
off on their great tides of sound, floating her, wide-eyed, toward
morning.' Repetitive, incantatory, this is actually one of the less
purple passages. It describes Mildred, Guy Montag's wife, in-
dulging in her favourite pastime of listening to her personal hi-fi.
Stupid, empty-headed woman, one is encouraged to think—and
yes, there is in this book, as in most sf novels of the 1950s, a rote
sexism, which once noted, I shall pass over perforce.

It is a rather simple-minded dystopia which Bradbury creates.
Everyone listens to the 'Seashells' and watches wall-to-wall TV.
Pedestrians are arrested; even to drive as slowly as forty miles an
hour is considered an offence. All books are banned and conver-
sation is a truly forgotten art. Suicide and juvenile delinquency
are rife, the world is overpopulated, and states are gearing themselves up for yet another war. Montag works as a 'fireman'; his
duty is to burn books, the former owners of which are carted off
to prison or the mental home. In spite of himself, Montag has
intellectual and poetic yearnings, and when he meets a fey seven-
teen-year-old girl who teaches him to appreciate trees and

flowers and rain he is moved to rebel against his job and his society. He reads Matthew Arnold's 'Dover Beach' and becomes aware of the ignorant armies clashing by night all around him. He makes contact with a secret underground of readers who are keeping literary culture alive by stealth. But eventually he is found out, and the fire engine arrives at *his* front door.

Fahrenheit 451 is a very straightforward book, a scream of rage against the mass media and the whole 20th century communications landscape. Television, pop music, comic books, digests, theme parks, spectator sports—Bradbury is agin 'em all, and if he had been writing this book thirty years later he would no doubt have included video games, home computers and role-playing fantasies in his tirade. It is the litany of an old-fashioned, puritanical moralist; small wonder that the message of this novel has fallen sweetly on the ears of schoolteachers and other Guardians of Culture the world over. Wrapped up as it is in an exciting story with poetic overtones, that message has proved to be a very acceptable one. Bradbury's book has become a Set Text, and so he has done his bit against the steady spread of Marshall McLuhan's 'global village' and the growing network of vacuous entertainment and 'information'. As a tract for teenagers, *Fahrenheit 451* still has considerable merits, but it is scarcely a classic of *adult* science fiction. It is too unbalanced to be counted as a serious attempt to grapple imaginatively with the moral values of the media barrage.

First edition: New York, Ballantine, 1953 (hardcover and paperback)
First British edition: London, Hart-Davis, 1954 (hardcover)
Most recent editions: New York, Bantam, and London, Granada (paperbacks)

9

ARTHUR C. CLARKE
Childhood's End

A novel about transcendence, with a very apt title, this book was another particular favourite of mine when I was in my early teens. It is generally recognized as Clarke's first major work (he had already published *The Sands of Mars*, a humdrum novel about space colonization, in 1951), and it gained praise from C.S. Lewis, among others, for its deft blend of hard science and religious mysticism. Set in the immediate future, at a time when the first manned space rockets are about to be launched, it depicts the arrival on earth of vastly powerful alien beings who become known as the 'Overlords'. Despite that ominous name, this is not a horrific tale of invasion and violent takeover: Clarke's Overlords have come to do us good in spite of ourselves, and the novel convincingly demonstrates the way in which beneficent alien rulers might spread harmony over a warring planet. As a young reader I assented to the whole idea, though its implications now make me uneasy. Arthur Charles Clarke (born 1917) is an English writer who has chosen to live for the past several decades in the former British colony of Sri Lanka. In my more questioning moments I cannot help feeling that the Overlords are an idealized projection of the Foreign Office bureaucrats who once ran the British Empire.

But there is a twist: these Overlords are not white-skinned. For fifty years they hide from humanity, and when at last they do reveal themselves it comes as a shock. 'There was no mistake. The leathery wings, the little horns, the barbed tail—all were there. The most terrible of all legends had come to life, out of the unknown past. Yet now it stood smiling, in ebon majesty, with the sunlight gleaming upon its tremendous body, and with a human child resting trustfully on either arm.' That revelation knocked me sideways when I first read the novel. It comes just one-third of the way through, and the next section is an extended description of the scientific utopia that the Overlords have wrought, a world without poverty, happily united under one government; crime almost non-existent, everyone living in garden cities, with endless leisure to pursue the arts and science. It made me sigh with longing: how rational, how wonderful!

There is more to come. The children of this utopia begin to dream strange dreams; they have night-time visions of far suns, alien planets. Under the tutelage of the Overlords they are beginning to evolve into something which will seem incomprehensible to their parents. They are about to join the 'Overmind'. In a grand metaphysical climax, thrillingly described, the entire human race undergoes an 'inconceivable metamorphosis', giving up the flesh in order to become a free-floating, star-roving Platonic ideal of *mind*. The Overlords look on rather forlornly: they are midwives at this cosmic rebirth, and they are unable themselves to become part of the Overmind. Poor devils.

The prose now seems slightly juvenile, the characters very thin—but the story still moves me. It is a generalized religious 'myth' for a scientific age, the tale of a benign Last Judgement when the gates of the City of God are opened to all.

First edition: New York, Ballantine, 1953 (hardcover and paperback)
First British edition: London, Sidgwick and Jackson, 1954 (hardcover)
Most recent editions: New York, Del Rey, and London, Pan (paperbacks)

10
CHARLES L. HARNESS
The Paradox Men

This is one of the *schlock* classics of American magazine sf. It has been compared frequently with the fiction of A.E. van Vogt, a very popular though slapdash writer whose works I have not been able to include in this listing (van Vogt's most characteristic novels are *Slan*, 1946, and *The World of Null-A*, 1948). In my opinion, Harness's book is superior to anything by the better-known author. *The Paradox Men* was first published in a shorter magazine version in 1949, under the title 'Flight into Yesterday'. The alternative titles give us strong clues to the principal motif of the story: the paradoxes of time travel.

Alar the Thief, the man with no memory, is pitted against Haze-Gaunt, the Chancellor of America Imperial. The latter likes to fondle a pet tarsier, which stares from his shoulder with a perpetually terrified gaze. We are in the 22nd century; society has advanced technology and space travel, yet human slavery has been reintroduced and sword-fights are commonplace. Harness anticipates Frank Herbert's *Dune* in this respect—his Thieves are protected by 'body armour' or force fields, which only the relatively slow-moving sword or knife-blade can penetrate. The Society of Thieves is dedicated to the abolition of slavery, and to that end its members fight Haze-Gaunt's tyranny with stealth and swordsmanship. Against this unlikely background Harness builds an involuted story-line.

The hero, Alar, has no memory of who he was or what happened to him before he emerged from a wrecked spacecraft five years before. It seems that his faster-than-light craft did a complete circuit of the universe, travelling backwards in time as it flew, and arrived on earth five years prior to its launch. The tarsier, now Haze-Gaunt's pet, came from that spaceship too. Alar has strange powers; he appears to be a highly 'evolved' human being—and the tarsier is possibly a *de*volved human being. Who is Alar? Moreover, who is the tarsier? As the novel rushes towards its breathless climax, the launching of the spacecraft, these questions grow in importance until the fate of humanity depends upon their answers.

The Paradox Men is a short but surprisingly rich book. The imagery and ideas are extraordinary, even if the prose is undistinguished. Harness uses Einsteinian physics and Arnold Toynbee's cyclical theory of history to good effect. An inventive high point is the description of Alar's visit to the sun; the decisive sword-fight takes place on a drifting 'Solarion'—a refrigerated space station which sails the surface of a sunspot. This scenario stretches our credulity, to say the least, but it is presented with such joyous throwaway erudition that it is almost convincing. The ending of the novel—where Alar is transformed into a god-like intelligence which declares to the universe that 'All men are brothers!'—is even more fantastic, though heartwarming.

Charles L. Harness (born 1915) has never been a prolific writer. Besides *The Paradox Men*, he is best remembered for his novella 'The Rose' (1953), another complex and moving parable of human transcendence embedded in a melodramatic narrative. His later novel, *The Ring of Ritornel* (1968), is well worth reading, although it already seemed old-fashioned at its time of publication.

First edition: New York, Bouregy and Curl, 1953
(hardcover; as *Flight Into Yesterday*)
First British edition: London, Faber and Faber, 1964
(hardcover; as *The Paradox Men*)
Most recent editions: London, NEL (paperback) and New York, Crown
(hardcover; as *The Paradox Men*, which has now become
accepted as the official title)

11
WARD MOORE
Bring the Jubilee

'Although I am writing this in the year 1877, I was not born until 1921. Neither the dates nor the tenses are in error—let me explain.' So begins Ward Moore's delightful novel. Evidently it is another tale of time travel, but it is more than that. It is also one of the earliest, and finest, full-length examples of that sub-category of science fiction which has come to be known as the 'alternative world' story. The rationale for these works is more or less as follows. It is possible that many different universes branch off from ours at each moment in time, and thus there must be an infinitude of other worlds, other Earths, stemming from variants of the crucial turning-points in history. By setting stories in one or another of these alternative time-lines, the sf writer can ring innumerable changes on known history. For example, he can imagine a world in which the Chinese were the first to colonize North America, as did Murray Leinster in 'Sideways in Time' (1935), or where contemporary American society stems from successful mass settlement by the Vikings nine hundred years ago, which was what L. Sprague de Camp did in 'The Wheels of If' (1940). In *Bring the Jubilee* Ward Moore builds his fiction on just such a conceit, in his case the supposition that the South won the American Civil War.

The hero, Hodge Backmaker, is a lad who grows up in the shrunken, underdeveloped United States of the 1920s and 30s. At the age of seventeen he makes his way to the great metropolis of New York, a city of cobblestones, gas-lamps and balloons, streets crammed with bicycles, and almost a million people living among the ten-storey 'skyscrapers'. He does not realize it, but this New York is but a pale shadow of what it might have been had the Confederate States not won their independence in the 1860s. The Confederacy, which now embraces Mexico, is much the richest nation in North America, and Washington, St. Louis and 'Leesburg' are the truly great cities of the continent, leaving New York in the provincial doldrums.

Hodge goes to work for a bookseller, and in his spare time he immerses himself in historical learning. He reads such books as 'Causes of American Decline and Decay by the always popular expatriot historian, Henry Adams.' After six years he becomes a full-time scholar of history, taking as his specialty the 'War of Southron Independence'. For a further eight years he studies the campaigns of that long-ago war, writing monographs which 'were published in learned Confederate and British journals—there were none in the United States.' Meanwhile, some scientific colleagues have devised a means of time-travel, and Hodge is tempted to use it in order to visit the time and place of the battle which decided the outcome of the war that so fascinates him. Arriving on the battlefield of Gettysburg in 1863, Hodge inadvertently changes the course of history. He finds himself in a new timeline, in a world where the South is losing the Civil War . . .

It is a lovely story, exceedingly well told. Even those who know little of North American history should enjoy this novel, full as it is of humour, colour and atmosphere. Ward Moore (1903-1978) is another of those writers who produced all too few works of science fiction; his only other significant sf book is *Greener Than You Think* (1947), a comic novel about the world being overrun by a mutant strain of grass. But he will be remembered for *Bring the Jubilee*, an enduring minor classic.

First edition: New York, Farrar, 1953 (hardcover)
First British edition: London, Heinemann, 1955 (hardcover)
Most recent edition: London, NEL (paperback)

12

FREDERIK POHL & C.M. KORNBLUTH
The Space Merchants

This novel was first serialized in *Galaxy* magazine in 1952, under the title 'Gravy Planet'. It is short and sprightly, and its continual inventiveness and barbed humour are delights. In many ways it represents the quintessence of the 'social science fiction' of the 1950s, a style of writing particularly associated with *Galaxy* under H.L. Gold's editorship. In 1960 the novelist Kingsley Amis declared that *The Space Merchants* 'has many claims to being the best sf novel so far'. He was talking about American magazine sf as opposed to the more respectable British tradition of Wells, Huxley and Orwell, but it was nevertheless a high compliment. Does the book live up to Amis's praise? I believe so.

Frederik Pohl (born 1919) and Cyril Kornbluth (1922-1958) had started young as writers, scribbling many pseudonymous stories for the lesser sf magazines of the 1940s. They had been science fiction fans from childhood, which is to say that they were part of the American sf subculture of readers' clubs and amateur magazines. They had grown up with sf, living it and breathing it. They were also highly intelligent. Thomas M. Disch, himself a bright kid of twelve at the time *The Space Merchants* appeared, was later to describe them as 'a pair of magnificent smart-alecks'. Pohl had worked in advertizing, Kornbluth in journalism. They were to put their worldly-wisdom, and their familiarity with the tones and tropes of magazine sf, to excellent use in this, their first collaborative novel.

Mitch Courtenay works for Schocken Associates, a New York advertising agency of two centuries hence. In this world the ad agencies run *everything*, including the government of the United States. It is a densely-populated scene, with millions of consumers cowed by the outrageous, all-intrusive advertisements. Pitted against the *status quo* is an underground group of saboteurs known as the 'Consies' (short for 'conservationists'—bear in mind that environmental conservation was *not* a fashionable theme in the early 1950s). Courtenay is given the task of selling the planet Venus to unwilling emigrants. His company portrays it as a paradise, but it is of course a hell-hole. Before he can fulfil this dubious assignment, he is kidnapped by the Consies and his eyes are opened to the ghastly reality of things. It is a conventional slam-bang plot, full of action and reversals. One reads it with pleasure because of the wealth of incidental detail and the many sly jokes, not least for the implied criticism of the anti-communist crusade of Senator Joe McCarthy, at its height in 1952. In fact, *The Space Merchants* is not about the future at all, it is about mid-20th century Madison Avenue writ very large indeed. The 'feel' of the novel is absolutely authentic, despite its technique of comic exaggeration. By being so true to its own time, the book has succeeded in becoming more relevant to the decades that have followed.

No other writer has surpassed Pohl and Kornbluth's achievement in this particular vein. Their own subsequent novel *Gladiator-at-Law* (1955) comes close, but it rests a notch further down the scale. *The Space Merchants* is a work of great self-confidence, at once cocky and urbane. Ultimately, perhaps, it is a little too slick and self-satisfied in its wit, but it remains a testament to the all-too-brief period in which American magazine sf first achieved a kind of political maturity.

First edition: New York, Ballantine, 1953 (hardcover and paperback)
First British edition: London, Heinemann, 1955 (hardcover)
Most recent editions: New York, Del Rey, and London, Penguin (paperbacks)

13
CLIFFORD D. SIMAK
Ring Around the Sun

The 'ring' referred to in the title is a metaphorical hoop of planet Earths, each occupying a separate, parallel continuum of space and time. All these worlds, apart from our own, are virgin territory, untouched by humanity. Assuming, as Simak does in the novel, that one can travel between the parallel worlds, then we have the perfect dream of *lebensraum*—enough land for an indefinite expansion of the human race, without our being compelled to leave the surface of the planet that we know and love. It is an implausible daydream, but a seductive one.

The story is set in 1977, twenty-five years from the time of writing. The Cold War between the USA and the Soviet Union is still going on (one wonders how many of Simak's readers in 1953 believed that would be in the case), and it is an unhappy world, full of economic and military tensions. There are famines in Asia; meanwhile, the ordinary citizens of the USA escape into role-playing games. The central character, Jay Vickers, is a writer who leads a rather solitary life in a rural suburb of New York. Strange things start to happen, altering the fabric of his all-too-familar world. A mysterious new company begins to market everlasting razor-blades and light-bulbs; soon it is providing cheap housing and automobiles—and, most worrying of all, free food.

Ring Around the Sun is essentially a Tall Tale about the destruction of capitalism. Certain mutated human beings have discovered that they can gain access to parallel worlds by purely mental means. On one of these pristine planet Earths they have built automated factories which produce food, clothing, gadgets, cars and housing units of very high quality at tremendous speed. The mutants import the goods to our world and use them to undermine the economic system. Factories fall idle, whole industries crash, men and women are thrown out of work. The unemployed are then enticed to disappear from this world, to enter a parallel continuum and become pioneer settlers. All this is done for the good of humanity, to break the stalemate of the Cold War and to forestall a nuclear armageddon. Jay Vickers finds that he may well be a mutant himself: his means of reaching the first of the parallel Earths, the 'factory world', is to revisit a scene of childhood happiness and to hypnotize himself by watching a brightly-coloured spinning-top.

It is a Tall Tale indeed, and it becomes too complicated for its own good. Although his prose style is plain (in fact simple to the point of banality), Simak introduces a new plot twist in almost every chapter, so that the final impression on the reader is that this is a very ornate book—part mystery story, part satire on the McCarthyite era (with its fears of internal conspiracy), part pastoral meditation, part economic speculation, part gosh-wow adventure yarn of mutants and robots and wonderful technological panaceas.

Clifford Donald Simak (born 1904) has had a longer career than any other American sf writer. He published his first magazine story in 1931, and he is still producing novels in the 1980s. A sentimental countryman at heart, he has always shown an antipathy to cities, to the capitalist economic system (though he is an agrarian populist rather than a socialist), and to modern life in general. *Ring Around the Sun* was his third novel, and it is one of his best in that it reveals his obsessions to the full. For all its complexity and confusion, it is a deeply felt work.

First edition: New York, Simon and Schuster, 1953 (hardcover)
First British edition: London, World, 1960 (paperback)
Most recent edition: London, NEL (paperback)

14
THEODORE STURGEON
More Than Human

Freaks have always been a favourite subject for science fiction writers, perhaps because many of them felt lonely and alienated during their own childhoods. Theodore Sturgeon (born 1918) first came to fame in 1940 with a short story called simply 'It', about a hideous, misshapen but roughly humanoid monster which awakes deep in a forest and sets out to look for things to kill. Sturgeon's first novel, *The Dreaming Jewels* (1950), describes a troupe of circus freaks who are in communication with an alien intelligence. In his second novel, *More Than Human*, he is at it again, inviting us to empathize with the odd and the outcast. And we respond, for this is an intensely-written and very moving book.

It is in three parts. The first section, 'The Fabulous Idiot', is mainly about an indigent subnormal called Lone. Dumb, emotionless, almost insensate, he is jerked into awareness by telepathic contact with a young woman who is being persecuted by her insane father (no one in this novel is 'normal'). The girl dies, and Lone is taken in by a farming couple who pine for the son they never had. He spends eight years on the farm, gradually learning to speak. On leaving, he builds a hut in the woods and provides a home there for three runaway girls aged four to six, all of whom have spectacular mental powers. A mongoloid baby is born to the farming couple (the mother dies in childbirth) and Lone adopts it. He comes to realize that he, the baby and the three little girls constitute one being, a *gestalt* entity of tremendous latent abilities. The baby's brain is like a computer; the girls, with their various telepathic and telekinetic talents, provide the input and output; and Lone, the erstwhile idiot, controls and co-ordinates the whole. Together, they devise an antigravity mechanism for the old farmer's run-down truck. In a moment of high pathos Sturgeon describes how this is left to rot away in a muddy field: 'Powered inexhaustably by the slow release of atomic binding energy, the device was the practical solution of flight without wings, the simple key to a new era in transportation, in materials handling, and in interplanetary travel. Made by an idiot, harnessed idiotically to replace a spavined horse, stupidly left, numbly forgotten . . .'

The second part, 'Baby is Three', is the first-person narrative of Gerry Thompson, an orphan who joins the group at the age of eight. When Lone is killed by a falling tree, Gerry has to assume the leadership. He takes the children to live in the home of a rich spinster, but he ends up murdering their benefactress when he realizes that her influence prevents the group from 'bleshing', that is, from becoming one organism as it did before. Gerry visits a psychoanalyst in order to find out why he committed this crime, and during the session he reaches a full awareness of his own telepathic abilities, which are more powerful than Lone's.

The third section, 'Morality', tells of the coming of Hip Barrows, a young man who has no special psychic talents, but who is able to provide *Homo gestalt* with a code of ethics and a conscience. At the very end of the story the collective entity discovers that it is not alone in the world—there are others that have delayed welcoming this newcomer until it has gained a measure of maturity.

More Than Human still seems an extraordinary novel. Marred by occasional touches of sentimentality and sadism, perhaps weakened by a rather forced optimistic ending, it is nevertheless a most memorable fantasy about the next step in human evolution—and indubitably the best book of its kind.

First edition: New York, Farrar, Straus and Young, 1953 (hardcover)
First British edition: London, Gollancz, 1954 (hardcover)
Most recent editions: London, Corgi, and New York, Del Rey (paperbacks)

15

HAL CLEMENT
Mission of Gravity

This is a well-known example of 'hard' science fiction. It belongs
to that species of sf which takes its inspiration directly from
mathematics, physics and chemistry, and which is written by
someone who knows these disciplines at first hand. Indeed,
Mission of Gravity reads as though it was written with a slide-
rule close by the typewriter. Its author, whose full name is Harry
Clement Stubbs (born 1922), is a Harvard graduate and former
B-24 pilot who has worked for most of his life as a science
teacher. He first gained his reputation as an sf writer in the pages
of *Astounding*, where this novel was serialized in 1953. It has
proved to be a popular and long-lived work, one which has
appealed to an audience wider than the core of technologically-
minded adolescents who no doubt formed its initial readership.

It is a quest-narrative set on an alien planet, Mesklin, which is
discus-shaped (rather like a broad spinning-top). The planet is
very large and dense, and spins rapidly on its axis. Because of its
peculiar formation the surface gravity varies enormously, from
three times Earth-normal at the equator or 'Rim', to almost seven
hundred times Earth's gravity at the poles. Hal Clement imagines
intelligent life existing in this inhospitable environment: small
flat creeping things with immensely tough bodies and an inbuilt
fear of heights (towards Mesklin's poles a fall of a few inches
would be instantly fatal even to the hardiest organisms). Despite
the virtually two-dimensional quality of their lives, these Mesklinites have a developed society which indulges in long-distance
trade. The hero of the novel, a centipede-like creature called
Barlennan, is the ambitious and independent-minded captain of a
trading ship. Before the story opens he has been contacted by
aliens from outer space, who turn out to be frail human beings
from the planet Earth.

The Earthmen are in search of an unmanned rocket probe
which has crash-landed near one of Mesklin's poles. If its instruments can be retrieved, the readings might enable humanity to

build an anti-gravity machine. Charles Lackland, human ambassador to Mesklin's Rim and the man who has befriended Barlennan, explains this to the Mesklinite skipper as best he can: 'The poles of your world have the most terrific surface gravity of any spot in the Universe so far accessible to us . . . We wanted measures in that tremendous gravity field—all sorts of measures. The value of the instruments that were designed and sent on that trip cannot be expressed in numbers we both know . . . We *must* have that data . . .'.

Barlennan has his own motives for co-operating with the Earthmen. As the story progresses he comes to appreciate the value of *science*, which one day may allow his people to transform their vast world. Meanwhile he and his crew are obliged to undertake an odyssey of truly heroic dimensions, travelling by land and sea all the way from the Rim to an unknown region of the pole. They have to deal with monsters, storms, hostile natives and towering cliffs. Charles Lackland accompanies them on the first leg of their journey, until the steepening gravity becomes too much for him to endure even with the aid of an armoured suit. Thereafter he can only guide the Mesklinites by radio from an orbiting space vessel.

Of course the psychology is minimal, the characters wooden, the prose flat. All the same, *Mission of Gravity* is an impressive feat of world-building, and a rather touching adventure story. It is written with hearty conviction, which is what matters most. Even if there is something inherently absurd about following the progress of a band of centipedes across a totally imaginary landscape, we find ourselves in sympathy with the little creatures as their quest nears its end. Above all, we can sympathize with Barlennan, whose plea for knowledge seems universal: 'I want to know why a fire glows, and why flame dust kills. I want my children or theirs, if I ever have any, to know what makes this radio work, and your tank, and some day this rocket. I want to know much—more than I can learn, no doubt . . .'.

First edition: Garden City, Doubleday, 1954 (hardcover)
First British edition: London, Hale, 1955 (hardcover)
Most recent editions: New York, Del Rey, and London, Penguin (paperbacks)

16

EDGAR PANGBORN
A Mirror for Observers

Unusual for its period, this is a slow-moving, painstakingly atmospheric and decidedly 'literary' science fiction novel. Edgar Pangborn (1909-1976) was best known for his first sf story, 'Angel's Egg', which appeared in *Galaxy* in 1951, and for his picaresque post-holocaust tale *Davy* (1964). *A Mirror for Observers*, his second novel, brought him a measure of critical acclaim, although it has never been a very popular work with the general sf readership. One can see why. The various sections of the book begin with quotations from Plato, Santayana and Emerson, which are indicative of the sententiousness and high moral tone the author strives for throughout.

Martian observers have been living on Earth, unknown to us, for many centuries. They maintain several underground bases in remote parts of the globe, from which they emerge to mingle with humanity. Although they have immensely long life-spans, and hearts that beat just once a minute, they are able to pass for human. Their motives are generally benign, but one of their number, an embittered renegade called Namir, begins to take an unhealthy interest in the life of a certain human boy. Another Martian, Elmis, is given the task of spying on Namir and the boy. He must find out what is going on, and ensure that no harm is done.

The story opens in a New England town in 1963. The boy, twelve-year-old Angelo Pontevecchio, is an intellectual prodigy with a crippled leg. Elmis, in human guise, moves into Angelo's mother's boarding house and begins to make friends with the lad and the other tenants. Posing as a retired teacher, he gives Angelo books to read. 'He wallowed in Mark Twain and Melville; I knew he was startled by Dostoevski, and amused by the thin wind of fallacy that blew through the insanitary beard of Marx.' But Namir, the evil Martian, is also at work, encouraging Angelo to join a juvenile gang and learn how to wield a knife . . .

In the second half of the novel the action moves to New York in the year 1972. Elmis traces the runaway Angelo to the head-quarters of a political organization, the neo-fascist Organic Unity Party, which is secretly run by Namir. The story climaxes with the accidental release of a man-made plague which kills a quarter of America's population (the virus has been developed by a scientist who works for Namir). In the chaos, Elmis wins Angelo away from the opposition and encourages him to accept the love of a good woman—his former childhood sweetheart, now a successful concert pianist. The Organic Unity Party is discredited, and Angelo works selflessly for the relief of the plague-stricken. Elmis kills Namir, then disappears from human view to resume his Martian identity, full of a faith in 'the incorruptible promise of returning spring'.

A Mirror for Observers is an anguished parable of good versus evil told from a humanistic point of view—but perhaps inevitably it is often religiose in tone. It makes a commendable attempt to plumb the confused depths of the human heart, and to reveal humanity's capacity for sainthood as well as for mass destruction. In the end, however, one cannot help but feel that the device of the Martian 'observers' reduces the stature of Angelo and the other merely human characters in this drama.

First edition: Garden City, Doubleday, 1954 (hardcover)
First British edition: London, Muller, 1955 (hardcover)
Most recent editions: New York, Bluejay, and London, Star
(paperbacks)

17

ISAAC ASIMOV
The End of Eternity

He is one of the best-known sf writers in the world, so I felt I had to include something by Isaac Asimov (born 1920), though I confess I have little enthusiasm for his work. It was a choice between this novel of time travel, or his famous *Foundation Trilogy* (1951-53). The latter has always seemed to me to be over-rated; a long series of short stories and novellas from 1940s *Astoundings*, cobbled together into three volumes, it collectively resumes the narrative of Gibbon's *Decline and Fall of the Roman Empire* as projected on to a future galactic backdrop. Nor do Asimov's robotic detective novels, *The Caves of Steel* (1954) and *The Naked Sun* (1957) appeal to me. They may confirm his standing as the Agatha Christie of sf but, frankly, I would rather read Christie. That leaves *The End of Eternity*, which has the merits of being pure sf and a novel.

The hero, Andrew Harlan, is a native of the 95th century. At the age of fifteen he was recruited into the guardians of Eternity, and he now roves the time-stream, helping to keep human history balanced and serene. Despite that grand theme, there is surprisingly little detail and colour in the novel. Eternity itself is a sort of warren of grey corridors which stand outside Time (everything in this book has a capital letter). It runs from the 27th century, when men first attained the ability to set it up, to the remote period of futurity when the sun goes nova (that titanic explosion is the energy source which maintains Eternity). Andrew Harlan is first of all a Cub, then an Observer, then a Technician, answerable to the Allwhen Council. Others of the Eternals are Sociologists, Computers, and Life-Plotters. Their collective task is to engineer Reality Changes which produce the Maximum Desired Response for the Minimum Necessary Change. Thus they iron out all the unhappy wrinkles in the fabric of human society—if one century is suffering from too much crime or drug addiction or whatever, then a small but cunningly-crafted Reality Change will take care of the problem.

It is a monkish bureaucracy, devoted to the highest ideals of chastity and service. 'If there was a flaw in Eternity, it involved women': there are none, to speak of—until one day Harlan catches a glimpse of Noÿs Lambent, a girl of the 482nd century. The narrative promptly stutters into rhyming embarrassment: 'Harlan had seen many women in his passages through Time, but in Time they were only objects to him, like walls and balls, barrows and harrows, kittens and mittens. They were facts to be Observed. In Eternity a girl was a different matter. And one like *this*!' The author seems to be every bit as discomfited as his hero; one of the other characters describes Noÿs as being 'built like a force-field latrine', a simile which makes the mind boggle. Harlan swiftly Falls in Love, and this is the catalyst for the plot. From now on he will find himself in increasing conflict with Eternity until, many ingenious plot twists, exclamation marks and capital letters later, he has succeeded in destroying the whole set-up. Although she sincerely loves Harlan, it turns out that Noÿs has been acting as a Secret Agent on behalf of Change. The operations of Eternity have led the human race into soft decadence: 'Safety and security. Moderation. Nothing in excess. No risks . . .' Now, with Eternity wiped from existence, humanity will be free to go onwards and upwards and outwards—to build a Galactic Empire, no less. In the closing lines of the novel Noÿs assures Harlan that '*we* will remain to have children and grand-children, and mankind will remain to reach the stars,' It is 'the final end of Eternity. —And the beginning of Infinity.'

First edition: Garden City, Doubleday, 1955 (hardcover)
First British edition: London, Panther, 1959 (paperback)
Most recent editions: New York, Del Rey, and London, Granada (paperbacks)

18
LEIGH BRACKETT
The Long Tomorrow

In his *Encyclopedia of Science Fiction* (1979) Peter Nicholls has
an entry on 'Conceptual Breakthrough', which, he argues, is the
essential theme of most science fiction. The idea of arriving at a
whole new awareness of one's surroundings—of metaphorically
breaking through into another universe of concepts—lies at the
heart of many sf stories, and it may be the reason why science
fiction appeals especially to young readers: they actively seek
these 'breakthroughs' in order to help them to come to terms
with the world. Many sf works dramatize such moments of
intellectual realignment in a very literal fashion, and Leigh
Brackett's *The Long Tomorrow* is one of them.

The story takes place in the United States a couple of generations after an all-out nuclear war. At first glance it is a pleasant
pastoral scene. Cities have been outlawed; the surviving population is spread thinly on farmsteads and in hamlets; the religious
sect known as the New Mennonites has the chief say in government, and it preaches self-sufficiency, respect for the land, and
the virtues of honest toil. Young Len Colter and his cousin Esau
have grown up in this reasonably happy, well-fed, God-fearing
society—and they are restless. They dream of *machines*; they
listen to their grandmother's tales of big cities, artificial fabrics,
flight, and long-distance communication; they dream above all of
a possibly mythical place called Bartorstown, where the old
knowledge and technical ability have been kept alive.

The Long Tomorrow is the tale of Len and Esau's journey to
Bartorstown, and what happens to them when they get there. It
is the story of their struggle to escape from the miasma of funda-
mentalist ignorance and breathe the clear air of scientific reason.
It is a very pro-science novel and, in a way, it is almost 'a
collapsed history' of the USA, a retelling of the progression from
New England theology to Californian nuclear physics. It is also
strangely prophetic, in that the conservative born-again society it
depicts has some of the lineaments of the reactionary Christian

movement known as the 'Moral Majority' that has influenced American politics in the 1980s. It also puts one in mind of Ayatollah Khomeini's Iran. In this world people are stoned to death if they are discovered to possess a radio set. If any settlement grows above the ordained limit of two hundred buildings, the farmers will come and raze it to the ground. It is a society which does everything according to the Book, and in which science and all 20th-century technology are abhorred.

Leigh Brackett (1915-1978) was well known as a writer of film scripts in addition to sf stories—she co-scripted such movies as Howard Hawk's *The Big Sleep* and *Rio Bravo*. For the most part her sf output consisted of colourful adventure stories, of which *The Sword of Rhiannon* (1953) is perhaps the most memorable. She married the sf writer Edmond Hamilton, the author of numerous crudely-written space operas, and because of that relationship her work is sometimes regarded as though it were an extension of his. In truth, she was a vastly superior writer to Hamilton. *The Long Tomorrow* is a beautifully-written novel, full of sharply-realized physical detail, believable characters and convincing action. Somewhat underrated today, it remains one of the most readable sf novels of its decade.

First edition: Garden City, Doubleday, 1955 (hardcover)
First British edition: London, Mayflower, 1962 (paperback)
Most recent edition: New York, Del Rey (paperback)

19

WILLIAM GOLDING
The Inheritors

William Golding (born 1911) is now regarded as one of the greatest English writers. I have long believed *The Inheritors* to be his best book, and I am happy to say that it is also his most science-fictional. As I said in the introduction to this book, my definition of sf is a form of narrative fiction which exploits the imaginative perspectives of the modern scientific world view. *The Inheritors* is a good case to point to when I try to explain what I mean by those 'imaginative perspectives'. The novel was not published as sf, and is not generally perceived as such, yet to me it is a fine example of a certain easily-recognizable type of science fiction. It could not possibly have been written were it not for the the discoveries of palaeoanthropology, the study of Stone Age humanity through the bones and tools it has left behind. The perspective which *The Inheritors* imaginatively exploits is the dark backward and abysm of time, as it has been revealed to us by one branch of modern science.

It begins with a quotation from H.G. Wells' *Outline of History*: 'We know very little of the appearance of the Neanderthal man, but this . . . seems to suggest an extreme hairiness, an ugliness, or a repulsive strangeness in his appearance over and above his low forehead, his beetle brows, his ape neck, and his inferior stature . . .' Golding proceeds to flesh out Wells' picture of the Neanderthals, and, by doing so, to invert all the values implied by words such as 'ugliness', 'repulsive' and 'inferior'. These Neanderthals are *people*; we feel for them. They form a large family group: the old woman guards the fire, the old man decides when to travel from winter to summer quarters, the younger men and women hunt and gather, and they all care for the children. Among the younger men is Lok. He is big and agile and carefree, sweet-natured but not very bright. He laughs a lot, and is good with the little girl, Liku. We follow the family as it makes its way back to its summer cave near a waterfall. We experience the people's great sadness when the old man sickens and dies and is buried beneath the floor of the cave. Although they use few words, and everything is narrated in terms of deceptive simplicity, Golding makes us appreciate that the Neanderthal's culture is humane. They have a mother-goddess religion (Liku carries a twisted root, roughly female in shape—she calls it the Little Oa, or Little Goddess), and they are mainly vegetarian, feeling guilt when they occasionally eat carrion meat.

A new thing comes into their innocent lives. One of their number disappears, and they slowly come to realize that he has been killed by strangers. Men—impossibly thin and hairless men—have arrived in the area, equipped with canoes, spears, bows and arrows. They are the Inheritors, the first human beings of our own type (though we see them only through the Neanderthal's eyes until the very last chapter). One by one the Neanderthals are killed, until only Lok and the woman Fa are left. Although terrified, they try to rescue a baby from the new people. Fa too is killed and is carried away down the waterfall. There follows an extraordinary scene, in which we view poor solitary Lok from the 'outside' for the first time: 'The red creature stood on the edge of the terrace and did nothing . . . the bar of its brow glistened in the moonlight, over the great caverns where the eyes were hidden . . .' Lok weeps, for himself and for his species—and the reader feels like weeping too, for this one forlorn creature or for the Fall of Man. Whatever you chose to read into it, this passage, like the whole book, is intensely moving.

First edition: London, Faber, 1955 (hardcover)
First American edition: New York, Harcourt, Brace, 1962 (hardcover)
Most recent editions: London, Faber, and New York, Pocket (paperbacks)

20

ALFRED BESTER

The Stars My Destination

The title is misleading, for this is not a novel about flight to the stars. The action takes place within our solar system, and much of it on Earth. It opens in space, however, on a drifting, wrecked spaceship where one man survives. He is Gulliver Foyle, Mechanic's Mate 3rd Class, and he has been on his own for 170 days. Another space vessel, the *Vorga*, ignores his distress flares and passes him by. This casual act of inhumanity galvanizes Foyle; he changes from the 'stereotype common man' into a passionate angel of revenge, determined to survive, escape, and hunt down the owners and crew of the *Vorga*. He manages to bring his crippled ship to the Sargasso Asteroid, an orbiting junkyard inhabited by 'the only savages of the twenty-fourth century; descendants of a research team of scientists that had been lost and marooned in the asteroid belt two centuries before'. These people receive him happily, tattoo his face so that it resembles a Maori mask, and then attempt to marry him off to one of their girls. Obsessed with revenge, Foyle finds a working rocket ship and blasts away from the asteroid, heading for Earth.

The colourful culture which Bester portrays in this book is even more outrageous than the one he depicted in *The Demolished Man*. Teleportation by mental means takes the place of the ESP which featured in the earlier novel. The ability to transport oneself over short distances, using only the power of the mind, is supposed to have been discovered by a man named Jaunte; hence the act of teleportation is known as jaunting. It is a skill which has to be learned, but it leads to immense social changes. 'There were land riots as the jaunting poor deserted slums to squat in plains and forests . . . There was a revolution in home and office building, labyrinths and masking devices had to be introduced to prevent unlawful entry by jaunting. There were crashes and panics and strikes and famines as pre-jaunte industries failed . . . Crime waves swept the planets and satellites as the underworlds took to jaunting with the night around the clock . . . There came

) a hideous return to the worst prudery of Victorianism as society fought the sexual and moral dangers of jaunting . . .' It is extremely far-fetched, but again it makes for a good story.

On his return to Earth Gully Foyle learns how to jaunte. He learns many other things in the course of his quest for revenge on Presteign of Presteign, the powerful owner of the spacefleet which includes the *Vorga*. The scene changes swiftly, from Presteign's eccentric mansion in New York, haunted by his beautiful albino daughter who can see only in the infra-red, to a prison which is located in immeasurable caverns beneath the Pyrenees, to the 'Freak Factory' in Trenton where Foyle has his facial tattoos removed. At one point he is confronted by 'a shrieking mob of post-operative patients, bird men with fluttering wings, mermaids dragging themselves along the floor like seals, hermaphrodites, giants, pygmies, two-headed twins, centaurs and a mewling sphinx'. Bester's inventiveness is prodigious, his manic glee infectious.

The narrative builds up tremendous energy, with the action flitting from Earth to outer space and back to Earth; from Canberra to Shanghai to Rome and once more to New York as Foyle hunts his enemies, dealing one by one with the crew-members of the *Vorga*. The plot becomes ever more complex—impossible to describe in brief—and is finally resolved in a spectacular synaesthetic climax in which towers of drunken typography totter across the page. Earth is almost destroyed by the super-explosive PYRE, but Foyle puts an end to all war by distributing the dangerous stuff to the common folk, saying 'I've blown the last secret wide open. No more secrets from now on . . . I've handed life and death back to the people who do the living and dying.' He also becomes the first man capable of jaunting to the stars. A note of hope and idealism is sounded, a fitting conclusion to one of the most justly celebrated of all American sf novels.

First edition: London, Sidgwick and Jackson, 1956 (hardcover; under the title *Tiger! Tiger!*)

First American edition: New York, Signet Books, 1957 (paperback; as *The Stars My Destination*, which has since become accepted as the definitive title)

Most recent editions: London, Penguin (as *Tiger! Tiger!*), and New York, Berkley (paperbacks)

21
JOHN CHRISTOPHER
The Death of Grass

This is commonly perceived as another British Disaster Novel, school of John Wyndham. Indeed that is what it is, though it has a sharper edge—a more disturbing, cutting quality to it—than either *The Day of the Triffids* or *The Kraken Wakes*. John Christopher (real name Christopher Samuel Youd, born 1922) had already contributed a number of stories to the British and American sf magazines. With this novel he became a bestseller.

The book begins gently, introducing us to a comfortable, middle-class English family called Custance. One branch of the family owns a farm in a secluded valley of the Lake District; the other branch, headed by John Custance, lives in London. They have few problems, although they worry occasionally about 'the poor wretched Chinese'—'Chinks' as John calls them. There is a famine in China, where the rice crops have been destroyed by the new Chung-Li virus, and two hundred million people are dying. It all seems very far away, but soon John hears from a friend who works in government that the virus has mutated and spread. It now attacks all grasses, including wheat, oats, barley and rye—and it has reached Britain.

> 'Damn it!' John said. 'This isn't China.'
> 'No,' Roger said. 'This is a country of fifty million people that imports nearly half its food requirements.'
> 'We might have to tighten our belts.'
> 'A tight belt,' said Roger, 'looks silly on a skeleton.'

Within a year the whole world is affected, and all the scientists' attempts to curb the virus have come to nothing. Despite rationing, the British attempt to carry on as normal—until John hears from his friend that the army is about to seal off the major cities. Only one-third of the population can survive on root crops and fish; the government has decided that the city-dwellers must be eliminated. John gathers his family and begins a frantic car journey northwards from London, heading for the safety of his brother's farm. With the aid of a gunsmith who has joined their party, they shoot their way through a roadblock to escape the city. English civilization is crumbling very rapidly indeed.

It is a tense, exciting narrative. The bulk of it is taken up in describing the journey. The party is forced to abandon its cars in Yorkshire and walk the last ninety miles through open countryside. They witness rape, looting and murder. They are themselves obliged to rob and kill in order to survive. Middle-class morality has not prepared them for this ordeal, nor for the need to take ruthless life-or-death decisions at every turn. Yet they carry on. By the time they reach the valley it comes as no surprise to the reader when John's party, now swollen to thirty-four people, is refused entry. The happy valley has been barricaded from the world; John's brother, David, has his own band of mouths to feed. The outsiders decide to take the valley by force, using a route known only to John. In the ensuing fight David Custance is killed. The valley has been gained, John Custance's family is safe, but he compares himself bitterly with Cain.

There is no grand *deus ex machina*, no cure for the viral plague. It is a happy ending only insofar as the characters who have been our immediate concern throughout the novel succeed in reaching their haven. Civilization and common humanity have lost out. One could accuse John Christopher of cynicism, but one could also say that *The Death of Grass* blows a much-needed cold draught of reality through the cosy parlour of 1950s disaster fiction.

First edition: London, Michael Joseph, 1956 (hardcover)
First American edition: New York, Simon and Schuster, 1957
(hardcover, retitled *No Blade of Grass*)
Most recent editions: London, Sphere, and New York, Avon
(paperbacks)

22

ARTHUR C. CLARKE
The City and the Stars

'Like a glowing jewel, the city lay upon the breast of the desert. Once it had known change and alteration, but now Time passed it by. Night and day fled across the desert's face, but in the streets of Diaspar it was always afternoon . . .' Arthur C. Clarke writes an unusually pure form of science fiction. Many sf novels, especially the better ones, do not necessarily conform to the popular stereotype of what a good science fiction story should be (far-future setting, space travel, alien beings and wonderful machines). This one does, and moreover does it beautifully. Originally written in a shorter form in the 1940s and published under the title 'Against the Fall of Night', it reached its definitive shape in 1956, and I doubt whether Clarke has written a better novel since. His later works include the world-famous *2001: A Space Odyssey* (1968) as well as the highly-acclaimed *Rendezvous With Rama* (1973) and *The Fountains of Paradise* (1979), none of which I have chosen to describe in the present volume. It seems to me that the later works are inherently old-fashioned—good as they are in their way, they offer more of the same: yesterday's pleasures.

The City and the Stars has the simplicity and the resonance of a fairy tale. Diaspar is the last city on Earth, and it has endured for a thousand million years. It is completely self-contained, sealed off, run by miraculous machinery. Its citizens have no navels, for they are born by unnatural means. The 'pattern' for each individual is stored in the city's memory banks, and everyone is incarnated anew at intervals of several millennia. Nor do these people have any urge to explore, to leave Diaspar and brave the endless desert which now covers the planet. They have infinite amusement—games, sexual play, arts and sciences—immediately to hand. In any case, they have been conditioned to shun the outside—their legends say that humanity once ruled a galactic empire but was beaten back to the planet Earth by terrible Invaders from beyond. To venture into space once more, even to step outside the city's walls, would be foolishly to incur the wrath of these Invaders.

Our hero, Alvin, is a sport—the first completely new individual to have been 'born' in Diaspar for countless millions of years. He is consumed by an inexplicable urge to leave the city, and to this end he explores the air-vents and all other possible avenues of escape. From a high tower he is able to look out over the desert and to see the stars as night falls. It is a moment of epiphany. With the aid of the city's Central Computer, he discovers an underground railway system which still has one functioning line. At last he has found an exit. The automatic train carries him away to the vale of Lys, a forgotten oasis inhabited by a tribe of telepathic pastoralists, and thence he eventually makes his way to the stars.

As is usual in Clarke's fiction, the characterization is minimal, the dialogue embarrassingly stilted, but the story succeeds in evoking a childlike sense of wonderment. Alvin's is the archetypal science fiction quest: to break out of an enclosed world, to discover the true nature of reality, and to return with star-begotten gifts which will revitalize a stagnant society. Like Asimov's *The End of Eternity*, like numerous other sf novels before and since, Clarke's book ends with an optimistic surge: 'Elsewhere the stars were still young and the light of morning lingered; and along the path he once had followed, Man would one day go again.'

First edition: New York, Harcourt, 1956 (hardcover)
First British edition: London, Muller, 1956 (hardcover)
Most recent editions: London, Corgi, and New York, NAL (paperbacks)

23

ROBERT A. HEINLEIN
The Door Into Summer

In contrast to his earlier *The Puppet Masters*, this novel by Hein-lein is a mellow and charming work. It features time-travel, a little girl and a pussy-cat—but it is not nearly as twee as that thumbnail description makes it sound. Apparently written at great speed (not that it suffers for that), *The Door Into Summer* was originally published as a serial in the *Magazine of Fantasy and Science Fiction*—which, by the late 1950s, was overtaking *Galaxy* as the most important of the American sf periodicals.

The story opens in 1970 (the future!). The hero, Dan Davis, is a talented engineer, designer of the domestic robots 'Hired Girl' and 'Flexible Frank'. He is also a cat lover. Thwarted in business by a treacherous partner and betrayed by his fiancée, he decides to take the Long Sleep in search of a 'door into summer'. That is to say, he invests his money cannily, then allows himself to be frozen into suspended animation, to awaken three decades later with swollen investments and a fresh start in life. The only per-son he regrets leaving behind is little Frederica ('Ricky'), his part-ner's step-daughter: 'Ricky had been "my girl" since she was a six-year-old at Sandia, with hair ribbons and big dark solemn eyes. I was "going to marry her" when she grew up . . .' He also regrets leaving his puss, Petronius Arbiter.

His plans go awry. Dan finds himself a pauper in the year 2000. It is a highly-automated world, one which he helped to create with his robotic designs of thirty years earlier, yet he has no recognized place in it. He has been cheated out of his 'inheri-tance'. Desperate to put things right, he contacts the inventor of a top-secret time machine and succeeds in throwing himself back to 1970. As in most tales which involve the paradoxes of time travel, the plot is complex. It is also delightfully absurd. All ends happily, with Dan getting the money, the girl (her age suitably adjusted) *and* the damned cat—and they return to the 21st cen-tury to live blissfully ever after amidst the fruits of Dan's labour.

In short, the novel is a piece of flummery. Yet it is interesting in that it casts light on the central obsessions which run through all Heinlein's fiction. As is the case with his famous short story, '—All You Zombies—', a twelve-page epic of time-travel and sex change in which the protagonist becomes his own mother and father, this novel illustrates a kind of solipsism, the belief that one is alone in an unreal world and that the individual's only means of elevation is to pull himself up by his bootstraps. This gells with Heinlein's 'political' philosophy of self-reliance and rugged individualism, but it all seems rather sad, and ultimately futile. But Heinlein is full of contradictions: the *texture* of this novel is anything but sad; on the contrary, it is a light, bright, jolly read, perhaps the slickest in the author's entire canon. The engineering details are very well handled, and the narrative carries a surprising amount of conviction throughout. I recommend *The Door Into Summer*, for its texture rather than its substance, to anyone who has been puzzled by the extent of Heinlein's reputation. It shows a great popular writer, a 'natural', at the height of his powers.

First edition: New York, Doubleday, 1957 (hardcover)
First British edition: London, Panther, 1960 (paperback)
Most recent editions: New York, NAL, and London, Pan (paperbacks)

24

JOHN WYNDHAM
The Midwich Cuckoos

For this novel—written during the early rock'n'roll era when 'Teddy Boys' of menacing appearance were roaming the streets of Britain—Wyndham came up with a clever idea which resolves itself into the perfect nightmare image of that 1950s problem, the Generation Gap. Not that the novel has anything whatsoever to do with rock music or Teddy Boys: it begins as if it is another of Wyndham's 'cosy catstrophes' (apt phrase courtesy of Brian Aldiss), in a quiet pastoral English setting.

The narrator and his wife are returning to their home in the little village of Midwich. They are stopped by a policeman, as an army truck lumbers past. 'Revolution in Midwich?' jokes the narrator. In fact, something much more serious has taken place. An alien spacecraft has landed in the village, and for a night and a day it casts a mysterious spell on the place. As in the tale of Sleeping Beauty, all living things slumber. The affected area is a perfect circle, two miles in diameter, and anyone who attempts to enter it immediately loses consciousness. The army can do nothing, but when the spacecraft leaves everyone suddenly wakes up. There have been a few deaths from exposure, but otherwise everybody is apparently unharmed. The villagers come to call the experience the 'Dayout'.

The consequences of the Dayout take nine months to reach term. Every Midwich woman of childbearing age has become pregnant, suggesting that each of them has been inseminated by the alien visitors, who no-one even saw. All of them give birth to perfect, beautiful babies, who have one unusual feature— golden eyes. The next odd consequence is that a few mothers who have moved away from Midwich return there, carrying their babies. They say the infants have *compelled* them to return. It seems that this sleepy village is the adoptive nest for a clutch of superhuman 'cuckoos'. As the children grow, their frightening powers become ever more apparent. They communicate with each other telepathically, perhaps they even share a common consciousness.

By the time the children are nine years old they have the physical build of teenagers; they are tall, blonde, golden-eyed youths and maidens, who keep close together and seem to have a faintly menacing aura . . .

In due course these inscrutable juvenile delinquents begin to kill. A normal Midwich youth is compelled to drive his car into a wall; when his brother tries to take revenge, he ends up turning the gun on himself, forced to commit suicide by the alien children. The local people decide to take action, with the vicar giving philosophical support: 'They have the *look* of *genus homo*, but not the nature. And since they are of *another* kind, and murder is, by definition, the killing of one's *own* kind, can the killing of one of them by us be, in fact, murder? . . . Since they are another species, are we not fully entitled—indeed, have we not perhaps a duty?—to fight them in order to protect our own species?' But when a mob tries to attack the children, the latter simply use their suasive powers to make the villagers fight each other, leaving four dead. After this incident, even the most rational and humane of the normal folk are forced to the decision that the children should be destroyed. By devious means this brutal end is finally achieved.

It is a novel which poses an unpleasant moral dilemma, and comes to a harsh conclusion. At the finish one cannot help feel a pang of regret, despite the fact that Wyndham has been careful to keep the reader's sympathy on the side of the regular human race. If the book is read as a parable of the generation gap, though I doubt whether that is what the author intended, it becomes very frightening indeed.

First edition: London, Michael Joseph, 1957 (hardcover)
First American edition: New York, Ballantine, 1958 (paperback)
Most recent edition: London, Penguin (paperback)

25

BRIAN W. ALDISS
Non-Stop

The first thing that needs to be said about this book is that it owes an imaginative debt to 'Universe' (1941), a novella by Robert Heinlein. In that story we are introduced to savages living in a mysterious artificial environment; before the end we discover they are descendants of the original crew of a vast space-vessel which is embarked on a generations-long voyage to the stars. Aldiss's novel follows the same pattern, with significant new twists. Such Generation Starship stories have been written by other authors since Heinlein and Aldiss, and have become a recognized convention of modern sf. It was not the first, but *Non-Stop* is probably still the best treatment of the theme. It also happens to be the first published novel of Brian Wilson Aldiss (born 1925), who is one of the most considerable talents in contemporary British sf.

Non-Stop differs from most of the sf of its decade in that it has an anti-heroic tone. The central character, Roy Complain, seems petty, mean, vindictive, and a bit stupid, although he grows in moral stature as the narrative unfolds. But then *all* the characters are mean and petty, hemmed in by their peculiar circumstances. Like later novels by Aldiss, this is essentially a book about 'little people'; in this case we discover that they are little both metaphorically and literally, since few of the characters are over five feet tall. Roy Complain is a member of the Greene tribe, which dwells in a claustrophobic world of endless corridors and identical small rooms. The corridors are choked with a plant growth which thrives in the artificial light. These plants are called the 'ponics', and they are a principal source of food. There are no windows in this hellish environment, and the tribesfolk have only a hazy idea that there may be an 'outside'. They subscribe to a home-made religion, full of decayed Freudian jargon, which teaches them they are on board a 'Ship'—but no-one seems to know what a ship is.

The opening chapters are taken up with bickering and fighting.

The story begins to grip the reader only when Complain and a few of his comrades break free of the tribe and set out on a journey of discovery. Their trek through the ponics is fraught with danger. They encounter human mutants, mysterous 'Giants' who maintain the ship's mechanisms, and—most terrifying of all—mutated rats. A high point of the journey is their discovery of the Sea, an inexplicable, functionless sheet of water which is the most beautiful thing they have ever beheld. It is in fact a swimming pool. Eventually they reach Forwards, a fabled realm of civilization; here the ponics have been cut back and everything is relatively tidy and well-ordered. But even the educated inhabitants of Forwards are unaware of the true nature of their world.

The story proceeds through a series of ingenious revelations until the break-up of the ship in the last chapter. A marvellous epiphany occurs near the end when Complain and his new-found girlfriend, Laur, enter an airlock where there is a window. 'Beyond the window, with stars tossed prodigiously into it like jewels into an emperor's sack, roared the unending stillness of space. It was something beyond the comprehension to gaze upon, the mightiest paradox of all, for although it gave an impression of unyielding blackness, every last pocket of it glistened with multi-coloured pangs of light.' It is the moment of conceptual breakthrough, that magical moment which so much science fiction strives to capture.

Non-Stop offers a number of conventional sf pleasures, but it does more. Unlike the Heinlein novella, it refuses to resolve itself into a happy, wish-fulfilling ending. The characters discover that they are the victims of a cosmic joke: ironies abound, the struggle goes on.

First edition: London, Faber, 1958 (hardcover)
First American edition: New York, Criterion, 1959
(hardcover, as *Starship*)
Most recent editions: London, Pan, and New York, Avon
(paperbacks; the latter as *Starship*)

26

JAMES BLISH

A Case of Conscience

This book mixes elements of hard science (physics, biology and chemistry) with theological, sociological and even literary speculations. The author's range of intellectual reference is astonishing. Brian Aldiss was not exaggerating when he said that Blish had 'one of the most powerful intellects—and one of the most diverse stores of knowledge, I would say—ever to apply itself to science fiction.' This seems all the more surprising when one recalls that James Blish (1921-1975) was a *genre* sf writer who had cut his teeth in the American pulp magazines of the 1940s. But he also happened to have a degree in biology, and had worked for a large pharmaceutical company before becoming a full-time writer. Prior to *A Case of Conscience* he was best known for his rather pretentious space-operatic stories in the 'Okie' series, several of which were combined to form the book *Earthman, Come Home* (1955)

A Case of Conscience is about a planet called Lithia, and the central character, Father Ramon Ruiz-Sanchez, is a Jesuit biologist. Together with three other scientists, he has been sent to Lithia to determine whether the planet is suitable to serve as a way-station for human spacefarers. The world is inhabited by a highly-intelligent species of reptile. These Lithians grow to heights of twelve feet and resemble dinosaurs, but they are exceedingly well-mannered and peaceful. In fact, Ruiz-Sanchez is elated—and appalled—to discover that their society is, to all appearances, *perfect*; they have no crime, no inequality, no unhappiness—and no conception of God.

The Lithians live in pottery houses, surrounded by sea and jungle. Their world has never known an ice age, and dangerous wildlife is almost non-existent. Lungfish bark on the shores, while small jumping lizards and larger reptiles roam the forests. There are numerous insects and poisonous plants, rendering the environment uncomfortable to human beings, but the possibility remains that Lithia is in reality a Garden of Eden with unfallen, sinless inhabitants. There is even a Tree in this paradise—known to the natives as the 'Message Tree'. It is the centre of a sophisticated communications network, and provides the novel with its most memorable image: 'A sequoia-like giant . . . As the winds came and went along the valley, the tree nodded and swayed . . . With every movement, the tree's root system, which underlay the entire city, tugged and distorted the buried crystalline cliff upon which the city had been founded . . . At every such pressure, the buried cliff responded with a vast heart-pulse of radio waves . . .'

Ruiz-Sanchez comes to believe that the Lithians, and their whole world, are the creations of the Devil, a snare set for humanity by the Great Adversary. Blish does not endorse this view—the novel is a piece of hard sf, not a religious fantasy—but he explores his hero's agony of conscience with considerable delicacy. He states in a foreword: 'The author . . . is an agnostic with no position at all in these matters. It was my intention to write about a man, not a body of doctrine.'

It is a knotty, involving narrative, with a density of scientific and theological thought which is rare in American sf. Unfortunately, the creative pressure falls away in the second half, when the action moves back to Earth, though even here there are some splendid passages, such as the description of the growth to consciousness of Egtverchi, a Lithian 'baby', which is surely one of the finest pieces of science-fictional prose poetry ever penned. Blish's most notable later work is the historical novel *Dr Mirabilis* (1964), about Friar Roger Bacon. Despite the fact that Blish regarded it as a thematic sequel to *A Case of Conscience*, it can scarcely be claimed for sf.

First edition: New York, Ballantine, 1958 (paperback)
First British edition: London, Faber, 1959 (hardcover)
Most recent edition: London, Arrow (paperback)

27
ROBERT A. HEINLEIN
Have Space-Suit—Will Travel

It has an awful title, but it is a significant book. This is the twelfth and last of the series of juvenile sf novels which Heinlein published, one a year, from 1947 onwards. Intended for bright teen-agers, they have been read copiously by adults—indeed, most paperback reprints give no indication that the books were meant originally for children. Many admirers of Heinlein's writing believe that the better of these volumes are among his most satisfying works. Earlier books which stand out from the rest of the series include *Red Planet* (1949), *Starman Jones* (1953) and *Citizen of the Galaxy* (1957), but none of them is quite such a bravura masterpiece as *Have Space Suit—Will Travel*.

The setting is 'Centerville', USA, in the near future. The hero, Kip Russell, is an intelligent lad in his late teens who is obsessed with flying to the moon. His father tells him: 'A man almost always gets what he wants badly enough. I am sure you will get to the Moon someday, one way or another.' We hear the voice of Heinlein the pedagogue in the opening chapters of this book, advising the youth of America to *excel*. Like a latter-day Horatio Alger character, Kip works himself into a fine frenzy of ambition. When a soap company advertises a free trip to the Moon in return for a winning sales slogan, Kip sends in no fewer than 5,782 entries. But he fails to win outright, and receives the consolation prize of a second-hand space suit. Heinlein's lengthy description of this suit, and of Kip's heroic labours to make it fully functional, is remarkably engrossing: it almost adds up to a mini-*Zen and the Art of Space-Suit Maintenance*. But then, Heinlein knows whereof he speaks—he worked on the design of high-altitude pressure suits during World War II.

Soon Kip gets his reward. Before selling the suit in order to pay his college fees, he decides to wear it one last time, out in the fields at night. A flying saucer homes in on his suit radio; he is knocked unconscious and awakes to find himself halfway to the Moon. He meets Peewee, an eleven-year-old girl who corrects

Kip's grammar, uses phrases like 'semantic inadequacy', and describes herself as a genius. They have been kidnapped by menacing aliens. Also a prisoner on the ship is the 'Mother Thing', a sympathetic alien who converses telepathically with Kip and Peewee. A comforting presence, she is almost like a run-in for Spielberg's *E.T.*. Kip's space suit proves very useful when they reach the Moon: it is roomy enough for both him and the Mother Thing.

Every scene in the novel is vividly realized, a clever blend of humour, excitement and technical detail. The book is like a telescope, starting small but opening out in a succession of widening circles—first Centersville, then the Moon, then Pluto, then twenty-seven light years out to Vega (in a matter of hours—'Dr Einstein must be known as "Whirligig Albert" among his cemetery neighbours,' thinks Kip). Finally they travel right out of the Galaxy to the Lesser Magellanic Cloud, where Kip and Peewee have to stand trial as representatives of the entire human race. Needless to say, they acquit themselves well before the intergalactic court, and are duly returned to Earth by the Mother Thing, who, it turns out, is actually 'a cop on the beat'. Kip gets his place in college.

Have Space Suit—Will Travel may sound ridiculous in outline, but it is a wonderful story, beautifully told. It is the last Heinlein novel I have chosen to describe in the present volume. He has written many books since, including the bestselling *Stranger in a Strange Land* (1961), but to my mind his slimmer, less hectoring novels of the 1950s stand at the peak of his achievement.

First edition: New York, Scribner's, 1958 (hardcover)
First British edition: London, Gollancz, 1970 (hardcover)
Most recent editions: New York, Del Rey, and London, NEL (paperbacks)

28

PHILIP K. DICK

Time Out of Joint

We come to the late great Philip Kindred Dick (1928-1982), one of science fiction's cult authors. Although none of his books was a bestseller on first publication, he elicited an extraordinary loyalty and protectiveness from his many admirers—particularly in Europe, where he is viewed by some as the greatest American sf writer. But it took a long time for that reputation to grow. His early novels, including *Solar Lottery* (1955), *The World Jones Made* (1956) and *Eye in the Sky* (1957), were all issued as paperback originals and tended to get lost in the flow of pulp publishing. *Time Out of Joint* was his first hardcover book.

For the first third of its length it scarcely reads like science fiction at all. It seems to be a pleasant, mildly witty novel of everyday life in the contemporary United States. It is the story of Ragle Gumm, a man in his mid-40s who lives quietly with his sister and brother-in-law and their ten-year-old son. The only peculiar detail is the means by which Ragle earns his money. He spends each day filling in the entry form for a newspaper competition called 'Where Will The Little Green Man Be Next?'. He always wins the competition, and has done so without fail for three years. It has become a tiresome chore, but it is a steady living and he feels unable to stop.

Gradually, insidiously, the family's sense of reality begins to break down. Many of the incidents are humorous. For instance, Ragle finds a tattered magazine which features a photograph of 'A lovely blonde Norse-looking actress . . . She smiled in an amazingly sweet manner, a jejune but intimate smile that held him . . . The girl leaned forward, and most of her bosom spilled out and displayed itself. It looked to be the smoothest, firmest, most natural bosom in the world . . . He did not recognize the girl's name. But he thought, There's the answer to our need of a mother. Look at that.' He shows the picture to his brother-in-law, who also fails to recognize the actress. The reader is told that it is a photograph of Marilyn Monroe, but in this America of

1959 Marilyn does not exist . . .

Soon Ragle is picking up mysterious messages on his nephew's crystal radio set: they appear to be coming from invisible aircraft, possibly spaceships, overhead. He hears his own name, *Ragle Gumm*, and his feeling of paranoia rises sharply: 'I'm retarded—psychotic. Hallucinations . . . Infantile and lunatic. What am I doing, sitting here? . . . Imagining that I'm the centre of a vast effort by millions of men and women, involving billions of dollars and infinite work . . . a universe revolving around me.' The irony is that Ragle's surmise is exactly correct—this world *does* revolve around him. It is an artificial environment which has been expressly designed to keep him docile as he performs vital work of great military importance. In reality it is the year 1998, and he is in the midst of a war of attrition between the 'One Happy World' dictatorship and rebels on the Moon. Ragle's task, disguised as a Little-Green-Man contest, is to predict the pattern of incoming missiles, since he has an uncanny talent for guessing where the next strikes will take place. In order to prevent him from questioning the purpose of the war, and hence losing heart, the government has forced him into a 'withdrawal psychosis'—a retreat to the world of his childhood, a make-believe small-town paradise of 1959.

The predicament which is dramatized in *Time Out of Joint* is a metaphor for the workings of the US military-industrial complex. In some ways it is a prescient novel, a book about the 'home front' of the Vietnam war, written ten years ahead of its time. Many of the small details of Dick's imagined future are spot-on—his description of punk youths with spiky hair and tattooed cheeks for example. In this fiction, a cosy suburban scene is riven by nightmare, a nightmare which may have seemed far-fetched in 1959, but which now strikes us as strangely truthful.

First edition: New York, Lippincott, 1959 (hardcover)
First British edition: London, Science Fiction Book Club, 1961 (hardcover)
Most recent editions: London, Penguin, and New York, Bluejay (paperbacks)

29
PAT FRANK
Alas, Babylon

This story about a nuclear holocaust and its immediate aftermath
has long been a steady seller in the United States, though it
appears to have made little impression elsewhere. Perhaps this is
because it gives a very American (and now badly dated) picture
of atomic doom. It is an American pastorale, a hymn to self-
sufficiency and the virtues of small-town life. In this novel the
atomic war is *liberating*: it makes a man of you. That must be
morally repugnant to most Europeans in the 1980s, yet it is a
skilfully-written book, and a curiously compelling one.

The hero, Randy Bragg, is a privileged loafer who lives in a big
old house in Fort Repose, central Florida. His garden is 'bright
with poinsettias and bougainvillia, hibiscus, camellias, gardenias
and flame vine'. His neighbour, a spinster who operates the local
telephone system, believes him to be 'a hermit, and a snob, and a
nigger-lover'. One day Randy receives a telegram from his
brother, an intelligence officer in the Strategic Air Command. It
contains the code phrase 'Alas, Babylon', which means the Russians are about to launch a pre-emptive nuclear strike on the USA.

Randy spends a busy day laying in groceries (and booze),
alerting his girlfriend and a local doctor, and preparing for the
arrival of his sister-in-law and her two children. After collecting
his relatives from an airport some hours' drive away, he falls into
an exhausted sleep, to be awoken by a distant rumbling and
strange lights in the sky. The war has begun: Miami and various
other targets in Florida have already been hit. 'Gazing at the
glow to the south, Randy was witnessing, from a distance of
almost two hundred miles, the incineration of a million people.'
Another bomb goes off at closer range and one of the children is
temporarily blinded. Chaos ensues.

The author has a grim word to say about the inadequacy of
preparations for such a war: 'This chaos did not result from a
breakdown in Civil Defence. It was simply that Civil Defence, as
a realistic buffer against thermo-nuclear war, did not exist.

Evacuation zones for entire cities had never been publicly announced, out of fear of "spreading alarm".' Nevertheless, the inhabitants of Fort Repose are very lucky. Their main problems are caused by heart attacks, destitute refugees, escaped convicts, failed power supplies. Most of the radiation and serious fall-out seems to pass them by.

Now the pastoral idyll begins, and Randy comes into his own as a leader of men and women. He gives up drinking and gains is on physical fitness. It is not a bad existence, being head of his own small community in the wake of a disaster which has effectively destroyed central government. After all, there is no income tax to worry about. Randy eventually forms a vigilante troop to maintain law and order in Fort Repose. As the months go by, life settles into a peaceful round of hard work and simple pleasures: they hunt and fish, grow corn and oranges, search out a salt supply. Exactly a year after the Day of the Bombs they hear news from the outside world: America has won the war, but by now nobody cares. Pat Frank (real name Harry Hart, born 1907) narrates all this with great expertise. His book has something of the appeal of George Stewart's *Earth Abides*, although it lacks that work's sweep and grandeur. Fundamentally a cosy fantasy, *Alas, Babylon* belongs very much to its period. It would be impossible to write such a hopeful novel about nuclear war today.

First edition: New York, Lippincott, 1959 (hardcover)
First British edition: London, Constable, 1959 (hardcover)
Most recent edition: New York, Bantam
(paperback—41 printings by 1983)

30

WALTER M. MILLER

A Canticle for Leibowitz

Like James Blish, Walter M. Miller (born 1923) is a science fiction writer with a strong interest in Christianity, but he differs in that he is evidently a believer rather than an agnostic. *A Canticle for Leibowitz* remains his only novel. When it was first published it did not carry the 'sf' label despite the fact that its three parts had originally appeared (in shorter form) as stories in the *Magazine of Fantasy and Science Fiction*. Miller wrote a goodly number of short stories for the American sf magazines throughout the 1950s—the best of these are collected in *Conditionally Human* (1962) and *The View from the Stars* (1964)—but on the completion of his novel he ceased writing altogether.

The story opens in the former United States of America, six centuries after a devastating nuclear war. The first third of the novel concerns an exciting discovery made by Brother Francis Gerard, a novice monk. Scrabbling in some ancient ruins, he finds a fallout survival shelter which contains a few relics of the blessed I.E. Leibowitz, legendary founder of his Order. The most valuable item is the blueprint of a circuit design, although the relics also include a grocery list and racing forms (whatever they might be). Almost all books and documents have been destroyed during the 'Age of Simplification' which followed the nuclear war. Brother Francis's findings, fragmentary as they are, represent a treasure trove to the monks, who are slowly, painfully, almost blindly, trying to accumulate and preserve the scattered knowledge of the past. Francis spends fifteen years copying the precious blueprint and illuminating his copy with gold leaf, even though he is utterly ignorant of the document's meaning. He then departs on a pilgrimage to New Rome, and is robbed of his life's work along the way. But Leibowitz—one-time weapons scientist turned 'booklegger'—is canonized. Francis's discoveries have not been in vain.

It is a touching fable, full of pathos and humour. In the middle section of the book another six hundred years have passed. It is now a time of renaissance, and of wars between princelings. To the monastery of St Leibowitz comes the leading natural scientist of the day, a scholar-aristocrat called Thon Taddeo. He is astonished to find that the monks have built a workable electric arclight, powered by the muscles of novices. He is even more astonished when he examines the Leibowitz Memorabilia: ancient texts and blueprints, scraps of scientific papers, mathematical equations—all dating from the mid-20th century. On the basis of this material, and with confidence in his own coldly intellectual genius, Taddeo predicts: 'A century from now, men will fly through the air in mechanical birds. Metal carriages will race along roads of man-made stone. There will be buildings of thirty stories, ships that go under the sea, machines to perform all works.'

In the final part of the novel yet another six centuries have gone by, and Taddeo's foretellings have been surpassed. Once more the world is able to manufacture nuclear weapons—and to carry its wars into outer space. As the bombs begin to fall, the last abbot of the Leibowitzian Order arranges for a number of his monks to escape the planet aboard a starship, bearing with them on microfilm the much-augmented Memorabilia. History repeats itself: the abbot dies amid the debris of his monastery, while the monks of St Leibowitz, and the Christian faith, fly away to endure on the world of another star. It is a moving end to a beautifully-written novel, rich in character and ironic detail, at the same time funny and sad. Flawed for some readers by its unabashedly religious content, and in particular by its emphasis on the fallen nature of humanity, *A Canticle for Leibowitz* is nevertheless one of the greatest works of modern science fiction.

First edition: New York, Lippincott, 1959 (hardcover)
First British edition: London, Weidenfeld and Nicolson, 1960 (hardcover)
Most recent editions: New York, Bantam, and London, Corgi (paperbacks)

31
KURT VONNEGUT
The Sirens of Titan

Wry, sentimental, wacky and hilarious, Kurt Vonnegut (born 1922) is now one of America's bestselling novelists. Not so when this book slipped out, almost invisibly, as a paperback original. The author had published one previous novel, the satirical *Player Piano* (1952, and in my view of less interest than Bernard Wolfe's *Limbo* which appeared in the same year). It was with *The Sirens of Titan* that Vonnegut found his voice, and it remains the best of his several ventures into science fiction. That 'voice' is of prime importance. Vonnegut writes in a wide-eyed but knowing style, falsely innocent, which uses short sentences and one-sentence paragraphs, banal rhymes, occasional doodles and babytalk. It is not a voice which appeals to everyone—some find it too coy and cutesy—but millions of readers, particularly the young, have responded to it warmly.

The Sirens of Titan is the one about millionaire astronaut Winston Niles Rumfoord, who flies his spaceship into a chrono-synclastic infundibulum (a space/time warp in plainer sf-speak). He and his pet dog now exist as 'wave phenomena—apparently pulsing in a distorted spiral with its origin in the Sun and its terminal in Betelgeuse.' They also pulse through time, able to view everything that has ever been and will be.

It is the one about the Reverend Bobby Denton, crusading evangelist and opponent of space travel: 'You want to fly through space? God has already given you the most wonderful space ship in all creation! Yes! Speed? You want speed? The space ship God has given you goes sixty-six thousand miles an hour . . . He's given you a space ship that will carry billions of men, women and children! Yes! And they don't have to stay strapped in chairs or wear fishbowls over their heads. No!' This reminds one of the idea of Spaceship Earth, promoted by the ecology movement in the 1970s.

It is about Malachi Constant, son of a know-nothing billionaire who owes his business success to the Gideon Bible. Malachi feels that there must be more to life than endless Hollywood parties can offer, and that there is some significant truth about the universe which he is destined to find. He is duly press-ganged into Winston Rumfoord's private army on the planet Mars. His memory wiped clean, and answering to the name of 'Unk', he has sundry adventures in the caves of Mercury before returning to Earth and becoming an unwitting scapegoat of Rumfoord's new religion, the Church of God the Utterly Indifferent.

It is also about Salo, an alien being from the planet Tralfamadore in the Lesser Magellanic Cloud, whom Rumfoord encounters on Titan, one of Saturn's moons. Salo has been there for 200,000 years, awaiting a spare part for his grounded flying-saucer. His mission is to carry an important message across the universe. The text of this message is sealed in lead and hangs around his neck. When he reads it to Malachi and Rumfoord it turns out to be just one word: *'Greetings'*.

In short, *The Sirens of Titan* is a very funny novel about the Meaningless Of It All. The whole of human history has been guided by the Tralfamadorians with the express purpose of providing a replacement part for Salo's space vessel. Salo's galaxy-spinning mission is simply to say to whoever may be listening: 'Here I am, here I am, here I am.' What else is there to say? God, if He exists, is utterly indifferent to the sufferings of human beings and alien entities alike—and the only appropriate response to such an absurd universe is an explosion of laughter.

First edition: New York, Dell, 1959 (paperback)
First British edition: London, Gollancz, 1962 (hardcover)
Most recent editions: New York, Dell, and London, Coronet (paperbacks)

32
ALGIS BUDRYS
Rogue Moon

This novel is an oddity. It was highly original in its day, and in some ways it prefigures the 'New Wave' science fiction of the late 1960s with its disturbing emphasis on psychology rather than engineering. Algis Budrys (born 1931) was still in his twenties when he wrote the book, though he was already well-known to American readers for his near-future thriller *Who?* (1958).

Rogue Moon is about a scientist called Edward Hawks who has invented a matter transmitter. He works for a large corporation, and his research is funded by the US navy, which has seized on his invention as a means of sending men to the Moon and thus stealing a march on the Soviet manned space programme. (These events are supposed to be taking place, in secret, at the very time the novel was written.) Hawks and his team have succeeded in transmitting human beings instantaneously to the Moon, but they have now come up against a greater challenge. On the far side of the Moon, just out of sight of Earth's telescopes, is an object which has evidently been put there by some alien intelligence. It is a maze-like structure which kills all the volunteers who enter it. It has no apparent purpose; it is an unfathomable mystery.

The reader never does discover the provenance of the alien maze, for that is not the purpose of the book. Rather, it is a story of human endurance and the testing to destruction of men's spirits. It is a novel about death. Hawk's volunteers do not return from the Moon; they die there, inevitably. But what Hawks is able to do is to create a second replica of each individual at the moment of transmission; this 'additional copy' is kept in a state of sensory deprivation for a short while, during which time the subject's mind is in contact, by some unexplained telepathic means, with the mind of his other self on the Moon. Thus the man in the sensory deprivation tank on Earth experiences the death of his *alter ego* in space—a traumatic ordeal indeed. All the military volunteers emerge insane from the sensory deprivation

83

chamber, until Hawks decides to use Al Barker, a civilian eccentric who is more than half in love with death. In a sense Barker is already crazy, having tested himself to the limits in various sports and daredevil stunts. He is able to go to the Moon, run the alien maze, die, and reawaken on Earth with his mind intact. He does this over and over again, until the maze has been mapped and a trail blazed for the technicians who will follow.

Needless to say, Barker is an extremely dislikable character, as are several of the other people in the novel. Edward Hawks is the true hero, though he does not go to the Moon himself until the very end of the story. In his depiction of Hawks, Budrys gives us a portrait of the scientist as moral superman, an unflinching gazer into the void: 'Only one thing in the universe grows fuller, and richer, and *forces* its way uphill. Intelligence—human lives—we're the only things there are that don't obey the universal law. The universe kills our bodies . . . in the end, it kills our brains. But our *minds* . . . There's the precious thing; there's the phenomenon that has nothing to do with time and space except to use them—to describe to itself the lives our bodies live in the physical universe.'

Algis Budrys was born of Lithuanian parents in East Prussia, but has lived in the USA since childhood. It seems to me that his novel expresses an aggressively American view of the scientific mission, tempered by a degree of European pessimism.

First edition: New York, Fawcett, 1960 (paperback)
First British edition: London, Coronet, 1968 (paperback)
Most recent edition: London, Fontana (paperback)

33

THEODORE STURGEON
Venus Plus X

Sturgeon is among the most talented writers ever to have devoted themselves to science fiction. In fluidity of style and sheer command of language he towers over the likes of Asimov and Clarke and even Heinlein. Unfortunately, he has written relatively few novels. Apart from the classic *More Than Human*, his most satisfying work is to be found in his many short stories and novellas of the 1940s and 50s. Particularly good collections of them include *A Touch of Strange* (1958), *The Worlds of Theodore Sturgeon* (1972), *The Stars are the Styx* (1979) and *The Golden Helix* (1980). James Blish once described Sturgeon as 'the finest conscious artist science fiction ever had,' and more recently, Samuel R. Delany has said that 'Sturgeon is *the* American short-story writer.' Both are overstatements, but they are indicative of the enthusiasm this author is capable of arousing. His is not a 'hard' sf; it is mainly psychological in emphasis, and is given to exploring the varieties of human response to odd situations.

Venus Plus X is Sturgeon's last full-length novel to date, and one of his most interesting. Charlie Johns, a citizen of the contemporary USA, awakes to find himself mysteriously translated into another world. He is surrounded by beautiful men who have multi-coloured clothes and high fluting voices. They inhabit a delightful utopia known as 'Ledom' (read it backwards). Force-fields waft them from their lofty top-heavy towers to the perfect greensward below. They are peaceful and contented folk who devote their time to arts and sciences. Charlie assumes that these people are the successors to the *Homo sapiens* of his day. Imprinted with their language by some uncanny technological means, he is invited to wander the place and ask all the questions he can think of. Apparently, the citizens of Ledom have brought him to their paradise in order to view themselves afresh through his untutored eyes.

Charlie is profoundly shocked by the central fact of Ledom society: its inhabitants are not 'men' after all. They are neither male nor female, but hermaphroditic. Each is fully equipped with the reproductive organs of both sexes, and each is capable of bearing children. But Charlie is a progressive guy with a stronger-than-average imagination: 'Though he made no pretense of being a bigdome, [he] seemed always to have been aware that progress is a dynamic thing, and you had to ride it leaning forward a little, like on a surfboard, because if you stood there flatfooted you'd get drowned.' His present predicamant, however, takes a lot of getting used to.

Sturgeon has interspersed this narrative with a succession of short chapters set in the suburban USA of 1960. We see two couples do the shopping, look after their kids, go ten-pin bowling—it is a mundane contrast to the wonders of Ledom, but the main point is to show that even now, in our 20th century, the distinctions between the sexes are breaking down. Affluent suburban man is already part-way towards hermaphroditism, even if he/she does not yet realize it. *Venus Plus X* is a remarkable prefiguration of the feminist sf of the 1970s. It owes a small debt to Philip Wylie's *The Disappearance* (1951), a novel which imagined a world without men (and its converse, a world without women), but Sturgeon's book remains one of the most original of all speculations on the subject of gender. It is marred by moments of slightly sickly coyness, especially in the 'contemporary' scenes, but despite these lapses it is an intelligent and engrossing work.

First edition: New York, Pyramid, 1960 (paperback)
First British edition: Gollancz, 1969 (hardcover)
Most recent editions: London, Corgi, and New York, Bluejay
(paperbacks)

34

BRIAN W. ALDISS
Hothouse

'Obeying an inalienable law, things grew, growing riotous and strange in their impulse for growth.' I have always remembered that opening sentence; it encapsulates for me what Aldiss's fiction is all about: *fecundity*. His novels and stories are replete with images of burgeoning life, idiosyncratic growth and variety, fullness and multifariousness. We see it in his later works—in *Greybeard*, for instance, in which an abundance of natural life reconquers England, and in *Barefoot in the Head* (1969), where a torrent of language points up the theme, language grown as fantastic and intertwined as the woods and jungles of the earlier novels (and Aldiss's penchant for a pun is highly indicative of his imaginative bent: he revels in the serendipity of incongruous juxtapositions). But nowhere does his celebration of fecundity come across more strongly than in *Hothouse*, his story of the inconceivably remote future when the Earth has ceased to rotate and a giant banyan tree covers much of the sunny side. In the branches of that world-tree live the last human beings, small green-skinned creatures of limited mentality who have to compete for survival with a billion species of voracious plant and insect.

Aldiss coins scores of new names for these fabulous species: berrywhisk, tigerfly, dumbler, whistlethistle, trappersnapper, crocksock, leapycreeper, slashweed, dripperlip, oystermaw, wiltmilt, fuzzypuzzle . . . Most fabulous of all are the traversers, vast vegetable gasbags which are capable of flying through space, hauling themselves along the web-like strands of matter which hang between the Earth and the stationary Moon—an astronomical impossibility, but it makes for a lovely image. Human beings are able to stow away aboard these traversers and hence take passage for the Moon, which is now a slightly more hospitable environment for them than the Earth itself.

Hothouse is about the adventures of Gren, humanity's last questing hero. Carried by a suckerbird, he and a few members of his dwindling tribe are stranded in Nomansland, the dividing line between the banyan forest and the ravening weed-choked sea. There they must avoid the dangerous sand octopus and the killerwillow. Separated from the others, Gren is infected by a sentient fungus, the morel, which attaches itself to his head. This creature is able to penetrate Gren's brain, quicken his intelligence and draw upon his racial memories. In happy symbiosis, Gren and the morel embark on a picaresque series of adventures which eventually lead them deep into the frozen night-side of the stilled planet. There they meet an intellect greater than their own, and learn something of the future fate of the Earth, the Moon and the universe.

This is a novel of prodigious inventiveness and linguistic dexterity, marred by occasional whimsicalities and by a rather too loosely episodic structure which betrays the book's provenance—it was originally a series of separate short stories in the *Magazine of Fantasy and Science Fiction*. It is not Aldiss's most serious work, but it is surely his most joyous.

First edition: New York, Signet, 1962
(paperback; as *The Long Afternoon of Earth*)
First British edition: London, Faber, 1962 (hardcover)
Most recent editions: London, Granada, and New York, Baen
(paperbacks)

35

J.G. BALLARD

The Drowned World

The Drowned World was published in the USA in August 1962 as a scruffy paperback original, and attracted almost no attention. When the British hardcover edition appeared in January 1963, the reaction was completely different. Kingsley Amis wrote: 'We have something without precedent in this country, a novel by a science fiction author that can be judged by the highest standards . . . Mr Ballard may turn out to be the most imaginative of Wells' successors.'

James Graham Ballard (born 1930) spent his childhood in Shanghai, China, but has lived in England since the age of fifteen. He published his first short stories in 1956, and with *The Drowned World* he emerged as unquestionably the most powerful and original talent in British sf. The narrative is set in the 21st century, after fluctuations in solar radiation have caused the Earth's ice-caps to melt and the seas to rise. All low-lying land areas have become flooded, global temperatures have climbed, and civilized life continues only within the Arctic and Antarctic Circles. The novel is actually set in and around London, a city turned swamp. Dr Robert Kerans is a member of an expedition which is logging the flora and fauna of this new Triassic Age. A loner, he chooses to camp in the abandoned Ritz Hotel, among the bats and iguanas and ferns and moulds which are now its natural inhabitants. He begins to experience strange dreams which suggest that part of his mind is descending on a 'night journey' into the deep wells of humanity's remote biological past.

It is a haunting story, richly described in Ballard's dense parenthetical prose. It ends on an apparently perverse note which disconcerted some readers at the time—Kerans decides to travel deeper into the drowned world in search of the 'forgotten paradises of the reborn sun.' This is a course of action which will surely lead to his physical death, even if it first brings him to a psychological fulfilment. What Ballard has done is to invert the priorities of the 'classic' English disaster novel, such as

Wyndham's *The Day of the Triffids* or Christopher's *The Death of Grass*. In this text the disaster is welcomed because the landscape it has produced gells with the hero's state of mind. Keran's quest is a surrealistic one, in search of a psychic truth.

It is apt to mention surrealism, because Ballard has been marked by the painters of the Surrealist Movement to a larger extent than he has been influenced by any writer. The inundated London of this novel resembles one of Max Ernst's magical forests; the book might even have been called *Europe After the Rain*. At the same time, Ballard is very much his own man. As in the best of his early short stories—collected in *The Voices of Time* (1963) and *The Terminal Beach* (1964)—the language of this novel is distinguished by its vivid use of medical and biological terminology, and by its breadth of artistic and mythological reference. Ballard is one of the very few sf writers who has successfully fused influences from the sciences and the arts on a sentence-to-sentence level, in such a way that one of his subordinate clauses may carry all the thrill of a whole story by a lesser science-fictional talent. While he is not to everyone's taste, Ballard is the kind of author whose work generally proves addictive to the sympathetic reader, for his is indeed a unique voice.

First edition: New York, Berkley Books, 1962 (paperback)
First British edition: London, Gollancz, 1963 (hardcover)
Most recent edition: London, Dent (paperback)

36
ANTHONY BURGESS
A Clockwork Orange

John Wyndham's *The Midwich Cuckoos* gave us an image of the generation gap—in the guise of mutant children. Anthony Burgess's *A Clockwork Orange* gives us an alternative image of the same thing, but in a much more literal, straightforward way. This is a novel about juvenile delinquents in a near-future Britain. More deeply, it is a novel about conditioning and free will: the 'clockwork orange' of the title is a metaphor for that impossible entity, the perfectly programmed man. Burgess (full name John Anthony Burgess Wilson, born 1917) is a lapsed Catholic who seems to retain a strong belief in the doctrine of Original Sin, and this gives his novel something in common with William Golding's *The Inheritors*. In this fiction Burgess makes it clear that he is opposed to the kind of social engineering which will try to turn a sinner into a saint by mechanical means.

The story is told in the first person by its unlovely anti-hero, Alex. He and his three mates are given to mugging lonely pedestrians, robbing tobacconists' shops, and the like. The most notable feature of the book is the amazing language which Alex speaks; a futuristic juvenile slang, full of Russian loan-words. Here is Alex's description of a raid on a shop at the beginning of the novel:

'Mother Slouse, the wife, was sort of froze behind the counter. We could tell she would creech murder given one chance, so I was round that counter very skorry and had a hold of her, and a horrorshow big lump she was too, all nuking of scent and with flipflop big bobbing groodies on her. I'd got my rooker round her rot to stop her belting out death and destruction to the four winds of heaven, but this lady doggie gave me a large foul bite on it, and then she opened up beautiful with a flip yell for the millicents. Well, then she had to be tolchocked proper with one of the weights for the scales, and then a fair tap with a crowbar they had for opening cases, and that brought the red out like an old friend. So we had her down on the floor and a rip of her platties for fun and a gentle bit of the boot to stop her moaning. And, viddying her lying there with her groodies on show, I wondered should I or not, but that was for later on in the evening. Then we cleared the till, and there was flip horrorshow takings that nochy, and we had a few packs of the very best top cancers apiece, then off we went, my brothers.' It is easy to derive the sense of the invented words from the context: 'groodies'= breasts; 'rooker'= hand; 'rot'= mouth; 'millicents'= police; 'tolchocked'= hit; 'platties'= clothes; 'viddying'= seeing; 'nochy'= night, and so on. 'Cancers' for cigarettes is an obvious black joke, while 'horrorshow' serves as an all-purpose term of praise and/or disgust. Burgess sustains this *argot* brilliantly; it is very funny as well as frightening.

Alex and his three 'droogs' enter the house of a writer (who is working on a book called *A Clockwork Orange*), beat the poor man brutally, rape his wife, and get away with it. A few evenings later, however, Alex is arrested after breaking into another house. He has struck its elderly owner a little too hard, and realizes that he has committed his first murder. Meanwhile, we have discovered two surprising facts about Alex: he is a lover of classical music—Beethoven seems to inspire him to ever-greater height of ultra-violence—and he is just fifteen years old. He now undergoes an enforced reformation in prison, compelled to watch the most appalling torture films while under the influence of an emetic drug. One film, a documentary about Nazi atrocities, is accompanied by the music of Beethoven. This aversion therapy cures Alex of his violent impulses—and of his love for great music. On his release from prison he becomes the pawn of a protest movement dedicated to the abolition of forcible conditioning for violent criminals. By a horrid irony, it turns out that the man whose wife Alex raped, the author of *A Clockwork Orange*, is a leading activist in this movement. Burgess's novel is none too convincing as an exploration of the causes and consequences of juvenile delinquency, but it is written with great vigour and inventiveness, and adds up to a most memorable black comedy.

First edition: London, Heinemann, 1962 (hardcover)
First American edition: New York, Norton, 1962 (hardcover)
Most recent editions: London, Penguin, and New York, Norton (paperbacks)

37
PHILIP K. DICK
The Man in the High Castle

This work has many of the attributes of a social novel. It is about
the interactions of male and female characters in a realistically-
depicted society—in the year 1962, as it happens. It even contains
some pointed 'comedy of manners'. Nevertheless it is indubitably science fiction, belonging like Ward Moore's *Bring the
Jubilee* to the subcategory of 'alternative world' stories. The
donnée of *The Man in the High Castle* is that Germany and
Japan were the victors in World War II and that they have split
the territory of a conquered America between them. In *this* 1962
the German Reich is busy carrying out some ghastly final solution in Africa, even as it lays plans to send the first manned
rocket to Mars. Meanwhile, a comparatively benign Japanese
Empire administers the West Coast of the erstwhile USA, its officials obsessed with the folkways and pop-cultural artifacts of the
defeated Californians.

Robert Childan runs a memorabilia store, selling Mickey
Mouse watches, old movie posters, comic books and the like to
the more cultured of the Japanese overlords, who are willing to
pay high prices for these genuine Americana. Childan is only too
eager to please. In one of the novel's most effective and quietly
hilarious scenes he is invited to the home of a *chic* young Japanese couple who wish to play him some of their prized New Or-
leans jazz records. Childan misreads their motives and denigrates
the black music in conventionally—and in this world socially
acceptable—racist terms, before realizing he is committing a *faux
pas*. Thus in the early 1960s, at the very height of the post-war
American imperium, Philip K. Dick succeeded in creating a
plausible imaginary world in which Americans are obliged to
squirm with embarrassment, resentment and remorse; they bear
the full weight of cultural oppression which has been borne in
our time-stream by so many of the world's other peoples. It is a
salutary reversal.

The Man in the High Castle is not just Robert Childan's novel.

The viewpoint shifts continually: to Mr Tagomi, the sympathetic Japanese businessman; to Juliana Frink, the judo instructress who goes in search of the reclusive Hawthorne Abendsen; to Abendsen himself, the 'man in the high castle' of the title, who has written a science fiction novel called *The Grasshopper Lies Heavy* in which—you may have guessed—Germany and Japan are imagined as having *lost* World War II. So Dick carefully builds a complex narrative of many strands, much of it bound together by references to the *I Ching*, the ancient Chinese oracular work which all the characters consult at intervals. The novel questions our whole notion of 'reality', showing just how frail the consensus can be. Paradoxically, for a book which tears reality apart at the seams, the characters are very real indeed. One of Dick's greatest strengths was his power of characterization—not a quality one normally expects of an sf writer—and that power is fully applied in this fine, subtle novel. It is probably Dick's best work, and the most memorable alternative world tale, or fantasia of historical possibility, ever written.

First edition: New York, Putnam, 1962 (hardcover)
First British edition: London, Penguin, 1965 (paperback)
Most recent editions: New York, Berkley, and London, Penguin (paperbacks)

38
ROBERT SHECKLEY
Journey Beyond Tomorrow

Robert Sheckley (born 1928) is a peripatetic American who has often lived in Europe. Like Ray Bradbury and Cordwainer Smith, he is one of those writers who is not best represented by a novel. It was for his sparky, provocative short stories that he first became famous; they were collected in such volumes as *Untouched by Human Hands* (1954), *Citizen in Space* (1955) and *Pilgrimage to Earth* (1957). Of his early novels, *Immortality, Inc.* (1959) is the most notable. *Journey Beyond Tomorrow* is, however, a funnier book—and it is for his sharp humour that Sheckley's work is most prized. The story was first published as a 1962 serial in *Fantasy and Science Fiction* under the title of 'Journey of Joenes'.

The eponymous Joenes is a sweetly innocent young man of the early 21st century. Born of American parents, he has been raised on the tiny island of Manituatua in Eastern Polynesia. At the age of twenty-five, having read many books from his father's extensive library, he sets out to discover the wider world for himself. In particular, he wishes to see the United States of America, that fabled realm. Arriving at San Francisco docks, he immediately falls in with a drug-pushing hipster called Lum—and consequently lands in jail ('A commie, huh?' says the arresting cop, after Joenes has made a fine little speech about the flawed nature of human laws and the higher morality which stems from 'following the true dictates of the illuminated soul'). He is whisked before a Congressional Committee which happens to be in town. The chairman of this committee takes a good old-fashioned line: "Comrade," he asked, with simple irony, "are you at this present time a card-carrying member of the Communist Party?" Unable to convince his questioners that he is not a communist, Joenes (or 'Comrade Jonski' as the chairman insists on calling him) is sent to the east for a trial by computer—following which he is given a suspended sentence and decanted on to the streets of New York.

Many madcap adventures follow, filled with zany characters and tales-within-tales. Joenes meets Lum once more, in a home for the criminally insane. Then he is pressed into service as a university lecturer, his subject being the culture of the Southwest Pacific. He becomes the guest of a very strange utopian commune: its artificial language contains no words for 'homosexuality', 'rape' or 'murder', and therefore these things are deemed not to exist. Finally Joenes is recruited by the US government and goes to work as a spy for the Octagon. He makes a trip to Moscow, where he also has difficulty in persuading the authorities that he is not a communist, but on his return to America an automatic radar station identifies his plane as an invader—and triggers a nuclear armageddon. America blows itself to pieces, the east coast and west coast lobbing missiles at each other as well as the rest of the world. 'And soon the civilization of proliferating machinery had vanished from the face of the earth.' Joenes survives of course—with his luck how could he fail to? He escapes in a small boat together with his friend Lum, and they sail back to Polynesia, which is now destined to become the centre of world civilization, with the tales of Joenes and Lum as its treasured scriptures.

All of this is narrated in a very slick and amusing manner. Sheckley's targets for satire are all fairly obvious ones, and the book seems mild stuff these days—but at the time of its first appearance it was praised as refreshingly iconoclastic.

First edition: New York, NAL, 1963 (paperback)
First British edition: London, Gollancz, 1964 (hardcover)
Most recent edition: London, Sphere
(paperback; retitled *Journey of Joenes*)

39
CLIFFORD D. SIMAK
Way Station

'The southwestern corner of Wisconsin is bounded by two rivers, the Mississippi on the west, the Wisconsin on the north. Away from the rivers there is flat, broad prairie land, with prosperous farms and towns. But the land that runs down to the river is rough and rugged; high hills and bluffs and deep ravines and cliffs, and there are certain areas forming bays or pockets that are isolated. They are served by inadequate roads and the small, rough farms are inhabited by a people who are closer, perhaps, to the pioneer days of a hundred years ago than they are to the twentieth century.' So one character describes the scene of this novel—it is in fact the area where Simak was born and raised. It is a scene to which the author has returned, almost obsessively, in work after work—his own equivalent of William Faulkner's Yoknapatawpha County. If this seems oddly parochial, conservative and backward-looking in a science fiction writer—well, so it is. But Simak delights in a simple irony which he repeats over and over again: whenever he visits southwest Wisconsin in his imagination, he invests it with the other-worldly and the alien, turning this backwoods patch into a crossroads of the cosmos. Nowhere does he do this more effectively than in *Way Station*.

It is the story of a fabulous hermit, Enoch Wallace, who is 124 years old and a veteran of the American Civil War. In the late 1860s, sickened by the war, he retreated to his father's little Wisconsin farm. There he was approached one day by a tall and gangling stranger whose ears were 'just a bit too pointed at the top'. This visitor proved to be an extraterrestrial emissary— Enoch dubbed him 'Ulysses'—who was looking for a suitably secluded spot to set up a galactic way station. Now, almost a century later, the eternally youthful Enoch still lives on his untended farm, serving as a sort of station master for an inter-stellar civilization. His house has been rendered indestructible by means of alien technology, and it has been filled with teleportation equipment. Every so often an alien creature materializes therein, using Enoch's home as a staging post before travelling on to some other point in the galaxy. Frequently, Enoch shares food and coffee with his 'guests', and they reciprocate with outlandish gifts.

Once, an alien wayfarer died in transit and Enoch buried its body with great reverence in his family graveyard. A US government agent, who has been sent to investigate Enoch's miraculous longevity, finds the grave, opens it, and removes the alien remains. This action sets the plot of the novel in motion. The alien's kindred learn that the body has been moved, and they blame Enoch. Ulysses, the emissary from Galactic Central, warns him that the way station may be closed down. Meanwhile, Enoch is having trouble with his neighbours: a beautiful deaf-mute girl runs away from her brutal father, and Enoch gives her refuge in his house. He discovers she has the telepathic ability to activate one of his alien gifts, a small pyramid of rotating spheres which hitherto has remained inert. Perhaps this mysterious artifact will prove to be the key to galactic harmony and peace on Earth.

It may sound like an implausible farrago, yet this slow, meditative story has considerable charm. The rural setting is depicted with genuine feeling, and the theme of universal harmony is given an immediacy which is not too cloying. The message of the novel would seem to be: Sit still and ye shall know; just listen to the stars . . .

First edition: Garden City, Doubleday, 1963 (hardcover)
First British edition: London, Gollancz, 1964 (hardcover)
Most recent editions: New York, Del Rey, and London, Methuen (paperbacks)

40

KURT VONNEGUT
Cat's Cradle

This is the one about *ice-nine*, a laboratory-produced crystalline substance designed to help the American army fight its way out of mud-holes. The only problem with *ice-nine* is that a single chip of it will freeze all the water in the world, permanently.

It is about Dr Felix Hoenikker, 'father of the atomic bomb', inventor of *ice-nine*, and eccentric head of a very odd family. Hoenikker is dead before the action of the novel commences, yet he is one of the most important characters in the book. He is the perfect amoral scientist, totally uninterested in human beings, obsessed with his intellectual games.

It is also about Bokonon, real name Lionel Boyd Johnson, an aged black West Indian who founds the world's first calypso religion—which he cheerfully admits is a pack of lies. 'Live by the *foma* that make you brave and kind and healthy and happy,' says Bokonon. He defines *foma* as 'harmless untruths'.

It is about the Republic of San Lorenzo, the Caribbean home of Bokononism, a desperately poor island paradise where Dr Hoenikker's worthless son, Frank, becomes 'Minister of Science and Progress'. The unnamed narrator—'Call me Jonah'—travels to San Lorenzo to interview Frank and other people, and finds himself elevated overnight to the Presidency of the island.

It is also about Mona Aamons Monzano, the heartbreakingly beautiful half-caste daughter of a Finnish architect who built San Lorenzo's only hospital. She is adept in the practice of *Boko-maru*, the mutual foot massage which leads to the ecstatic mingling of souls through the soles. She converts the narrator to Bokononism, the only religion which makes sense of a crazy, crazy world.

It is about much more besides, for *Cat's Cradle* is one of Kurt Vonnegut's most continuously inventive and delightfully complex novels. It makes a mockery of science, religion, patriotism, sex—everything; and it concludes in the only way it possibly can, with the End of the World. Some *ice-nine* is accidentally cast into the sea off San Lorenzo, and everything freezes over to the accompaniment of worldwide tornadoes. The narrator survives for six months, occupied in writing his memoirs. Finally, all that is left for him to do is to follow Bokonon's last words of advice: to climb a mountain and lie down with his history of human stupidity for a pillow, to put some *ice-nine* to his lips, grin horribly, and thumb his nose at You-Know-Who.

Vonnegut's droll, and ultimately rather comforting, brand of nihilism eventually became very fashionable with the publication of his later novel, *Slaughterhouse-5* (1969). There was not much in that book which had not already been said—humorously, slyly, even movingly—in *The Sirens of Titan* and *Cat's Cradle*, and in the excellent non-sf novel *Mother Night* (1961). I doubt that Vonnegut is a sage, but he is certainly one of the most original entertainers of our time.

First edition: New York, Holt, Rinehart and Winston, 1963 (hardcover)

First British edition: London, Gollancz, 1963 (hardcover)

Most recent editions: New York, Dell, and London, Penguin (paperbacks)

41
BRIAN W. ALDISS
Greybeard

Parts of this novel remind me of *After London* (1885), a small masterpiece by the Victorian nature writer Richard Jefferies. In Jefferies' book—which we may regard as one of the earliest English disaster novels—London has been swept away by some ill-defined cataclysm, and nature has long since reclaimed its own. The opening section of the story is a lovingly detailed description of the wild plants and animals which flourish in the abandoned Home Counties. In Brian Aldiss's *Greybeard* the human race has been struck by a terrible plague of infertility: no children have been born for several decades, and the population shrinks by a process of natural wastage until the landscape comes to resemble that imagined by the earlier writer:

> Wild life swarmed back across the Earth as abundantly as it had ever done . . .
> The Earth had great powers of replenishment . . . It had supported many different kinds of life through many different ages. As far as that outcast spit of the European mainland called the British Isles was concerned, its flora and fauna had never entirely regained the richness they enjoyed before the Pliocene. During that period, the glaciers descended . . . But the ice retreated again; life followed it back towards its northern strongholds . . . like the opening of a giant hand, a stream of life poured across the lands that had recently been barren. The ascendency of man had only momentarily affected the copiousness of this stream.
> Now the stream was a giant tide of petals, leaves, fur, scales, and feathers. Nothing could stem it, though it contained its own balances. Every summer saw its weight increasing as it followed paths and habits established, in many cases, in distant ages before *homo sapiens* made his brief appearance . . .

They greybeard of the title is Algy Timberlane, one of the youngest men left in the world—despite the fact that he is over fifty years old. He was born just before the 'Accident' of 1981, when nuclear weapons were exploded in Earth orbit, which is the cause of the universal sterility. It is now the year 2029, and Algy

101

and his wife, Martha, live in the little village of Sparcot by the banks of the Thames. They have been there for over a decade, during which time the world has grown wild and woody. The remaining members of the population are all aged sixty or over— most of Algy's contemporaries died in childhood from radiation-induced diseases—and they view their surroundings through a haze of superstition and fear. There are rumours of sprites and goblins, marauding Scotsmen, ravening hordes of stoats, and wild badger children. Despairing of Sparcot, Algy and a small group of others decide to go on a boat trip down the river to the sea. It seems safe to travel once more, now that the country has become quiescent and senescent. This will be the last voyage of discovery.

The novel is beautifully structured. As Algy wends his way down the Thames the story of his past life is told in alternating chapters, in reverse order of events. Thus, when he reaches his journey's end we have also reached back into his childhood. Along the way the party meets various bizarre old folk, such as Norsgrey, who they mistake for a gnome, and the quack doctor Bunny Jingadangelow, who peddles rejuvenation serums and has a booth at Swifford Fair where he displays a 'youth'—in reality a castrated oldster, cunningly made up. They reach Oxford, where a few elderly scholars still eke out a life of 'learning', and then they travel on across the inland Sea of Barks. The book ends on a note of hope. The legends of wood sprites are borne out: a few human children survive in the wilderness. Sadly, Algy realizes that they must be allowed to live in their own way, well removed from a fast-decaying civilization which will only imprison them and exploit them as sideshow freaks.

Brian Aldiss has written many sf novels since *Greybeard*. With such works as *Report on Probability A* (1968) he became closely identified with the British 'New Wave'. Just recently, he has been producing his *magnum opus*, a science fiction trilogy beginning with *Helliconia Spring* (1982), the final part of which has still to be published at the time of writing.

First edition: New York, Harcourt, Brace and World, 1964 (hardcover)
First British edition: London, Faber, 1964 (hardcover)
Most recent editions: London, Granada, and New York, NAL (paperbacks)

42
WILLIAM S. BURROUGHS
Nova Express

The blurb on my paperback edition describes this book as 'an hallucinatory interplanetary cops and robbers game with the Nova Police on one side and the Nova Mob (among whom, Izzy the Push, Hamburger Mary and the Subliminal Kid) on the other.' Clearly, all of American pop culture—and much of its high culture—is grist to William Burroughs' word-mill. Science fiction has its place therein, along with the private-eye novel, the horror comic, the western, and the shapeless beat 'confession'. In fact, sf looms larger than most other *genres* in Burrough's ramshackle but very telling mythology. He used great gobbets of science-fictional imagery in *The Naked Lunch* (1959), *The Soft Machine* (1961) and *The Ticket That Exploded* (1962)—and he is on record as being an admirer of various sf authors from Theodore Sturgeon to J.G. Ballard. In *Nova Express* he founds an entire book on an sf conceit.

The basic idea is this: there is a group of entities which Burroughs calls the Nova Mob, and their purpose is to take control of this planet by manipulating the strings of *addiction*—not just drug addiction, but the human dependence on sex, on violence, and on language itself. They are in cahoots with 'the all-powerful boards and syndicates of the earth', and they offer us the Garden of Delights, Immortality, Cosmic Consciousness, and the Best Ever in Drug Kicks. As Burroughs' spokesman says: '*Listen:* Their Garden of Delights is a terminal sewer . . . Their Immortality Cosmic Consciousness and Love is second-run grade-B shit—Their drugs are poison designed to beam in Orgasm Death and Nova Ovens—'.

Pitted against the Nova conspiracy are the good guys, Inspector J. Lee (that is, Burroughs himself) and the Nova Police. They offer nothing but 'total austerity and total resistance'. Their object is to expose the Nova criminals who, by extension, are all the forces of capitalism and bureaucratic control, and to 'occupy The Reality Studio and retake their universe of Fear Death and

Monopoly . . .' It is a simple, Manichean view of things, and it is clear that Burroughs utterly believes in it. The bulk of the book consists of an avalanche of metaphors which in differing ways— funny, horrific, enlightening, disgusting—give power to this straightforward message. There is no plot, no linear narrative. Instead we have a tumble of brilliant and disturbing images, and a continuous rhetoric of subversive outrage interspersed with hilarious 'routines' which feature the most bizarre characters (for example, Uranian Willy, the Heavy Metal Kid, who visits a café where 'two Lesbian Agents with glazed faces of grafted penis flesh sat sipping spinal fluid through alabaster straws').

We are introduced to the Insect Brains of Minraud, and to the Venusian Fish People: 'The green boy-girl climbed out on a ledge . . . He squirmed towards the controller with little chirps and giggles—The controller reached down a translucent hand felt absently into the boneless jelly caressing glands and nerve centres—The green boy-girl twisted in spasms of ingratiation—'. We are taken on a tour of the Amusement Gardens, and of the Biologic Courts: 'Swarming with terminal life forms desperately seeking extension of cancelled permissos and residence certificates . . . Holding up insect claws, animal and bird parts, all manner of diseases and deformities . . . Shrieking for compensations and attempting to corrupt or influence the judges in a thousand languages living and dead . . .'.

These vivid, ungrammatical ramblings are rather more than crazed hallucinations. They amount to an alternative mythology of our time, deployed in a moral cause. William Seward Burroughs (born 1914), much loved and much imitated by poets and punk musicians as well as by certain of the younger sf writers, is the greatest demonologist of the science fiction era.

First edition: New York, Grove Press, 1964 (hardcover)
First British edition: London, Cape (hardcover)
Most recent editions: New York, Grove, and London, Granada
(paperbacks)

43
PHILIP K. DICK
Martian Time-Slip

The Mars of this novel 'is exactly and vividly drawn', writes
Brian Aldiss in his introduction to the British edition; 'it is
neither the Mars of Edgar Rice Burroughs—an adventure play-
ground, nor the Mars of Ray Bradbury—a parallel of Pristine
America; this is Mars used in elegant and expert fashion as a
metaphor of spiritual poverty.' Which is not to say it is a realistic
portrayal of the bleak Mars we known from the findings of NASA
probes: on the contrary, Dick uses a number of traditional ingredients—a network of canals, a long-decayed Martian civilization—which are sheer fantasy, but he reworks them to fit his
personal vision of a near future in which the wonders of space
travel and advanced technology have failed to transform the
human condition. In this book, Earth's colonists on Mars lead an
existence which is meagre (a favourite adjective of Dick's); they
have to contend with dust and boredom, with broken-down
machines and an untrustworthy water supply. A typical canal is
'a sluggish and repellent green . . . it showed the accretions of
time, the underlying slime and sand and contaminants which
made it anything but potable. God knew what alkalines the population had absorbed and built into its bones by now. However,
they were alive.'

There are many people in the book, but none of them, in the
last analysis, is a hero or a villain. The most sympathetic character, Jack Bohlen, is a handyman, a fixer of gadgets; he worries
about a recurrence of the schizophrenia which once afflicted him,
but he muddles along as best he can. The least sympathetic character is Arnie Kott, a corrupt trade union boss, who refers to the
Bleekmen (the apparently primitive Martian natives) as 'niggers'.
The plot involves a land deal which will transform an area of
wilderness—holy territory to the Bleekmen—into a vast housing
tract for a new wave of colonists from Earth. Bohlen and Kott
both become involved with a ten-year-old autistic boy whose
father has committed suicide. It may be that this boy has the

ability to see the future, and has been terrified into his autistic state by a prevision of his own far-off death. It turns out that the Bleekmen are the only people who can 'heal' him.

Boredom, schizophrenia, suicide, corruption, death: a dismal litany indeed—but the surprising thing is (and it is a paradox we come to expect of Philip K. Dick) that the novel is frequently amusing, and sometimes downright funny. A small example of Dick's humour: there is a psychiatrist in *Martian Time-Slip* who has been slighted by Arnie Kott and wishes to take revenge. Concerned about his own motives, he assures himself that he is not 'the anal-expulsive or . . . the oral-biting type . . . long ago he had classified himself as the late genital type, devoted to mature genital strivings.' Characters in Dick's novels are always analyzing themselves—and forever taking psychological pratfalls.

In addition to the humour there is tenderness. At the end of the novel Kott gets his come-uppance: while trying to stake a fraudulent claim in the Martian mountains he is shot by a small-time smuggler. Jack Bohlen (who at one point Kott has tried to kill) is at his side: 'The realization that Arnie Kott was dead filled him, to his incredulity, with grief . . . Silently, they continued on back to Lewistown, carrying with them the body of Arnie Kott; carrying Arnie home to his settlement, where he was—and probably always would be—Supreme Goodmember of his Water Worker's Union, Fourth Planet Branch.' There are no heroics here, no great victories: life just goes on.

First edition: New York, Ballantine, 1964 (paperback)
First British edition: London, NEL, 1976 (hardcover)
Most recent editions: New York, Del Rey, and London, NEL (paperbacks)

44

PHILIP K. DICK
The Three Stigmata of Palmer Eldritch

Philip Dick was extraordinarily prolific during the mid-60s. In 1964 alone he published five novels, including the aforementioned *Martian Time-Slip* and three minor but very interesting paperback originals, *The Simulacra*, *Clans of the Alphane Moon* and *The Penultimate Truth*. His last novel of 1964, and perhaps the most significant, was *The Three Stigmata of Palmer Eldritch*. This was the book which turned me on to Dick (I use the phrase advisedly) when I first discovered it at the age of sixteen. I did not fully understand it then, and I am not sure that I comprehend it all now, for it is Dick at his wildest and strangest. Among other things, it is a novel about drugs, which made it seem very appropriate to its decade.

It opens in the manner of a Pohl-and-Kornbluth satire. Barney Mayerson is a 'precog'; he has the ability to foresee the future to a limited degree. He works as a 'Pre-Fash' expert for a New York company called Perky Pat Layouts, Inc., where his task is to foretell fashions in dress, ornaments and interior design. P.P. Layouts manufactures dolls and dollhouses for the users of a drug known as Can-D. Anyone who consumes the drug is able to enter the world of Perky Pat and similar dolls, to lead an illusory life of leisure and erotic play. This escapist hobby is especially appealing to the bored and homesick colonists on Mars. Although he is one of the best precogs in the business, Barney has his problems. He feels threatened by his new assistant, Roni Fugate (the two of them go to bed together after a few hours' acquaintance: 'You're both precogs,' his computer psychiatrist explains to him the following morning. 'You previewed that you'd eventually hit it off, become erotically involved. So you both decided . . . why should you wait?'). He has also received his draft notice—the demand that he becomes a Mars colonist—and hence is carrying the suitcase-sized psychiatrist, Dr Smile, around with him wherever he goes, in the hope that it will make him neurotic enough to fail the emigration test. Meanwhile New York swelters in a permanent 180-degree heatwave (presumably caused by the Greenhouse Effect—this is the 21st century), and the bulk of the population lives in vast 'Conapts' where they have to pay a fortune in cooling bills.

Barney's boss, Leo Bulero, is one of the privileged few who can afford to have Evolution Therapy in a German clinic, and this is gradually turning him into a 'bubblehead'. He boasts: 'Because I take that E Therapy I've got a huge frontal lobe; I'm practically a precog myself, I'm so advanced.' This is of little use to him when he hears that a rival industrialist, Palmer Eldritch, has returned from a ten-year voyage to Proxima Centauri with some alien lichens which may be the source of a new drug to rival Can-D. Bulero flies to the Moon to confront Eldritch, and to kill him if needs be. But he is too late: a corporation has already been set up to market Eldritch's wonder-drug, Chew-Z; shipments of the stuff are beginning to arrive on Mars. Unlike Can-D, Chew-Z is supposedly non-addictive; it has been approved by the United Nations, and soon everyone will be taking it, on Earth as well as on Mars and the various unhappy moons of the solar system. But the new drug is vastly more powerful in its effects than Can-D: as Bulero and Barney Mayerson discover, it may even plunge one into a *permanent* world of illusion, a world which is controlled by Palmer Eldritch (whose 'stigmata' are an artificial hand, mechanical eyes and steel teeth), or by some demonic entity who is working through Eldritch.

The novel is not so much a satire as a metaphysical black comedy which becomes more and more nightmarish. Towards the end, it is hard to distinguish illusion from reality; and that, no doubt, is the point. *The Three Stigmata of Palmer Eldritch* is a mystifying but brilliant book.

First edition: Garden City, Doubleday, 1964 (hardcover)
First British edition: London, Cape, 1966 (hardcover)
Most recent editions: London, Granada, and New York, NEL (paperbacks)

45

FRITZ LEIBER
The Wanderer

If I were writing a volume about the *The Hundred Best Fantasy Novels* Fritz Leiber (born 1910) would deserve at least three entries. He has produced fewer notable works of science fiction than he has of supernatural horror and sword-and-sorcery, and of the few his short novel *The Big Time* (1961) is often cited as the best. I prefer *The Wanderer*, which is a long novel, an ambitious one, and eminently readable.

It begins with an eclipse of the Moon. All over the world people are looking at the sky and, in rapid succession, we are introduced to dozens of them: amateur astronomers, science fiction fans, flying saucer enthusiasts, others—all sharply drawn, quirkily individualized. It is a narrative of many strands. The main one concerns Paul Hagbolt and Margo Gelhorn, and their cat Miaow, who are out for an evening drive in Southern California. They fall in with an open-air gathering of UFO-spotters. Suddenly the stars flicker to one side of the darkened Moon, and a new planet swims into view. It is the Wanderer, four times the size of the moon, its visible face patterned like a Yin-Yang symbol, half gold, half purple: a vast unidentified object beyond the wildest dreams of the flying saucer nuts—an artificial world which has travelled through hyperspace and stopped off in our solar system to refuel itself from the Moon.

The Wanderer's abrupt arrival causes catastrophic gravitational effects. Don Merriam, an American astronaut on the lunar surface, manages to escape in a small spacecraft just as the Moon begins to crack down the middle and split in two. He is drawn to the Wanderer's surface and discovers that it is a hollow planet inhabited by all manner of intelligent beings. Meanwhile, California is riven by earthquakes, and oceans the world over begin to swell with tidal waves. Many people die. Paul and Margo and their pet cat are about to be engulfed by a *tsunami* when a 'flying saucer'—a miniature version of the Wanderer itself—descends and saves them. Paul and the cat are whisked away. The flower-filled, mirror-lined vessel is piloted by a beautiful feline creature (Paul comes to call her Tigerishka) who has mistaken Maiow for an intelligent being. Realizing her mistake, and learning English by telepathic means, she refers to Paul contemptuously as a 'monkey'. Nevertheless a kind of friendship grows between the man and the cat-woman, which culminates in an act of physical love. Tigerishka explains where the Wanderer has come from and why: it is a rogue planet on the run from an intergalactic civilization which has become overcrowded and decadent. She provides a disturbing vision of the cosmos:

> A pond can fill with infusoria almost as quickly as a ditchwater puddle. A continent can fill with rabbits almost as swiftly as a single field. And intelligent life can spread to the ends of the universe—those ends which are everywhere—as swiftly as it grows to maturity on a single planet.
>
> The planets of a trillion suns can fill with spaceship-builders as quickly as those of one. Ten million trillion galaxies can become infected with the itch of thought—that great pandemic!—as readily as one.
>
> Intelligent life spreads faster than the plague. And science grows more uncontrollably than cancer.

Eventually Paul is united with Don Merriam from the Wanderer, and the two are returned safely to Earth, before the artificial planet flees back into hyperspace just three days after its arrival.

The Wanderer is part disaster novel, part space opera. Leiber enriches the book by cramming in countless references to mythology, religion, the arts—and sf. The characters talk incessantly. Despite its grab-bag plot, this is no slickly-written piece of bestseller fiction, but a richly eccentric, almost encyclopaedic work, a summation of its author's wide-ranging interests and obsessions. Although it was popular with sf readers at the time of its first publication, *The Wanderer* has become a neglected novel, hardly ever mentioned in critical studies of science fiction. I believe it is Leiber's *chef-d'œuvre*, and overdue for revaluation.

First edition: New York, Ballantine, 1964 (paperback)
First British edition: London, Dobson, 1967 (hardcover)
Most recent editions: London, Penguin, and New York, Tor (paperbacks)

46

CORDWAINER SMITH
Norstrilia

'Cordwainer Smith' was a pseudonym for Dr Paul M.A. Line-barger (1913-1966), a rather remarkable American whose achievements included the authorship of a prominent work on psychological warfare. *Norstrilia*, his only science fiction novel, was initially published in two halves as *The Planet Buyer* (1964) and *The Underpeople* (1968). A unified, corrected version was eventually issued in 1975, well after its author's death. The title refers to the planet, Old North Australia, whence the hero comes. This is extravagant, far-future sf which imagines a universe thickly populated by humanity and other intelligent beings, including the so-called underpeople, animals that have been turned into the semblance of men and women by latter-day avatars of Dr Moreau. The interstellar imperium is ruled by the mysterious Lords of the Instrumentality, a sort of scientific priesthood which also figures in many of Cordwainer Smith's short stories. In fact, almost all the stories which Smith published in the sf mgazines between 1950 and the year of his death are set in the same future cosmos as *Norstrilia*, and references to the characters and events of those stories abound in the novel. The tales—which tend to have whimsical sing-song titles such as 'Alpha Ralpha Boulevard' and 'Golden The Ship Was—Oh! Oh! Oh!'—are Smith's finest works, and they have been reprinted in several overlapping volumes. *The Best of Cordwainer Smith* (1975) is an excellent selection.

The novel's hero is a youth called Rod McBan, scion of an ancient family on the rugged and deeply conservative planet Norstrilia. Originally settled by Australians from Old Earth, Rod's world has become immensely wealthy, thanks to a disease of the local sheep. The farmers' hideously bloated sheep are the source of a drug, *stroon*, which confers near-immortality on human beings. It is impossible to manufacture the drug arti-ficially, or to export the lucrative disease to other planets, so Norstrilia remains the sole provider of this life-giving substance.

The natives guard their farms jealously, and cull their own population to prevent overcrowding and degeneration. At the opening of the story Rod undergoes a test to determine whether he shall live or die. There is reason to doubt his future, since he suffers from an incapacity to communicate telepathically, as can all his neighbours. He passes the test, but he also makes a dangerous enemy, and it seems that his best course of action is to leave the planet of his birth. With the aid of an age-old (and illegal) computer he gambles his inherited wealth on the galactic stock market. Overnight he becomes the richest man in the universe, and the effective owner of humanity's homeworld. He is now free to travel across space and claim his own—to see for the first time the 'mad wild faraway skies of Old Earth'.

On Earth Rod finds a society of daunting complexity. He becomes involved with the underpeople, and with the 'Rediscovery of Man'. This last is a movement which has been launched by certain members of the Instrumentality in order to bring to an end the sybaritic stagnation which ensnares the majority of humankind: 'Earth had no dangers, no hopes, no rewards, no future except endlessness . . .'.

It is a rich, colourful, and at times irritating narrative, full of veiled religious overtones. Although somewhat fragmentary in its effects, it serves to confirm that Cordwainer Smith was one of science fiction's most original writers, and also one of its most eccentric. John Sladek once wrote a parady of Smith which he entitled 'One Damned Thing After Another—A Co-ordainer's Myth'. Indeed, *Norstrilia* is a book which contains one damned thing after another—but many of those things are vividly drawn and wonderfully suggestive.

First editions: *The Planet Buyer*, New York, Pyramid, 1964;
The Underpeople, New York, Pyramid, 1968;
Norstrilia, New York, Ballantine, 1975 (all paperbacks)
First British editions: *The Planet Buyer*, London, Sphere, 1975
The Underpeople, London, Sphere, 1975
(both paperbacks)

47
PHILIP K. DICK
Dr Bloodmoney

Bob Dylan once sang 'You can be in my dream if I can be in yours', and essentially that is what this book is all about. The 'Dr Bloodmoney' of the title is Bruno Bluthgeld, a German-born scientist who works for the US military. The time is the 1980s, the place California, and Bluthgeld is cracking up. Ten years ago he was responsible for a dreadful miscalculation which led to many people being contaminated by nuclear radiation. Now he has an irrational conviction that he is disfigured, his face covered in blotches. He also believes he is being hounded by an 'international communist conspiracy'. Contrasted with the dangerously paranoid Bluthgeld are various other characters (it is a richly-peopled novel): Stuart McConchie, a black salesman of stereo TV sets; Hoppy Harrington, a young thalidomide victim, armless and legless, who works as a repairman in the TV shop; Walt Dangerfield, a wisecracking astronaut—'a sort of Voltaire and Will Rogers combined'—who becomes trapped in an endless orbit around the Earth; and Bonny Keller, flighty enchantress, who will give birth to a little girl who carries a Siamese twin inside her stomach.

The novel opens on the day that World War III breaks out. San Francisco is destroyed, but life goes on in West Marin County, to the north. The surviving characters make their way there, and over a period of several years they build a rural barter economy. Superficially, the situation resembles that in Pat Frank's *Alas, Babylon*; however, as one might expect of a Philip K. Dick novel, the development is anything but conventionally realistic. This post-bomb pastoral society is held together by the wit and wisdom of a disc jockey. Walt Dangerfield, the astronaut who was launched into space on the day the bombs fell, is equipped with 'a million miles of video and audio tape', and he broadcasts endless music and readings of classic books to the folk down below—Somerset Maugham's *Of Human Bondage* proves particularly popular.

This relatively happy state of affairs is threatened by the two characters who wish to remake the world in their own cracked moulds. Bruno Bluthgeld believes that he was responsible for the H-bombs—which in a sense is true. At first he lives quietly under an assumed name, protected by Bonny Keller, who is the only person aware of his true identity. When others begin to suspect that he is the terrible Dr Bloodmoney, Bluthgeld's madness returns, stronger than ever. He threatens to blow the world up once more. The other character with megalomaniac ambitions is Hoppy Harrington, the limbless handyman. Hoppy propels himself around in a mechanical cart of his own design; he fixes things by telekinetic means. In this crazy world of biological freaks Hoppy's talent grows immensely. He is able to reach out to the orbiting satellite and take control of Walt Dangerfield's tape machines; mimicking Dangerfield's voice, he intends to broadcast his own messages to the world. He clashes with Bluthgeld, killing him by tossing him into the air. The only remaining character who can deal with Hoppy and prevent him from becoming a dictator is Bill Keller, Bonny's unsuspected seven-year-old son, who leads an invisible unborn life inside his sister's belly . . .

It is a loopy book, grotesque and endearing. At one point the sympathetic Stuart McConchie, who makes a living after the war by selling small-animal traps, meets a man who tells him about his pet rat—a mutant, like so many of the creatures in the novel: 'He's smart; he can play the flute. I'm not putting you under an illusion, it's true. I made a little wooden flute and he plays it, through his nose . . . it's practically an Asiatic nose-flute like they have in India.' This image of a rat that plays the nose-flute is somehow central. It epitomizes Dick's comic vision of life persisting in a million unexpected ways, despite the 'bad dreams' of a Hoppy Harrington and a Dr Bloodmoney.

First edition: New York, Ace, 1965 (paperback)
First British edition: London, Arrow, 1977 (paperback)
Most recent editions: London, Arrow, and New York, Bluejay (paperbacks)

114

48
FRANK HERBERT
Dune

Why has *Dune* been such an enormously popular novel? Its British paperback publisher asserts that it is 'the finest, most widely acclaimed Science Fiction novel of this century.' Hmm. It is a fat book, as bestsellers tend to be, and it contains many well-tried ingredients. It is part 'hard sf', part Ruritanian romance, part family saga. It embraces everything from cynical *realpolitik* and courtly intrigue to religious aphorisms and mystical rhapsodies. It has a large cast of characters, including a youthful hero and a strong feminine presence (the hero's mother). It ranges from high estate (counts, princes, emperors) to low (the noble savages known as the Fremen). It has an exotic setting—the desert planet Arrakis with its giant sandworms— and it encompasses a great deal of action, from individual swordfights to vast armoured battles. It contains hints of torture and sexual depravity. It depicts the use of drugs in order to expand the powers of the human mind, a theme which undoubtedly helped make it popular with the campus readership of the late 1960s. And with its emphasis on hierarchy, messianic leadership and militaristic virtues it gives off a faint musk of fascism—an aroma which, I regret to say, does make for popularity.

Above all, it is a *yarn*. It moves along for almost five hundred pages, building a world for the reader to get lost in. The book has many complexities, perhaps even some profundities, which make certain intellectual demands upon the reader, yet at times it is crudely written:

> A chuckle sounded beside the globe. A basso voice rumbled out of the chuckle: 'There it is, Piter—the biggest mantrap in all history. And the Duke's headed into its jaws. Is it not a magnificent thing that I, the Baron Vladimir Harkonnen, do?'
> 'Assuredly, Baron,' said the man. His voice came out tenor with a sweet, musical quality.
> The fat hand descended on to the globe . . . 'I invite you to observe,' the basso voice rumbled. 'Observe closely . . .'

That is Hollywood fustion at its most 'orrible. To be fair, the passages which deal with the hero, Paul Atreides (known as Muad'Dib), are usually better written than those which describe the villains, but *Dune* remains an odd blend of the vulgar and the genuine highflown. Blood-and-thunder clichés jostle with ingenious speculations, and I suppose that very mixture goes a long way towards explaining the book's commercial success.

There is no need for me to attempt an explanation of the plot here. Personally, I detest all the courtly-intrigue stuff—it is as though Herbert wants his readers to live in an eternal Middle Ages of the mind. For me, the book comes to life when Paul and his mother get out into the desert and begin to roam with the Fremen. The hard-sf element of the novel, the careful construction of the ecology of Arrakis, its landscapes and wildlife, is appealing, and of course the sandworms are marvellous. I wish the book told us more of the worms and less of the Harkonnens. It was probably this invented ecology, with all the details of still-suits, ornithopters and spice-gathering, which held an attraction for the readers of *Analog* (as *Astounding* was retitled in its long declining years) where the novel was originally serialized in 1963-65. Frank Herbert (born 1920) was considered a fairly minor American sf author before *Dune* took off as an underground bestseller. He was remembered for his first novel, *The Dragon in the Sea* (1956), a futuristic submarine thriller. Since *Dune* he has written a number of interesting but flawed sf novels—notably *Destination: Void* (1966), *The Santaroga Barrier* (1968) and *Hellstrom's Hive* (1973), which in various ways explore the subject of human transcendence. But the success of *Dune* has trapped Herbert into the writing of endless sequels to that famous book. It has become a 'saga', as unstoppable as the interstellar Jihad which Paul Muad'Dib foresees with such sorrow.

First edition: Philadelphia and New York, Chilton, 1965 (hardcover)
First British edition: London, Gollancz, 1966 (hardcover)
Most recent editions: London, NEL, and New York, Berkley (paperbacks)

49
J.G. BALLARD
The Crystal World

Dr Edward Sanders, an expert on leprosy, arrives at Port Matarre in West Africa. He has been summoned by a friend, who has sent him fragmentary reports of a jungle which is turning into crystal. Before travelling upriver, Sanders encounters several odd characters, including a priest who is apparently tortured by guilt, and a moody architect who carries a gun. For different reasons, all are drawn towards the mysterious transformation which is taking place inland. A military cordon surrounds the affected area, but eventually Sanders is permitted to see what is going on. He finds that the vegetative and animal life of the forest has been frozen, by a disease of time, into something resembling a vast crystalline grotto. The author's descriptions of this phantasmagorical landscape are hallucinatory in their power.

In truth, the plot of *The Crystal World* is of little consequence. The book's strength lies in its visual imagery, the set-pieces at which Ballard excels: a crashed helicopter crystallized into the semblance of a fabulous dragon; a jewelled crocodile; a man torn from the jungle in a half-crystallized state, staggering bloodily back into the affected zone with a wooden spar across his shoulders; Father Balthus adopting a cruciform stance as he begins to be crystallized into the nave of his church; the lepers transformed into a joyful band of harlequins; a black gunman dressed in a crocodile skin fusing into something part man, part beast. Ostensibly a disaster novel and a completion of the loose trilogy begun by *The Drowned World* and *The Drought* (1964), this book is in fact a metaphysical thriller about the human impulse to seek a world beyond time, and about the need to negate oneself in order to enter such a world. The ending of the novel, in which Sanders travels upriver once more to lose himself in the crystalline forest, embodies a fulfilment rather than a defeat.

The Crystal World was first published in shorter form as a serial in *New Worlds*, a British magazine which, in the mid-1960s, became the platform for a 'New Wave' in science fiction writing. There was a shared belief that sf had become over-conventionalized, ossified, decadent, and that it was time to find a new subject matter and new means of expression. No one played a more important part in creating this climate of feeling and endeavour than J.G. Ballard. He did not invent the 'New Wave' label (which critics came to use by analogy with the *nouvelle vague* of the French cinema represented by the films of Truffaut, Godard and Resnais), but he was soon perceived as its leading British champion. 'The biggest developments of the immediate future will take place, not on the Moon or Mars, but on Earth,' wrote Ballard in a *New Worlds* guest editorial, 'and it is *inner* space, not outer, that needs to be explored. The only truly alien planet is Earth.' In *The Crystal World* Ballard successfully evokes the alien-ness of our own planet, just as he does in his brilliant short stories of the period, which are collected in such volumes as *The Disaster Area* (1967), *Vermilion Sands* (1971), and his most 'experimental book', *The Atrocity Exhibition* (1970). All these works prove him to be the most original and wayward of modern sf writers.

First edition: London, Cape, 1966 (hardcover)
First American edition: New York, Farrar, Straus, 1966 (hardcover)
Most recent editions: New York, Avon, and London, Granada
(paperbacks)

50

HARRY HARRISON

Make Room! Make Room!

Science fiction is not so much a trend-setter as a dedicated follower of fashion. It plunders ideas from the sciences, from popular sociology and from the Sunday supplements, working them over and exaggerating them into nightmare images of The Future. The 1950s was the great decade for Bomb stories— almost every other sf novel seemed to be set in the aftermath of a nuclear war—whereas in the 1960s the fashion was for tales of Overpopulation and Pollution. In the mid-60s it became a commonplace that the world's population would double by the year 2000, and this notion struck a horror into many hearts. Harrison's *Make Room! Make Room!* is one of the classic expressions of that horror (another is John Brunner's *Stand on Zanzibar*, which I shall come to later). Harrison appends to his novel a list of some forty 'Suggestions for Further Reading', nonfiction works ranging from Malthus to Vance Packard and J.K. Galbraith. Of such stuff are science fiction stories born.

His narrative is set in New York in the year 1999, a city where 35 million people compete for water and space. The hero, Andy Rusch, is a policemen. Despite his regular income, he is obliged to share his one-room apartment with another man, the 75-year-old Sol Kahn. Sol is something of a homespun philosopher, and one cannot help feeling that he is a stand-in for the author (Harry Harrison will be in his middle 70s in 1999). When a teenage boy kills a local racketeer, Rusch becomes involved in the murder hunt. He has an affair with the dead man's former girlfriend, and eventually the girl moves into his tiny apartment. Sol dies, after participating in an 'Eldsters'' street riot. Rusch goes on searching for the boy, eventually finding him long after the trail has gone cold. There is no sense of triumph. The woman leaves, and Rusch has to live on without her or Sol, lonely in the midst of a teeming city. It is a simple story, lacking in sensationalism or heroics, and narrated in a dignified fashion with much careful—and moving— detail. It is not a mystery novel, for the reader knows the identity of the killer from the first, but it uses the crime story format in order to build up a picture of a city in long-drawn-out crisis. It is rather more than Ed McBain in a *fin-du-millenium* setting.

Harrison's New York, where everyone lives on soylent burgers and Ener-G oatmeal, and collects water from a standpipe in the street, is probably not far removed from the realities of a Third World city like Calcutta in the 1960s. It is a salutary experience to see such verities projected into the future of the world's richest nation. Even if 1999 in New York turns out to be nothing like Harrison's imaginings, this will remain a truthful novel.

Harry Harrison (born 1925) is best known for his humorous adventure stories, like *The Stainless Steel Rat* (1961), and for his spoofing sf romps such as *Bill, the Galactic Hero* (1965) and *The Technicolor Time Machine* (1967). In *Make Room! Make Room!* he produced his most serious and heartfelt work. It is a great pity that when it was filmed, as *Soylent Green* (1973), the story was trivialized by the introduction of cannibalism and other gruesome elements which are not present in the book. An impressive sf novel became just another mediocre movie.

First edition: Garden City, Doubleday, 1966 (hardcover)
First British edition: London, Penguin, 1967 (paperback)
Most recent edition: New York, Ace, and London, Penguin (paperbacks)

51
DANIEL KEYES
Flowers for Algernon

This is the best-known of a triptych of modern American sf novels which deal with the enhancement of intelligence in human beings. The others are Poul Anderson's *Brain Wave* (1954), which I had intended to list in this volume until I discovered on re-reading it just how ill-written and patchy it is, and Thomas M. Disch's *Camp Concentration*, which I describe later. The forcing of an individual's intelligence quotient to giddy new heights is a natural theme for science fiction, given the *genre*'s leaning towards tales of conceptual breakthrough. Indeed, many stories of extra-sensory perception and other unlikely mental powers can be read as dealing with precisely this theme in slightly disguised form. To tackle the subject head-on, though, is a demanding imaginative task. How does own describe transcendent intelligence? Even if the writer has the ability to do it, how can he or she retain the reader's understanding of, and sympathy for, the character concerned? Daniel Keyes' remarkable achievement in *Flowers for Algernon* was to discover a rhetoric, a ploy, for attaining those ends.

It is the story of Charlie Gordon, a 32-year-old of subnormal intelligence who sweeps the floor in a bakery. He comes to the attention of Alice Kinnian, a teacher at a school for retarded adults, and she recommends him to some university researchers who are looking for someone to experiment on. These men have found a way to boost human intelligence by surgical means, and Charlie becomes their first subject. He makes the acquaintance of Algernon, a laboratory mouse that has already undergone the operation. Charlie is asked to keep a diary, and the novel is cast in the form of his daily 'progris riports'. At first these are very childlike, full of fear, bewilderment and spelling errors. After the operation Charlie's perceptions, and his prose style, begin to improve slowly and steadily. We see him grow to full intelligence—and onwards and upwards until he reaches genius level. He loses his job at the bakery and has an unhappy affair with

Alice Kinnian. He rebels against the university and his role as a laboratory subject. He remains fascinated by the mouse, Algernon, and when its behaviour becomes erratic, its intelligence apparently *decreasing*, Charlie foresees his own sad end . . .

It is a narrative *tour-de-force*, very moving, beautiful and remorseless in its simple logic. A human mind is brought out of the darkness and into the light; after a short spell of vision and intense awareness it is consigned to the darkness again. Anyone can identify with poor Charlie Gordon; his story is a parable of the human condition.

Daniel Keyes (born 1927) wrote a handful of sf short stories during the 1950s. One of them was a brief version of *Flowers for Algernon*. After its first appearance in the *Magazine of Fantasy and Science Fiction* in 1959, it was reprinted widely and adapted for television. The story's success encouraged Keyes to produce his definitive novel version, since when the tale of Charlie Gordon has been made into a film and, believe it or not, a stage musical. No doubt it will appear in other forms in years to come, for it is one of the universally appealing stories of our time.

First edition: New York, Harcourt Brace Jovanovich, 1966 (hardcover)
First British edition: London, Cassell, 1966 (hardcover)
Most recent editions: New York, Bantam, and London, Pan
(paperbacks)

52
ROGER ZELAZNY
The Dream Master

Back in the mid-60s, Roger Zelasny (born 1937) was a real dazzler. He was acclaimed as the first of the American 'New Wave' writers, one who brought an unexpected sophistication and slyness to his reworkings of well-worn *genre* materials. There was little that was new in the substance of his tales; it was the manner of their telling that counted. Short stories such as 'A Rose for Ecclesiastes' (1963) and 'The Doors of His Face, The Lamps of His Mouth' (1965) amazed the readers of *Fantasy and Science Fiction*. They may have had conventional settings (a dry Mars in the one case and a watery Venus in the other—backgrounds which were already out of date) but they were narrated with such pzazz, with such a deftly-assured blend of sentiment and hard-boiled knowingness, that they charmed almost everyone. Zelazny's triumph was very much a triumph of style, and now that the novelty of his style is no longer immediately perceptible it suffers somewhat in retrospect. Younger New Wave contemporaries such as Thomas M. Disch and Samuel R. Delany have long since overtaken him in terms of substance, or intellectual weight, if not in popularity. Zelazny remains a butterfly.

The Dream Master was his second novel to be published in book form—although a shorter version, entitled 'He Who Shapes', had appeared in a magazine in 1964, over a year before Zelazny's first novel, *This Immortal*. The dream master, or Shaper, of the title is Dr Charles Render, whose profession is 'neuroparticipant therapist'. Using the electronic technology of the 1990s, an 'Omnichannel Neural Transmission and Receiver Unit', he is able to enter his patients' dreams, shape them to his will, and reveal hidden matters which will help in the cure of their neuroses. Like all psychotherapists, Render has been analyzed himself, 'analyzed and passed upon as a granite-willed, ultra-stable outsider—tough to weather the basilisk gaze of a fixation, walk unscathed amidst the chimera of perversions, force dark Mother Medusa to close her eyes before the caduceus of his art.' In other words he is a hard man, and a supremely talented one. He enjoys a rich standard of living, and although he has a regular mistress, he spurns close emotional ties ('It was after the auto wreck, after the death of Ruth and of Miranda, their daughter, that he had begun to feel detached'). This cold hedonistic detachment is soon to end. Render meets an attractive blind woman, also a therapist, who enlists his help in enabling her to 'see'. With the aid of his cunning machine he builds a colourful dream-world for her to share, a visual realm full of trees and leaves and living creatures, all things bright and beautiful.

The Shaper does not remain in control. He becomes obsessed with the blind doctor, and finds himself drawn into fantasies that *she* controls. The dream master yields to the dream mistress. It is an intriguing and well-told story, but much of the success of the novel is due to its background detail. Zelazny sketches a highly-mechanized near-future world in which suicide is fast becoming the major cause of death. There are animals of enhanced intelligence: one of the more important characters in the book is the heroine's guide-dog, a vocal beast called Sigmund, who takes a dislike to Render. Road traffic is automated, and people are in the habit of going for 'blind-spins'—they punch map coordinates at random, then whiz aimlessly through the night like so many mindless fireflies.

First edition: New York, Ace, 1966 (paperback)
First British edition: London, Hart-Davis, 1968 (hardcover)
Most recent editions: New York, Ace, and London, Methuen
(paperbacks)

53
JOHN BRUNNER
Stand on Zanzibar

An even longer novel than Frank Herbert's *Dune*, Brunner's best-known work is in sharp contrast to the earlier book in almost every other respect. What is impressive about this particular tome is that it does *not* try to create a completely fanciful world from scratch; instead it attempts the much more difficult task of describing what our actual world may be like just three or four decades hence. Brunner shows us planet Earth on the threshold of the 21st century: overcrowded, unstable, dominated by giant corporations and the mass media. He focuses on the United States, though important segments of the narrative are set in Africa and the Far East, demonstrating—a little schematically—the differences between developed, developing and underdeveloped countries. This is an enormously ambitious novel; the execution may falter at times, but the author deserves full marks for effort. Before *Stand on Zanzibar*, John Brunner (born 1934) was best known for the space operas which he began writing prolifically at an early age, but he had also produced some rather more serious novels—for example *The Brink* (1959), a near-future thriller about nuclear war, *Telepathist* (1964), about a deformed youth with amazing mental powers, and *The Squares of the City* (1965), a long book with a complex plot based on a chess game.

In terms of its structure, *Stand on Zanzibar* owes a great deal to the left-wing novelist John Dos Passos, best remembered for his trilogy of books collectively entitled *U.S.A.* (1930-36). Dos Passos had tried to deal with the totality of American life during the early years of this century, borrowing techniques from the cinema, the popular press and sociological research to give depth and modernity to his fictions. John Brunner emulates Don Passos's methods with considerable success. *Stand on Zanzibar* is interwoven with numerous short chapters which bear the running headings 'Context', 'The Happening World' and 'Tracking with Closeups'. These serve to fill in the details of the intricate society which Brunner depicts. Many of the 'Context' chapters consist of quotations from the imaginary pop sociologist Chad C. Mulligan. Coming on like a hip blend of Marshall McLuhan and Alvin Toffler, Mulligan provides an often witty and sometimes outrageous commentary on 21st-century humankind. He is the most memorable character in the novel.

The principal characters, however, are two men who share the same New York apartment. Norman House is black, and works for General Technics, a mighty international corporation. Donald Hogan is white, and is employed as a secret government agent. The main strands of the plot follow these men as they become involved in scientific breakthroughs and the consequent political imbroglios in Africa and Asia. Their world is over-populated and violent: the title of the novel refers to the supposition that by the year 2010 the entire human race might just be able to stand shoulder-to-shoulder on the 640-square-mile island of Zanzibar. City streets are made hazardous by 'muckers'—people who run amok—and riots flare periodically. Meanwhile General Technics has built a super-computer called Shalmaneser which may help find a genetic solution to human problems. Some aspects of the story now seem outdated. Shalmaneser is like a cybernetic dinosaur, an extrapolation from the big mainframe computers of the 1950s and 60s, bearing small resemblance to the actual developments in computing power during the past fifteen years. Nevertheless the book gives a rich, overpowering sense of desperation and decadence. Among other things it deals with eugenics, race relations, sex, drugs, juvenile delinquency, the pervasiveness of the media, international conflict, brainwashing and pollution. It is still one of the mightiest chunks of 'future reality' which any sf writer has given us to chew over.

Readers may be surprised to discover that John Brunner is a British author. His later novels, such as the dark vision of environmental degradation entitled *The Sheep Look Up* (1972), also tend to have American characters and international settings. Clearly he is one of those rare Englishmen, like Arthur C. Clarke or Ian Watson, who is not parochially obsessed with the state of the weather in his own country.

First edition: Garden City, Doubleday, 1968 (hardcover)
First American edition: London, Macdonald, 1969 (hardcover)
Most recent editions: New York, Del Rey, and London, Arrow (paperbacks)

54

SAMUEL R. DELANY

Nova

It is an appropriate title. Although he was barely twenty-five when he wrote it, *Nova* was Samuel Delany's eighth novel in a short space of time. It was also the first to appear in hard covers. His previous two paperback originals, *Babel-17* (1966) and *The Einstein Intersection* (1967), had won great praise, and Algis Budrys was moved to describe Delany as 'the best science fiction writer in the world'. It is hardly too extravagant to say that he burst upon the American sf scene like an exploding star. In effect, Delany *was* the American New Wave. Readers may not have foreseen it at the time, but *Nova* proved to be his summation. It was followed by a longish period of silence, and by the time that came to an end with the publication of his ponderous novel *Dhalgren* (1975) it was clear that he had gone off on a very different tack. One has to return to *Nova* to appreciate the young Delany at his peak—all flash and filigree, a master of movement and excitement.

Set against an interstellar background, *Nova* is an updating of the pulp-magazine space opera. It concerns the quest of Captain Lorq von Ray to find a new source of the immensely valuable heavy metal, Illyrion. He believes he can achieve this by plunging his spaceship into a star which is on the point of going nova. In the stillness at the heart of the firestorm he will find his unlimited supply of treasure. With this wealth he will change the economic structure of the known galaxy and break the tyranny of the autocratic Prince Red, scion of the Red-shift corporation. To accompany him on this crazy mission he gathers together a motley crew of vividly-drawn characters. Chief among them is a gypsy boy called the Mouse, who improvises wonderful 'melodies' on an instrument known as a sensory-syrinx. Delany's greatest admirer, Algis Budrys, has pointed out that the Mouse is another incarnation of the author's favourite hero type, the 'magic kid', ripe with innate talents and a streetwise intelligence. Samuel Ray Delany (born 1942) was himself a magic kid, a black undertaker's son from Harlem, New York, whose greatest gift is his ability to communicate the sheer liberatory *joy* that science fiction represented for him.

The plot-business, though strong and well-handled, is of less importance than the rich and integrated backdrop to the action. The novel successfully portrays a vast, complex, teeming and fundamentally *hopeful* future society. It is, in fact, utopian, although without the static, over-organized qualities that make one queasy in the face of utopian visions. It conveys a sense that the future may turn out to be a marvellous place for 'ordinary folk' such as disinherited gypsies, blacks, women, albinos and freakish intellectuals: for this band of the meek have inherited the universe. The book communicates the feeling that the future will be *different*, in a million-and-one ways that we can scarcely comprehend at present. Incidental action spills off the page in profusion. Instead of the bland, metallic corridors of the future cities envisioned by Asimov and Clarke, Delany shows us an interstellar metropolis which is like an immense bazaar. It encompasses dirt, smell and chaos, but when seen through the eyes of the magic kid it offers wonder and delight, quickening the imagination to a fever.

The most appealing sf notion in the novel is that of the surgically-implanted sockets with which all the characters are equipped. These enable Delany's people to 'plug in' to any machine, any system, and to control it directly by nerve impulses from the brain. Happy, fulfilling relationships between human beings and machines are an important part of this utopia. Everyone is now a 'cyborg' or cybernetic organism—the machines have become a part of humanity, but humanity has not become machine-like, and the human mind is always in control. It is a vision which inspires, a consummation devoutly to be wished.

First edition: Garden City, Doubleday, 1968 (hardcover)
First British edition: London, Gollancz, 1969 (hardcover)
Most recent editions: New York, Bantam, and London, Sphere (paperbacks)

55

PHILIP K. DICK

Do Androids Dream of Electric Sheep?

This is the last of the several novels by Philip Dick which I have chosen for mention in the present volume. I could have gone on to mention his *Ubik* (1969), *Flow My Tears, the Policeman Said* (1974), or *A Scanner Darkly* (1977), all of which have much to commend them. I even considered including his late novel *VALIS* (1981), which some people to find unreadable but which I believe to be a painfully funny and honest self-revelation. One has to draw the line somewhere. *Do Androids Dream of Electric Sheep?* has become Dick's most widely-read novel since it formed the basis of the fine science fiction movie *Bladerunner* in 1982. It is also one of his best.

The hero, Rick Deckard, is a bounty hunter whose task is to shoot rogue androids. These sophisticated machines are almost identical to human beings; it is only by applying certain psychological tests that Deckard can be sure that they *are* androids. (The wavering boundary between the natural and the artificial is the main subject of the book, as it is in much of Dick's work.) The androids have been manufactured for use on other planets of the solar system, but a few of them have escaped the colony worlds and are illicitly roaming the Earth. It is a decaying, underpopulated Earth of several decades hence: World War Terminus has come and gone, and now almost all animals are extinct, killed by radioactive dust. Most of surviving humanity has migrated off-world, and vast empty apartment blocks clutter the Californian landscape, full of dust and dead television sets and all the entropic detritus which the other main character, J.R. Isidore, calls 'kipple'. As Isidore explains, kipple consists of 'useless objects, like junk mail or match folders after you use the last match or gum wrappers or yesterday's homeopape. When nobody's around, kipple reproduces itself. For instance, if you go to bed leaving any kipple around your apartment, when you wake up the next morning there's twice as much of it. It always gets more and more.' Isidore is crazy, a 'chickenhead', but there is wisdom in his simplicity.

In fact, this whole run-down world is crazy. Rick Deckard keeps an electronic sheep on the roof of his apartment building. Because genuine animals are so scarce, status is measured by animal-ownership, and fakes abound. Related to this near-worship of animals is a strange new religion, Mercerism, to which all the characters subscribe: they experience visions while clutching the handles of an 'empathy box'. Most of these details, which make the book much more than a violent story of pursuit and mayhem, are missing from the film *Bladerunner*. Good though that movie is in its way, it is also lacking in the most characteristic Dickian element: humour. For example, Deckard and his wife (he is married in the novel, unlike the macho loner of the film) overcome their sorrows by using a 'Penfield mood organ'. They keep this ingenious device by their bedside, and it programmes their moods for the day. Perversely, Deckard's wife schedules a 'six-hour self-accusatory depression' for herself. He remonstrates with her, suggesting she dial the number for 'the desire to watch TV, no matter what's on it,' or, better still, 'pleased acknowledgement of husband's superior wisdom in all matters.'

The action of the novel takes place over a twenty-four hour period, and the plot concerns Deckard's hunt for a group of dangerous 'Nexus-6' androids. He eventually traces the last of them to J.R. Isidore's lonely apartment, and kills them—but first he has the disturbing experience of falling in love with a female android, the beautiful Rachael Rosen (whom he allows to go free). He has 'retired' six androids in a day, but it gives him no joy. He returns home, and as he falls into bed his wife sets the mood organ for 'long deserved peace'.

First edition: Garden City, Doubleday, 1968 (hardcover)
First British edition: London, Rapp and Whiting, 1969 (hardcover)
Most recent editions: London, Granada, and New York, Del Rey (paperbacks)

56
THOMAS M. DISCH
Camp Concentration

The sf New Wave was cresting on both sides of the Atlantic by the time this marvellous novel appeared. Thomas Michael Disch (born 1940) straddled the waters. He was an American who had chosen to live in England for a while; *Camp Concentration*, his fourth sf novel, first appeared as a 1967 serial in the British magazine *New Worlds* (edited by the remarkable Michael Moorcock, who was of an age with Disch). His earlier works—*The Genocides* (1965), *Mankind Under the Leash* (1966) and *Echo Round His Bones* (1967)—were sprightly, witty, sardonic; but it was with the outrageously titled *Camp Concentration* that he really made his mark.

In a sense it is part of the literary response to the Vietnam war. It projects a world, some decades on from the 1960s, in which the USA is fighting an endless war against Third World guerrillas on almost every front. The narrative is not directly concerned with this struggle, however, since the protagonist is a conscientious objector. Louis Sacchetti, a rather overweight poet, is imprisoned along with a score of other misfits in an underground military establishment, 'Fort Archimedes', somewhere in the Midwest. There he becomes an unwitting subject of a perverse scientific experiment: he is infected with a germ, a mutated form of the syphilis bug, which has the effect of raising human intelligence. It also has unfortunate side-effects: physical decay and death.

Disch tackles this demanding subject matter head on, no holds barred. The story is told in the first person, in the form of a prison diary which Sacchetti is encouraged to keep. Already an intelligent man at the outset of the novel, he turns into a genius—with the reader, as it were, inside his head. It is a difficult feat to bring off, and indeed the book falters at times, but the degree to which Disch succeeds is nevertheless astonishing. The narrative is dense with literary references, particularly with references to the major versions of the Faust story from Marlowe to Thomas Mann. A character called Mordecai Washington plays

Mephistopheles to Sacchetti's Dr Faustus. He is Disch's most entertaining creation: almost an illiterate prior to the commencement of the experiment, he has gained a formidable understanding of all Western culture in a period of just six months (Fort Archimedes has a well-stocked library), and he is now the tacit leader of the camp's inmates. He becomes preoccupied with the study of alchemy, much to Sacchetti's bafflement.

Meanwhile Sacchetti has his own obsessions to indulge. As his body begins to fall apart he is inspired to heights of creativity, producing long and fiendishly knotty poems full of devastating new insights (Disch, himself an accomplished poet as well as an sf writer, wisely refrains from quoting more than a few lines of Sacchetti's masterpieces). His efforts culminate with a drama called 'Auschwitz: A Comedy'—after which he goes through a period of silence, followed by some poetic ravings. The story ends with a return to lucidity, in which we learn the surprising outcome of Mordecai's alchemical research (it was all a front to deceive the prison's authorities) and the precise form of heavenly grace which is to be Louis Sacchetti's salvation.

Camp Concentration is the novel of a very gifted young man. He is stylish, extremely intelligent, and inclined to show off. There can be no doubt, though, that he has created a memorable work of art.

First edition: London, Hart-Davis, 1968 (hardcover)
First American edition: Garden City, Doubleday, 1968 (hardcover)
Most recent editions: London, Granada, and New York, Bantam (paperbacks)

57

MICHAEL MOORCOCK
The Final Programme

Parts of this novel first appeared in *New Worlds* in 1965 and 1966. Michael Moorcock (born 1939), best known at that time for his sword-and-sorcery tales about Elric of Melniboné, had written it in the space of a month. Despite the speed of composition, it was his first 'serious' novel, and appropriately enough his first humorous one, but it took him several years to find a willing book publisher. It must have seemed a zany work, even an incomprehensible one, to those who read it in manuscript. Nevertheless, when the book eventually reached a British hardcover edition *The Times Literary Supplement* pronounced: 'The total effect has—of what other science-fiction catastrophe novel could one use the word?—charm . . .' Readers have continued to be charmed by *The Final Programme*, and by its three progressively more ambitious sequels, *A Cure for Cancer* (1971), *The English Assassin* (1972) and *The Condition of Muzak* (1977). The four books were later published, in America only, as a single volume entitled *The Cornelius Chronicles*.

The first edition of *The Final Programme* contained this dedication: 'To Jimmy Ballard, Bill Burroughs, and the Beatles—who are pointing the way through.' That mix of names is indicative of the novel's flavour. The main character, Jerry Cornelius, is a long-haired, pill-popping young man of ambivalent sexuality. He is reputed to be a former Jesuit, and has written a book called *Time-Search Through The Declining West*. He likes fast cars and power boats, and appreciates rock music by The Who, The Moody Blues, and The Animals ('Jerry played only the best'). He carries a 'needle gun', and is not loth to use it. An apparently amoral fantasy-figure, Jerry Cornelius is Moorcock's conscious attempt at the creation of a larger-than-life hero who is fit for the times. He is chameleon-like and impossible to pin down, moving insouciantly through a world in chaos.

The first third of the book is a fast-moving, violent account of a raid on Jerry's former home in Northern France. Jerry, in league with the dangerous Miss Brunner, pursues a vendetta against his vile brother, who is holding their sister prisoner. In the second part the action moves back to London, where Jerry is truly at home: 'It was a world ruled these days by the gun, the guitar, and the needle, sexier than sex, where the good right hand had become the male's primary sexual organ . . .' It is very macho, and redolent of a kind of knowing innocence which seems highly characteristic of the 1960s. The plot, which makes no sense at all (quite deliberately so), now involves Jerry in a trip to Lapland, where Miss Brunner is building a computer in underground caverns abandoned by the Nazis. This machine will run the 'final programme', integrating the sum total of human knowledge. In London once again, Jerry throws a party which is the set-piece of the third section of the novel. The party lasts for months and is attended by 'Turkish and Persian lesbians with huge houri eyes like those of sad, neutered cats', as well as a pop group called The Deep Fix and 'a self-pitying albino' (in-references, these), and many, many others.

The book ends with the creation of a new, artificial Messiah—a hermaphroditic fusion of Jerry and Miss Brunner—which leads the population of Europe to its doom in the sea. 'A tasty world,' the Messiah reflects when the job is done, 'a very tasty world.' One can only attempt to describe *The Final Programme*, not to analyze it. Much of it, particularly the last two-thirds, is richly entertaining even if it is utterly baffling. It is not really a satire, nor does it seem cynical: it is a comedy of desperation, a Pop-Art novel, all surfaces and appearances, which captures the mood of its day beautifully.

First edition: New York, Avon, 1968 (paperback)
First British edition: London, Allison and Busby, 1969 (hardcover)
Most recent edition: London, Fontana (paperback)

58
KEITH ROBERTS
Pavane

Most science fiction writers like to enlighten us (or dazzle us) with a certain amount of technical knowledge, be it a knowledge of astrophysics, sociology, psychology or whatever. Keith Roberts (born 1935) is no exception, but in his case the technicalities are of an unexpected sort: 'On the bench in front of the monk lay a slab of limestone some two feet long by four or more inches thick. Beside it were boxes of silver sand; Brother John was engaged in grinding the surface of the stone, pouring the sand through wells in a circular iron muller which he afterwards spun with some dexterity, whirling an emulsion of water and abrasive across the slab. The job was both tiring and exacting; when finished, the stone must have no trace of bowing in either direction. From time to time he checked it for concavity, laying a steel straight-edge across its surface. After some hours the slab was nearing completion, and its most critical stage. The grained texture imparted by the muller must also be free of blemish . . .'

Brother John is preparing the slab for use in a lithographic printing press—a press which turns out handbills and advertisements, such as the one which shows 'a drawing of a buxom country girl holding a sheaf of barley, and the inscription *Harvesters Ale; brewed under licence at the monastery of Saint Adhelm, Sherborne, Dorset.*' A lovingly-described but old-fashioned technology abounds elsewhere in the book, notably in the opening section (or 'First Measure'), which introduces us to Jesse Strange, the proud owner of a fleet of steam locomotives. These are engines which run on roads, not rails, and they are the main form of heavy transport in this England of AD 1968: 'Maybe one day petrol propulsion might amount to something . . . But the hand of the Church would have to be lifted first. The Bull of 1910, *Petroleum Veto*, had limited the capacity of IC engines to 150cc's, and since then the [steam] hauliers had had no real competition. Petrol vehicles had been forced to fit gaudy sails to help tow themselves along . . .'

Readers will gather from this odd blend of ancient and modern, of the cloistered and the commercial, that *Pavane* is yet another alternative-world novel. It is set in a time-stream where Queen Elizabeth I was assassinated in the year 1588, Philip II of Spain conquered England, and the consequent 'War of The Three Henrys ended with the Holy League triumphant, and the Church restored once more to her ancient power.' The central fact of this world is the oppressive power of the Catholic Church, a power which has stifled scientific enquiry and technical progress. Nevertheless, change has been taking place, if slowly, and men like Jesse Strange and Brother John are its agents. The struggle between the Church and the inchoate forces of material progress is coming to a head.

The novel does not consist of a single consecutive narrative, but of six long stories together with a prologue and coda (the individual parts first appeared in the short-lived British sf magazine *Impulse*, of which Keith Roberts was managing editor). The 'Measures' of the book are precisely detailed and intensely felt, each a masterpiece in miniature. They progress like a vividly-costumed stately dance, or *pavane*. The 'Coda' is very revealing. In a future era of monorails and electric power stations—long after the protracted battle has been won and the Church forced to retreat—we are given a brief glimpse of our own time-stream with its frenetic pace of change. It is suggested that the Church had foreknowledge of our world, and set out—successfully—to prevent its coming into being: 'The Church knew there was no halting Progress; but slowing it . . ., giving man time to reach a little higher towards true Reason; that was the gift she gave this world. And it was priceless. Did she oppress? Did she hang and burn? A little, yes. But there was no Belsen. No Buchenwald. No Passchendaele.'

First edition: London, Hart-Davis, 1968 (hardcover)
First American edition: Garden City, Doubleday, 1968 (hardcover)
Most recent editions: London, Penguin, and New York, Ace
(paperbacks)

59

ANGELA CARTER

Heroes and Villains

'Marianne lived in a white tower made of steel and concrete. She looked out of her window and, in autumn, she saw a blazing hill of corn and orchards where the trees creaked with crimson apples; in spring, the fields unfurled like various flags, first brown, then green. Beyond the farmland was nothing but marshes, an indifferent acreage of tumbled stone and some distant intimations of the surrounding forest which, in certain stormy lights of late August, seemed to encroach on and menace the community . . .' And in that forest, which fills most of this wild terrain of the not-so-distant future, live Barbarians, terrifying men and women decorated with tattoos, war paint and crude ornaments. Dangerous animals also roam there, over the broken remains of pre-War roads and buildings. From a few small clues, we learn that the scene is set in the aftermath of a nuclear cataclysm (Marianne's nurse has six fingers on each hand: she is obviously a mutant). The soldiers who defend the community have guns, and there are still a few petrol-driven trucks, but these details are of small importance. It is essentially a stripped-down, almost primal setting for an intensely-written tale of love and hate, civilization and barbarism, order and chaos, heroes and villains, as these things are perceived by one young woman.

Angela Carter (born 1940) is a distinguished British novelist, not normally associated with the field of science fiction. All her writing is highly imaginative, and pushes its subject matter to extremes. *Heroes and Villains* is prefaced by a quotation from the critic Leslie A. Fiedler: 'The Gothic mode is essentially a form of parody, a way of assailing clichés by exaggerating them to the limit of grotesqueness.' This could well stand as a justification for every novel by Angela Carter, especially her later fantasies such as *The Infernal Desire Machines of Dr Hoffman* (1972) and *The Passion of New Eve* (1977). Her work is of a piece. Nevertheless I single out *Heroes and Villains* for mention here because it is her closest approach to a formal sf text.

Marianne runs away from the dully oppressive community of the Professors—evidently the remains of an old university, where a now meaningless literacy is kept alive in flickering fashion. She takes up with a young Barbarian called Jewel. He leads her through the woods to a camp which is centred on a ruined building: 'This house was a gigantic memory of rotten stone, a compilation of innumerable forgotten styles now given some green unity by the devouring web of creeper, fur of moss and fungoid growth . . . The forest perched upon the tumbled roofs in the shapes of yellow and purple weeds rooted in the gapped tiles, besides a few small trees and bushes. The windows gaped or sprouted internal foliage, as if the forest were as well already camped inside, there gathering strength for a green eruption which would one day burst the walls sky high back to nature.'

Jewel rapes Marianne. Life in the Barbarian tribe is harsh and disease-ridden. But it turns out that Jewel has a 'tutor', an exiled Professor with whom Marianne has learned conversations. She asks why he has not taught Jewel to read, and the man replies: 'Literacy would blur his outlines.' Eventually Marianne is married to Jewel, not unwillingly, in a bizarre and elaborate ceremony ('The ancient chapel was full of wild people in rags and fur'). Perhaps the whole thing should be read as an allegory of relations between the sexes in contemporary society—a most un-genteel alternative to the conventional domestic novel. But unlike the general run of allegories, this book is notable for the brilliant immediacy of its images. There is a startling clarity to its visions, and a complex depth to its eroticism, which make it much more than just another fey literary fantasy.

First edition: London, Heinemann, 1969 (hardcover)
First American edition: New York, Simon and Schuster, 1969 (hardcover)
Most recent editions: London, Penguin, and New York, Pocket (paperbacks)

60
URSULA K. LE GUIN
The Left Hand of Darkness

Here we have yet another famous novel which began life as a humble paperback original—it has since been through several hardcover editions and has sold by the hundreds of thousands in paperback. Ursula Kroeber Le Guin (born 1929) published her first short story in 1962 and followed it up with three slim sf novels which went almost unnoticed (the best of them is *City of Illusions*, 1967). In 1968 a successful children's book brought her a measure of fame, and in 1969 she consolidated that spectacularly with *The Left Hand of Darkness*. By the mid-1970s Le Guin was the most frequently discussed, the most intensively *studied*, of contemporary sf writers. There had been a number of women novelists in the male-dominated field of American science fiction (C.L. Moore, Leigh Brackett, Judith Merril, Zenna Henderson and Anne McCaffrey, to name a few), but Le Guin was the first to gain indisputable major status—the first to become, in effect, a guru; an inspiration to younger writers of both sexes, as well as to readers.

Appropriately enough, *The Left Hand of Darkness* deals with the subject of gender. It is a rich, romantic, philosophical novel about life on a far planet known as Gethen, or Winter. The inhabitants of Gethen are human beings who differ from ourselves in one important respect: they are hermaphrodites. More exactly, they are sexless for much of the time but they develop male or female attributes when they are in *kemmer* (that is, in season). During *kemmer* each person may become sexually active as a man or a woman, according to circumstances. The novel's central character, Genly Ai, is an Earthman, black-skinned as it happens: 'Gethenians are yellow-brown or red-brown, generally, but I have seen a good many as dark as myself.' He has come to Gethen as an envoy of the Ekumen, the interstellar federation of worlds. He has difficulty in accustoming himself to the uncertain sexuality of these people: 'My efforts took the form of self-consciously seeing a Gethenian first as a man, then as a woman, forcing him into those categories so irrelevant to his nature and so essential to my own.'

Gethen is gripped by an ice age—and its political institutions are frozen too. Genly Ai has to cope with separate nations, monarchs, prime ministers, bureaucrats. When his most trustworthy acquaintance, a 'man' called Estraven, is banished from the kingdom of Karhide, Genly decides to follow him into exile. Much of the narrative is taken up with an account of his journeyings and his slow-growing appreciation of Gethenian customs and religion. Many details are conveyed to the reader through the medium of folk tales (beautifully done by Le Guin) which Genly records during his travels. Eventually he meets up with Estraven once more, and after various vicissitudes the two are imprisoned. They escape, and make a heroic trek across the ice-cap to Karhide, their starting-point.

The ice journey is the high point of the novel, a tremendous piece of descriptive writing. During their trek, Genly, the man from Earth, and Estraven, the manwoman of the planet Winter, grow to understand each other and to love each other. 'Light is the left hand of darkness,' Estraven quotes from one of his world's poets, 'and darkness the right hand of light': it is an expression of wholeness, so alien from the Earthman's obsession with duality. At the journey's end Estraven is killed by border guards. Broken-hearted, Genly carries on to a successful completion of his mission: the king of Karhide is persuaded to join the Ekumen. Delicate yet daring in its handling of sexual themes, narrated with immense *gravitas*, *The Left Hand of Darkness* remains Ursula Le Guin's masterpiece.

First edition: New York, Ace, 1969 (paperback)
First British edition: London, Macdonald, 1969 (hardcover)
Most recent editions: New York, Harper and Row (hardcover);
New York, Ace, and London, Futura (paperbacks)

61

BOB SHAW

The Palace of Eternity

In 1966 Bob Shaw made a considerable impact on the readers of
Analog magazine with his short story, 'Light of Other Days',
about slow glass, a substance which impedes the passage of light
by days or weeks or even years, allowing one to view the past.
The story was later incorporated into the novel *Other Days,
Other Eyes* (1972). His first two novels, *Night Walk* (1967) and
The Two-Timers (1968), were solidly enjoyable science fictions
of a traditional sort. Appearing during the heyday of the sf New
Wave, they attracted little attention from critics. With the publication of *The Palace of Eternity*—the first which I read and my
favourite among his early novels—it became clear that Shaw had
emerged as a very dependable writer of the second rank in British
sf. He did not attempt to push back the boundaries of the *genre*,
as did Aldiss, Ballard or Moorcock, but he was able to produce
effective work within discreetly updated versions of the conventions that had been laid down during the 1940s and 50s.

It is a story of interstellar war. The hero, Mack Tavernor, lives
on a colonized world known as Mnemosyne, the 'poets' planet'.
An ex-army man, tired of the forty-year war against the alien
Syccans, he has come to this beautiful world for respite. It seems,
however, that the war will follow him there. Tavernor is horrified when a military force arrives on Mnemosyne and reduces his
beloved forest to 'a shimmering, glass-smooth plain'. He has seen
something very like this on another planet, where the increasingly tyrannical forces of Imperial Earth had turned their advanced
weapons against human rebels:

> Tavernor spent a day walking across the green-and-silver lakes
> of cellulose. Towards evening he found an area where the flux had
> run clear.
> And from below the amber surface a dead woman's face looked
> up at him.
> He knelt on the glassy surface for a holy moment, staring down
> at the pale, drowned ovoid of her face. The black swirls of her hair

were frozen, preserved, eternal . . .

This is a haunting image, of a sort which is not uncommon in Shaw's fiction.

The plot quickens as Tavernor takes to the wild with a group of renegade poets and artists. Mnemosyne is being transformed into a military base; people's homes are destroyed, the environment despoiled, and Tavernor is forced into the role of guerrilla leader. All of these action sequences are excitingly done, told with imaginative flair. Suddenly, almost two-thirds of the way through the narrative does a surprising flip: Tavernor is killed, to be reborn in outer space as an 'egon'. He is one of millions of such entities, 'organized clouds of energy' which feed on sunlight. The egon-mass surrounding Mnemosyne forms a 'world-mind', and it is gradually being destroyed by the passage of the faster-than-light spacecraft which the human race uses to prosecute its war against the Syccans. The collective mind of the egon-mass decides that Tavernor should be reincarnated as his own son . . .

It is a curious blend of hardware and metaphysics. Some readers may find the novel broken-backed: the extravagance of the later episodes does not gell with the 'realism' of the opening scenes. Bob Shaw (born 1931 in Northern Ireland) is slightly reminiscent of the American writer Clifford Simak, in that he is essentially a teller of tall tales which are often excessively re-complicated. *The Palace of Eternity* has something of the silliness and seductiveness of a 1950s novel such as *Ring Around the Sun*. But it has more besides, for Shaw is a better writer than Simak: his characterization is more than adequate, his scientific and engineering speculations are convincing, and above all his images and metaphors are memorable.

First edition: New York, Ace, 1969 (paperback)
First British edition: London, Gollancz, 1970 (hardcover)
Most recent edition: London, Pan (paperback)

62
NORMAN SPINRAD
Bug Jack Barron

This notorious novel of the US New Wave was serialized in *New Worlds* in 1968. It caused quite a fuss. A leading British distributor refused to sell the magazine because of it, and a Member of Parliament asked the Government why the Arts Council was funding a magazine which produced such filth. In fact, *Bug Jack Barron* could *only* have been published in Moorcock's *New Worlds*: no American sf magazine would have dared to touch it. In contrast to that previous *New Worlds* serial, Disch's *Camp Concentration*, which represented American New Wave sf at its most urbane and witty and 'civilized', Spinrad's novel was raw meat. It is a story about politics, big business and television in the USA of the near future, and it has some tough things to say about power and corruption—but what made it seem so innovative was that it was the first sf novel to use four-letter obscenities profusely and to describe sexual acts in explicit detail. Norman Spinrad (born 1940) described the book as an attempt at 'a coherent *Nova Express*'. This was undoubtedly self-flattery, for his images do not have William Burrough's unnerving clarity. Nevertheless . . .

Jack Barron, one-time student radical, is the compère of a live TV show called 'Bug Jack Barron'. Using the video-telephone system, viewers call in with their grouses and grumbles, and Jack attempts to resolve their problems on the air before an audience of a hundred million. He phones politicians, high officials, corporation presidents, and the like, challenging them to answer the points that have been raised. He sits at the centre of an electronic web which spans a continent, wielding immense media power—and it has made him cynical and manipulative. His left-wing ideals have decayed, worn away by a rich lifestyle, yet he finds himself being forced to take up a stance against an evil multi-millionaire called Benedict Howards. Jack becomes the gallant knight once more, tilting at the bad guys. Howards owns the Foundation for Human Immortality, an outfit which freezes the dead body of any American able to pay $50,000 for the privilege. The Foundation carries out research into longevity—immortality is an obsession of Howards'—and, unknown to the public, it has already achieved a degree of success, but at a terrible human cost, involving the irradiation of certain glands in young black children and transferring those glands to older bodies.

A very conventional sf plot lurks beneath the surface of the book—but then the surface is what matters most. Spinrad uses a breathless slangy style which is an extrapolation of the 'hip' speech of 1960s America, headlong and adjectival:

> Watching the commercial fade into his own face on the monitor, Barron felt a weird psychedelic flash go through him, the reality of the last week compressed into an instantaneous image flashed on the promptboard of his mind: Sitting in the studio chair, electronic feedback-circuitry connecting him with subsystems of power—Foundation power, S.J.C.-Democrat-Republican power, hundred million Brackett Count power—he was like the master transistor in a massive satellite network confluence circuit of power, gigantic input of others' power feeding into his head through vidphone circuits, none of it his, but all feeding through him, his to control by microcosmic adjustment; for one hour, 8-9 P.M. Eastern Standard Time, that power was de facto *his*.
>
> He felt his subjective head-time speeding up, like an alien drug in his bloodstream, at the focus of forces far beyond him yet at his command as letters crawled across the promptboard an electric-dot message that seemed to take ten million years: 'On the Air'.
>
> 'And what's bugging you out there tonight?' Jack Barron asked, playing to the kinesthop-darkness shapes double-reflected (backdrop off desktop) in his eye hollows ominous with foreknowledge of the shape of the show to come. 'What bugs you, bugs Jack Barron,' he said, digging his own image on the monitor, eyes picking up flashes as never before ·. . .

This is a novel about living in a media landscape, and the prose is intended to convey the all-embracing, ever-changing qualities of the electronic media. Frequently over-the-top, occasionally sentimental, for the most part it works surprisingly well.

First edition: New York, Avon, 1969 (paperback) and New York, Walker, 1969 (hardcover)
First British Edition: London, Macdonald, 1970 (hardcover)
Most recent editions: London, Granada, and New York, Berkley (paperbacks)

63

POUL ANDERSON
Tau Zero

In his introduction to a short-story collection called *The Best of Poul Anderson* (1976), Barry Malzberg refers to Anderson's 'magnificent novel, *Tau Zero*,' which, he says, 'has long struck me as the only work published after 1955 or so that can elicit from me some of the same responses I had towards science fiction in my adolescence—a sense of timelessness, human eternity, and the order of the cosmos as reflected in the individual fate of every person who would try to measure himself against these qualities . . . The novel builds to an overpowering climax, yet has a decent sense of humility . . . *Tau Zero* suggested to me that it was not my own sense of wonder but that of the science-fiction field itself that had flagged within the last twenty years.'

Well, it is not quite as good a book as Malzberg suggests, but many people have responded to it in similar terms. It is a traditional sf novel in several ways: a space story, conceived on an intergalactic scale, and a sense-of-wonder tale which exploits the perspectives of modern cosmology to bring about a marvellous sequence of conceptual breakthroughs. Its characters fail to convince me, and Anderson's purple prose is sometimes embarrassing, but as an exercise in hard sf, yes, it is second to none.

Poul Anderson (born 1926) studied physics at university before turning to full-time sf writing while still in his early twenties. He has been a prolific purveyor of the goods ever since, praised for such novels as *Brain Wave* (1954) and *The High Crusade* (1960). I have always enjoyed his time-travel stories, for example *Guardians of Time* (1960) and *The Corridors of Time* (1965), but he is perhaps at his most characteristic when writing of spaceships and far planets. Anderson is known to hold conservative views (an exponent of free enterprise to the stars), and when *Tau Zero* appeared in 1970 it was regarded as something of a comeback for the Old Guard of American sf—the New Wave, which had crested in the late 60s, was perceived by hostile critics as being pessimistic, anti-scientific, muddle-headed and dangerously liberal.

What happens in the novel is this: in the 23rd century fifty men and women set out from Earth aboard an interstellar space-craft called the *Leonora Christine*. Their destination is a planet some thirty light-years distant. The ship scoops up hydrogen as it flies through space, burning it in a fusion reaction which will bring the vessel close to the speed of light. Aboard the ship sub-jective time slows (as Einstein predicted it should) so that the journey of several decades will seem to be of just a few years' duration to the travellers. In the mathematics of relativity there is a factor known as *tau*. The closer *tau* comes to zero, when the vessel's speed would theoretically equal that of light, the more massive the ship becomes—and the more stretched out its sub-jective time—in relation to the rest of the universe. Nine light-years out from Earth an accident occurs: the *Leonora Christine* strikes a cloud of interstellar dust. Aside from some bad buffet-ing, there is no immediate adverse effect on the flight—accelera-tion continues towards light-speed. However, the crew soon dis-cover that their deceleration system has been wrecked: they are unable to stop, and they carry on gaining velocity as the *tau* fac-tor creeps inexorably towards zero. The upshot of this is that within a short (subjective) time the ship is speeding through whole galaxies in the blink of an eye; millions of years pass in the outer universe as the ship grows ever more massive, devouring interstellar matter at a colossal rate. The consequences, for the ship's crew and for the fabric of reality, are ingeniously worked out— 'mind-boggling' seems much too mild a term to describe them.

First edition: Garden City, Doubleday, 1970 (hardcover)
First British edition: London, Gollancz, 1971 (hardcover)
Most recent editions: New York, Berkley, and London, Coronet
(paperbacks)

64
ROBERT SILVERBERG
Downward to the Earth

Robert Silverberg (born 1935) has been the most prolific of all science fiction writers. A professional author by the time he was twenty-one, he used to turn out at least a million words a year. Leaving aside the reams of non-sf, one still has to choose from among dozens of his science fiction novels, many of them surprisingly good. The books which he wrote between *Thorns* (1967) and *Shadrach in the Furnace* (1976) are generally reckoned to be his best, with *Dying Inside* (1972) often cited as his masterpiece. I am not fond of that bitter novel, well-written as it is. It strikes me as being a solemn and self-conscious version of Philip Roth's *Portnoy's Complaint*—with telepathy taking the place of masturbation. I much prefer *Downward to the Earth*, which is sf of a purer kind, done with feeling.

It is about an Earthman's quest for enlightenment on an Edenic alien planet. Edmund Gundersen has returned to the former colony-world of Belzagor after eight years away. He is driven by an obscure guilt. Belzagor has now gained its independence from Earth's empire, and its two intelligent species—the *nildoror*, who look rather like horned mastodons, and the *sulidoror*, who resemble abominable snowmen with long tails—have allowed most of the human colonial settlements to fall into decay. A few Earth-people linger on there, catering for a small tourist trade, but the *nildoror* and the *sulidoror* have no use for human things—for money, gadgets, or even buildings—and there is no real commerce. Theirs is an amazingly peaceful, pastoral society. The climate is very warm and the plant-life lush, but it is difficult for Earthmen to understand how intelligent beings can be so placid, so indifferent to material progress. The natives of Belzagor seem to be interested in just one thing—the religion which both species share, with its hidden rites of 'purification' and 'rebirth'.

Gundersen's guilt springs from the fact that once, years before when he was working as a colonial administrator, he forcefully prevented some *nildoror* from travelling into the Mist Country to visit their sacred mountain and participate in the all-important ceremony of rebirth. At that time Gundersen held the natives in contempt, as did most members of Earth's administration. Now he has come back to atone, if that is at all possible, and to discover just why it is that rebirth means so much to the *nildoror*. He sets out on a lonely pilgrimage to the Mist Country, visiting a few scattered Earth-folk along the way—such as his former girl-friend, Seena, and her husband Kurtz, who, it turns out, has himself penetrated the alien holy-of-holies and has been hideously transformed. The name Kurtz alerts us to the fact that this novel is in part a science-fictional recension of Joseph Conrad's *Heart of Darkness*. Silverberg has stated that he wrote the book shortly after a visit to Africa, and that he had Conrad's powerful novella of psychological horror very much in mind.

Although to some extent a self-conscious book—an *exercise*, like so much of Silverberg's work—*Downward to the Earth* builds its own power. The alien jungles and plateaux are very well described, and there are several pieces of memorable grotesquerie: the 'milking' of serpents; the ritual dances of the elephantine *nildoror*; an unfortunate couple from Earth who have become horribly infested by alien parasites; and the climactic scenes set inside the mountain of rebirth, where Gundersen is eventually vouchsafed a vision of the meaning of life.

First edition: Garden City, Nelson Doubleday (Science Fiction Book Club), 1970 (hardcover)
First British edition: London, Gollancz, 1977 (hardcover)
Most recent editions: London, Pan, and New York, Bantam (paperbacks)

148

65

WILSON TUCKER
The Year of the Quiet Sun

Arthur Wilson Tucker (born 1914) is a minor American sf writer who has tended to specialize in tales of time travel. One of his best-remembered novels is *The Lincoln Hunters* (1958), about men of the future who travel back to the mid-19th century in search of Abraham Lincoln. By contrast, *The Year of the Quiet Sun* is about an exploration of the very near future via time machine. The story opens in the 1970s. Its reluctant hero, Brian Chaney, is an expert on ancient Palestine, and author of a book called *From the Qumram Caves: Past, Present and Future*. He is recruited by a beautiful young woman, Katrina von Hise, who works for the US Bureau of Standards. They are to participate in a survey of the year 2000, a *physical* survey using the newly-invented and top-secret Time Displacement Vehicle.

Chaney has translated an old document, 'Eschatos', from the Hebrew. It foretells the end of civilization, but Chaney believes not a word of it, regarding it as a piece of *midrash*, or Biblical fiction. However, he does have a gloomy faith in the long view of human affairs: 'I can predict the downfall of the United States, of every government on the North American continent . . . I mean that all this will be dust in ten thousand years. Name a single government, a single nation which has endured since the birth of civilization—say, five or six thousand years ago . . . Nothing endures. The United States will not. If we are fortunate we may endure at least as long as Jericho.' Chaney makes this prophecy to the director of the project before he embarks in the one-man time machine. His first foray takes him just a couple of years into the future. He has been ordered to discover the results of the next presidential election, and this he does, though he is disconcerted to find that Chicago has been torn in two by bloody race riots and that a makeshift wall divides the city.

The main expedition into the future now follows. One man is sent to July 1999, and another to November 2000. The first dies, the other returns badly injured. Chaney travels further ahead, to the year 2009. He finds a bleak, desolate landscape. America has become divided on racial lines, and has ruined itself in a protracted civil war. Chaney sees a group of ragged people and hails them: 'They stood motionless, frozen by fear, for only a tick in time. The woman cried out as though in pain . . . she ran to protect the child. The man sprinted after her—passed her—and caught up the child in a quick scooping motion . . . They ran from him with all the speed and strength they possessed, the child now crying with consternation. Fear ran with them . . . Chaney picked up the rifle and turned away . . . He had never known anyone to run from him—not even those beggar children who had squatted on the sands of the Negev and watched him pry into the sands of their forgotten history. They were timid and mistrustful, those Bedouin, but they hadn't run from him . . . He walked with the taste of wormwood in his mouth.' We discover, for the first time, that Chaney is black (the ragged people were whites). It seems that thirty years, not three thousand, have been enough to obliterate the United States of his own day. The Year of the Quiet Sun, foretold by an old Hebrew prophet in the Dead Sea scroll which Chaney translated, has already come.

It is a simple book, old-fashioned in tone and at times crudely written, but nevertheless quite moving in its conclusion. Chaney finds Katrina, now a middle-aged woman. He realizes that he has always been in love with her. Unable to return to his own time, he settles down to watch the long slow end of the world.

First edition: New York, Ace, 1970 (paperback)
First British edition: London, Hale, 1971 (hardcover)
Most recent editions: Boston, Gregg Press (hardcover),
and London, Arrow (paperback)

66
THOMAS M. DISCH
334

This book, which I still believe to be Disch's masterpiece, received little attention when it was first published as a British hardcover (apart from a review in the *Birmingham Evening Mail* which described it as 'Brave New Worldy, four-letter-wordy, and frighteningly fascinating'). Its first American edition did not appear until 1974, and then only as a paperback original. Disch was truly a prophet without honour in his own country.

It is a novel in six sections, five of which were originally published as separate short stories or novellas. Yet it adds up to more than a 'story cycle', for the pieces are closely related and cunningly interwoven. Together they constitute a social novel of rare power and beauty. I use the phrase 'social novel' advisedly, for the book is about the relationships of realistically-drawn characters in an invented setting which has all the stubbornness of actuality. It concerns people living in New York fifty years in the future (the title refers to the number of the huge apartment block which houses most of them). The world Disch creates is no crude dystopia, but it is infused with a great sadness. In many ways *334* is an image of what the future will be like if things go comparatively well: the population explosion has been controlled by strict family planning, automation has reduced the need for unskilled labour, and a welfare state ensures that no-one starves. In fact, Disch's world of the early 21st century is a social planner's paradise, full of technological wonders. But it has a heart of stone.

The author concentrates on the losers in this utopia. They are people like Birdie Ludd, who fails his REGENTS test (the reference is to the Revised Genetics Testing Act of 2011) and tries to recoup by writing an essay on 'Problems of Creativeness'—a painful business—but ends up becoming a US Marine instead. Or Chapel, the hospital porter who spends all his off-work hours watching soap operas on TV. Or Alexa, the social worker who reads Oswald Spengler and indulges in drug-induced daydreams of the late Roman Empire—as she gradually cracks up. Or Boz Hanson, happily married to Milly, who wants to fill his time by becoming a mother which—with a little medical help, he is able to do. Or Mrs Hanson, mother of many, who is evicted from her apartment, makes a bonfire of her belongings in the street, and then begs for death: 'You've *got* to approve my application. If you don't, I'll appeal . . . My whole family was a smart family, with very high scores. I never did much with my intelligence, I have to confess, but I'll do this. I'll get what I want and what I have a right to.'

For the most part, Disch's characters are the unemployed, the ageing, those of low IQ, the frustrated and the unfulfilled—the folk who are shunted from one social service department to another, whose path through life is a circuitous route from the orphanage to the old folk's home. They have hopes, fantasies, ambitions, but at every turn they are balked by a society which is beyond comprehension and beyond compassion. Apparent power is in the hands of the planners, administrators and 'experts': however benign their intentions they seem to end up treating people as things. The result is an enormous mute suffering as millions are pushed to the margins of the meritocracy. Much science fiction is about winners; its characters are clever and capable, at home in their technological world or at least confident in their fight against it—if they lose they lose nobly, articulately. Not so in *334*. Disch has written a book about the forgotten people, and in doing so he has produced a fine, subtle and moving novel.

First edition: London, MacGibbon & Kee, 1972 (hardcover)
First American edition: New York, Avon, 1974 (paperback)
Most recent edition: London, Methuen (paperback)

67
GENE WOLFE
The Fifth Head of Cerberus

Imagine a big old house, its entrance guarded by a statue of Cerberus, the mythical three-headed dog. Picture a sensitive boy growing up in this house of mystery. He and his brother are tended by tireless servants, and watched over by an eccentric aunt who seems to float noiselessly along the mansion's many corridors. A distant, authoritarian father summons the boys to his study at dead of night, where he performs meaningless psychological experiments on them. 'I have a dim memory of standing—at how early an age I cannot say—before that huge carved door. Of seeing it swing back, and the crippled monkey on my father's shoulder pressing itself against his hawk face, with the black scarf and scarlet dressing gown beneath and the rows and rows of shabby books and notebooks behind them, and the sick-sweet smell of formaldehyde coming from the laboratory beyond the sliding mirror.' Is this man really the boys' father? The young hero is also the narrator of this deceptive tale: we are not told his name, but his father addresses him as 'Number Five'. The central impulse of the narrator's life is to discover his origins, to unravel the mystery of his parentage.

All this sounds like the purest Gothic, and so it is. Yet the book is also pure science fiction, for the setting is an alien solar system in a spacefaring future. The twin planets of Sainte Croix and Saint Anne have been colonized by French-speakers from Earth. The House of Cerberus, or *Maison du Chien*, is situated in the main city of Sainte Croix, and it is in fact a high-class brothel. The narrator and his brother are looked after by a robot tutor, a wise machine called Mr Million, which carries the brain-pattern of a man long dead. The boys' aunt really does float on air, because she has an electrical levitation device beneath her skirts to compensate for her withered legs. And the narrator's 'father' is not really his father in any normal sense of the term: he is actually the hero's clone-brother, number four in a nightmarish series of self-replications. Tales of cloning—artificial

153

asexual reproduction from the cells of a single 'parent'—became fashionable in the sf of the 1970s; this is perhaps the best of them.

The author has a remarkable talent for combining futuristic motifs and themes with a deep, dank, overwhelming sense of the *past*. Here the technologies are old and redolent of evil, and the brave new interstellar society is like something out of the ancient East: 'Mr Million insisted on stopping for an hour at the slave market . . . It was not a large one . . . and the auctioneers and their merchandise were frequently on a most friendly basis—having met several times previously as a succession of owners discovered the same fault. Mr Million . . . watched the bidding, motionless, while we kicked our heels and munched the fried bread he had bought at a stall for us. There were sedan chairmen, their legs knotted with muscle, and simpering bath attendants; fighting slaves in chains, with eyes dulled by drugs or blazing with imbecile ferocity; cooks, house servants, a hundred others . . .'

Gene Wolfe (born 1931) is a veteran of the Korean War and a former engineer. He was a late starter as a writer of fiction, with his first short stories appearing towards the end of the 1960s. *The Fifth Head of Cerberus* was his first book of substance, and a truly extraordinary work it is too. Consisting of three novellas, different in tone but closely linked, it is one of the most cunningly wrought narratives in the whole of modern sf, a masterpiece of misdirection, subtle clues, and apparently casual revelations. It was appropriately described by Malcolm Edwards in *The Encyclopedia of Science Fiction* as 'a richly imaginative exploration of the nature of identity and individuality'.

First edition: New York, Scribner's, 1972 (hardcover)
First British edition: London, Gollancz, 1973 (hardcover)
Most recent editions: New York, Ace, and London, Arrow (paperbacks)

68

MICHAEL MOORCOCK
The Dancers at the End of Time

'The cycle of the Earth (indeed, the universe, if the truth had been known) was nearing its end and the human race had at last ceased to take itself seriously. Having inherited millennia of scientific and technological knowledge it used this knowledge to indulge its richest fantasies, to play immense imaginative games, to relax and create beautiful monstrosities. After all, there was little else left to do.' So begins this comic trilogy, consisting of *An Alien Heat* (1972), *The Hollow Lands* (1974) and *The End of All Songs* (1976). Full of charm and silliness, the tripartite tale is about the time-travelling adventures of Mr Jherek Carnelian, who hails from the End of Time, and Mrs Amelia Underwood, who comes from Bromley in Kent (AD 1896). Carnelian is evidently an avatar of Moorcock's best-known hero, Jerry Cornelius, though the links between this trilogy and *The Cornelius Chronicles* are of small importance.

The End of Time is an inconceivably remote future era when the universe is dying and the few remaining human beings have apparently unlimited powers of creation. By twisting a few power-rings, and thus drawing on the energy and the incomprehensible technology of the 'rotted cities', the inhabitants of this world can make anything they wish—oceans, landscapes, a sun to give them warmth, an artificial paradise to mask the surface of a barren planet. They lead an amoral but fundamentally innocent existence, and much of the fun-and-games of the trilogy arises from the clash between their languid *fin-du-cosmos* ethos, personified by the decadent but curiously childlike Carnelian, and the stern morality of the Victorian time-traveller, Mrs Underwood, whose head is stuffed with notions of duty, suffering and sacrifice.

With their endless fancy-dress parties, for which they are apt to change sex (or even bodies), and their menageries packed with bizarre creatures, including human specimens from different periods of history, the citizens of the End of Time are profoundly shocking to Amelia Underwood. She has been plucked from the 19th century at the whim of these people, and she is not amused. As soon as possible she has herself sent back to whence she came, but not before Jherek Carnelian has fallen in love with her—an emotion which seems a bright novelty to the bored Jherek. He pursues her down the time-lines, searching for that fabulous place, 23 Collins Avenue, Bromley, in April 1896. Needless to say, Jherek is very confused when he arrives in the suburbs of Victorian London. He is exploited by an East-End crook called Snoozer Vine, is imprisoned, and ends up on the gallows. At the critical moment he is saved by the 'Morphail Effect' (which causes all travellers from the future to revert to their proper eras). In the second volume he is off in search of Bromley again. This time he stumbles into the Café Royale, where he meets a Mr Frank Harris and a Mr Herbert Wells. Riotous events ensue. In the third volume Jherek and Amelia are marooned on a Palaeozoic beach, at the very dawn of the planet's life. They escape to the End of Time with the aid of certain members of the Guild of Temporal Adventurers (characters from other Moorcock novels: *The Warlord of the Air*, 1971, and *The Land Leviathan*, 1974). All ends happily, with a mass wedding and the commencement of a whole new cycle in the universe's history.

This unlikely blend of Wells, Wilde and Wodehouse is primarily a romp, frequently very funny if a bit long-drawn-out. Moorcock uses many 19th-century rhetorical devices to good comic effect, and if one chooses the whole thing can be viewed as a veiled satire on the inadequacy of the traditional English novel to deal with present-day realities (never mind the realities of the End of Time!). After all, the trilogy's title does seem to be a mocking echo of Anthony Powell's novel sequence *A Dance to the Music of Time*, much praised by Britain's literary establishment.

First editions: An Alien Heat, London, MacGibbon & Kee, 1972 (hardcover); *The Hollow Lands*, New York, Harper & Row, 1974 (hardcover); *The End of All Songs*, New York, Harper & Row, 1976 (hardcover)
Most recent edition: The Dancers at the End of Time, London, (paperback; the three novels combined in one volume)

69

J.G. BALLARD
Crash

Its author has described this book as 'an example of a kind of terminal irony, where not even the writer knows where he stands.' He has also said that it is 'an extreme metaphor at a time when only the extreme will do.' There is no doubt that *Crash* is a terrible novel, and a devastating one. It is perhaps the most disturbing work of fiction to have been written in the past twenty years, and—with the possible exception of William Burroughs' *Nova Express*—it is surely the most outrageous of my choices for the present volume. Is it science fiction? Some people think not, but the author believes it to be sf, and I would agree with him. It is a book about technology, represented—obsessively—by the automobile: the motor car as 20th-century icon. But it is more than that: it is about humanity's relationship with technology, about what technology has done to us, and about what we have done to ourselves through technology. More still: it is about the coming of a new world, a mediatized landscape where nothing is 'real', everything is possible. It is about the dark side of the present, about the hidden desires which lurk below the glossy surfaces of a brightly-lit consumer society. It can be read as a dystopian nightmare—not projected on to the future, or another planet, but realized *here*, right now, no further away than your nearest motorway or airport (and perhaps even closer to home than that). Ballard has taken some of the familiar furniture of the early 1970s and made it seem very alien indeed. Moreover, he has refused to moralize about it: he presents us with the material, and it is for us to grapple with it as best we can.

Everything is shockingly bright and vivid, as though the entire action is taking place under the arc-lights of a film crew. There is no vagueness here, no fuzziness, no darkly-muttered warnings. The narrator, a director of TV commercials, is involved in a car crash in which the driver of the other vehicle is killed. As he recovers in hospital, the narrator is overwhelmed by sexual fantasies about the nurses and doctors around him, the crashed cars, and the dead driver's wife. On his release from hospital he immediately takes to the roads again, revisiting the scene of the accident, inspecting his wrecked car in the breaker's yard. He becomes aware that he is being followed by a man with a camera. This is Dr Robert Vaughan, 'one-time computer specialist . . . one of the first of the new-style TV scientists,' who 'projected a potent image, almost that of scientist as hoodlum.' Vaughan is obsessed by car crashes, and spends much of his time photographing them. He and the narrator form an uneasy friendship: they drive around together, become voyeurs of road accidents, share the services of the same airport prostitutes. They watch simulated car crashes at the Road Research Laboratory, and Vaughan confides that it is his ambition to die in an automobile accident with the film star Elizabeth Taylor. Events reach a climax when the narrator and Vaughan cruise the motorways while under the influence of a hallucinogenic drug:

> The daylight above the motorway grew brighter, an intense desert air. The white concrete became a curving bone. Waves of anxiety enveloped the car like pools of heat off summer macadam . . . The cars overtaking us were now being superheated by the sunlight, and I was sure that their metal bodies were only a fraction of a degree below their melting points, held together by the force of my own vision, and that the slightest shift of my attention to the steering wheel would burst the metal films that held them together and break these blocks of boiling steel across our path. By contrast, the oncoming cars were carrying huge cargoes of cool light, floats loaded with electric flowers being transported to a festival. As their speeds increased I found myself drawn into the fast lane, so that the oncoming vehicles were moving almost straight towards us, enormous carousels of accelerating light. Their radiator grilles formed mysterious emblems, racing alphabets that unravelled at high speed across the road surface.

It is an intense, visionary piece of writing which goes on for many pages. Soon afterwards, Vaughan dies in a deliberate car smash, leaving the narrator to mourn—and to 'design the elements' of his own coming death.

First edition: London, Cape, 1973 (hardcover)
First American edition: New York, Farrar, Straus & Giroux, 1973 (hardcover)
Most recent edition: London, Granada (paperback)

158

70

MACK REYNOLDS
Looking Backward,
From The Year 2000

In the 1950s and 60s it seemed that the dream of utopia had died. Science fiction did not give us many visions of future societies which were both radically different and *good*. From *The Space Merchants* to *Stand on Zanzibar* the dystopia was the norm, reflecting modern disenchantment with the possibilities of science and human nature (there were of course a few exceptions, Sturgeon's *Venus Plus X* being one). A surprising feature of the 1970s was the re-emergence of utopia as a serious subject matter for sf. The feminist and ecological movements helped kindle this new enthusiasm, but a refurbished *technophilic* utopianism was also apparent in the work of some minor American authors. Reynolds' *Looking Backward* is the most interesting book of the latter type, a paean of praise to high economic growth and the burgeoning of communications technology.

It is a latter-day rewrite of Edward Bellamy's once-famous *Looking Backward* (1888). Bellamy's hero, Julian West, fell asleep in 1887 and awoke in the year 2000, to find himself in a highly-mechanized socialistic utopia of canned music and egalitarian bliss, a steam-driven paradise which now seems comically out of date. Mack Reynolds set himself the task of recasting the story in a form suitable for the 1970s. Reynolds' version of Julian West is suffering from incurable heart disease, so he has himself 'frozen' until such time as medical science has advanced sufficiently to cope with his problem. He awakes just over thirty years later, at the beginning of the 21st century, in a world utterly transformed. Like Bellamy's, it is an egalitarian society, organized on the principle of 'from each according to his ability, to each according to his need.' It differs from Bellamy's imagined world in that it is an electronic, post-industrial society where the vast majority of the population is unemployed.

Much of the book is taken up with extended dialogues between West and his 'host', Dr Leete. West, a rich and privileged man in his previous incarnation, is disconcerted to find that *everyone* is now wealthy. Even those who do no useful work are assured of a high income. As Leete explains, they are all heirs to millennia of human ingenuity: each individual has a moral right to enjoy the fruits of his ancestors' labour. Goods are produced in automated underground factories; the surface of the Earth is park-like and beautiful, dotted with vast apartment blocks; most people pass the time as eternal students, plugged into the international computer banks which keep them abreast of all human knowledge. That knowledge has increased exponentially: almost the first thing Leete explains is that during the lapse of thirty years 'science' has grown sixteen-fold. Most human endeavour is bent to the task of simply *keeping up*. It is a free and equal and materially bountiful society, but its intellectual demands prove daunting to the unfortunate Julian West.

One could pick at many implausibilies, but the book's main weakness is that it does not show how humanity got from *here* to *there* (somehow, it all 'just happened'). Nevertheless, the author pulls the threads of his utopia together quite effectively, and it makes for a pleasurable read. Dallas McCord Reynolds (1917-1983) was an anomalous figure in American sf. As a prolific author of poorly-written action novels about spies and mercenaries and gladiators he was especially popular with the readership of *Analog*, that most right-wing of sf magazines. Yet he was also the man who wrote of himself: 'I was born into a Marxian Socialist family. I am the child who, at the age of five or six, said to his parent, "Mother, who is Comrade Jesus Christ?"... While still in my teens, I joined the Marxist Socialist Labor Party and remained, very active, in it for many years . . . I have been a lifelong radical . . .' In *Looking Backward* he tried to reconcile his political beliefs with the technophilia of *Analog*-type sf—and it is that unholy mixture which makes the book fascinating.

First edition: New York, Ace, 1973 (paperback)
First British edition: Morley, Elmfield Press, 1976 (hardcover)

71

IAN WATSON
The Embedding

Although he had published a couple of short stories in *New Worlds*, Ian Watson (born 1943) was virtually unknown to sf readers until he arrived with a bang in 1973. The noisy event was the publication of his first novel, *The Embedding*. A fast, slightly confusing but very invigorating book, it heralded a renewed concern in British sf with ideas, politics and current intellectual fashions. It seemed to deal with everything: anthropology, linguistics, despoliation of the environment, consciousness-raising drugs, space travel, alien contact, Latin-American liberation movements, the CIA, you name it.

Watson writes with energy and panache, whipping a large cast of interesting characters around an all-too-real world of the near future. The novel opens in a British research institute where linguist Chris Sole is teaching a strange form of language to four children who live in an artificial environment. The language is English, but gramatically restructured by computer: a 'self-embedded' English which no normally-socialized person can speak. The object of the experiment is to find out whether normal grammar is inherent in the human brain, or whether individuals can be trained to think in more complex grammars, thus opening up new possibilities for the mind. Meanwhile, down in Brazil, a friend of Chris Sole's is studying an Indian tribe known as the Xemahoa. Their territory is threatened by flooding as a result of a vast dam built by the Brazilian military government with financial and technical assistance from the USA. The anthropologist Pierre Darriand is elated by his discovery that the Xemahoa speak two kinds of language: their everyday speech, and a second, rhapsodic, tongue which is spoken under the influence of a drug. This 'Xemahoa B' is a self-embedded language with apparently incomprehensible syntax, akin to the artificial speech which Sole is teaching the children back in England.

A third element enters the story. A large alien spacecraft arrives in Earth orbit, and Chris Sole is flown to the USA to help establish communication with the craft's occupants. The aliens call themselves the Sp'thra. They learn English very swiftly, and indeed it turns out that language is their overriding interest: they wish to trade various items of technology in return for a number of live human brains 'programmed' to speak different terrestrial languages. They become very excited when they hear about Pierre Darriand's discoveries in the Amazon basin, and the US government finds itself in the embarrassing position of having to put a stop to the flooding which is taking place there.

The narrative increases in tension and intellectual excitement as everything begins to go disastrously wrong. Some of the closing scenes are shockingly unexpected. The book ends with the human race triumphant—after a fashion. Sadly, the Machiavellian side of human nature has frustrated a possible human transcendence. *The Embedding* was a brilliant debut for Ian Watson, and it won him high praise: J.G. Ballard called him 'the most interesting British sf writer of ideas—or, more accurately, the only British sf writer of ideas'. The two novels which followed— *The Jonah Kit* (1975) and *The Martian Inca* (1977)—proved to be almost as good as the first, if a trifle more mechanical in their application of Watson's new-found formula: they too employ near-future settings, in countries such as Japan and Bolivia, and ingenious plots spun from up-to-the-minute scientific speculations. It seemed, in the mid-1970s, that the world was Ian Watson's oyster.

First edition: London, Gollancz, 1973 (hardcover)
First American edition: New York, Scribner's, 1975 (hardcover)
Most recent edition: London, Granada (paperback)

72
SUZY McKEE CHARNAS
Walk to the End of the World

'The men of the Holdfast had long treated with contempt the degenerated creatures known as 'fems'. To give themselves the drive to survive and reconquer the world, the men needed a common enemy. Superstitious belief had ascribed to the fems the guilt for the terrible Wasting that had destroyed the world. They were the ideal scapegoat.' So runs the cover blurb on this novel's first edition. The 'fems' are of course women, here imagined as the abject slaves of men in a post-catastrophe landscape ('pollution, exhaustion and inevitable wars among swollen, impoverished populations have devastated the world, leaving it to the wild weeds'). It is a savage novel, not only in the angry, political sense, but in terms of the uncompromising quality of unfettered imagination which Charnas displays. William S. Burroughs has praised the book, and one can appreciate why.

In the shrunken land of the Holdfast, which ekes out a living by farming hemp and seaweed, the males are totally, pathologically dominant. Women do all the heavy and dirty work. Normally they are kept in compounds, guarded by young men with whips, and they are exploited and debased in every conceivable way. Even their hair is taken from them to be woven into fabrics. Unsurprisingly, the men who run this horrible system have peculiar psychological quirks: for instance, they are terrified of the moon in the night sky since they believe it to be 'the mistress of all fems and of the evil in them'. All males are raised together in the communal Boyhouse, and no man knows who his own father is, much less his mother. No man, that is, except for one, a rebel called Eykar Bek: he sets out to find and kill his father, and thus to challenge the whole basis of his crazy society.

It is a bright, shocking, and at times rather crude scenario, as vivid and grotesque as a first-rate comic strip. A *reductio-ad-absurdum* story certainly, but one which touches many raw nerves. Eykar Bek is aided in his quest by his homosexual lover Servan dLayo, known as the DarkDreamer. In search of allies wherever they can find them, these men even penetrate the dank underworld of the fems. A crone who is unofficial leader of the women makes them a gift of a young female called Alldera. This girl has been illegally 'speed-trained' (her leg muscles are well developed) and Bek comes to suspect that she has an unusual intelligence. After much travelling and much violence, Alldera and Bek grow to understand each other. Their relationship is not one of 'love'—nothing so sentimental can possibly happen in this novel—but Bek is forced to a realization that Alldera is after all an independent being with her own kind of dignity. This happens shortly before Bek, in a final suicidal frenzy, locates his father and slays him, bringing destruction to a whole town and to much of the Holdfast. Alldera survives, a 'free fem', and runs off into the wilds where one day she will encounter the tribes of the horsewomen. Her further adventures are recounted in Charnas's second novel, *Motherlines* (1978).

Walk to the End of the World is a prime example of the feminist science fiction which burgeoned in America during the 1970s, fed both by the women's movement and by the example of Ursula Le Guin's writing. Suzy McKee Charnas (born 1939) has a tougher imagination than Le Guin. Her novel is a comment not only on the sexist nature of present-day society but on the tradition of the sf adventure story itself, that 'entertainment for boys' which will never seem quite the same after one has read this book.

First edition: New York, Ballantine, 1974 (paperback)
First British edition: London, Gollancz, 1979 (hardcover)
Most recent editions: New York, Berkley, and London, Coronet (paperbacks)

73

M. JOHN HARRISON
The Centauri Device

Michael John Harrison (born 1945) is one of the finest writers ever to have served an apprenticeship in the sf magazines (he was particularly associated with *New Worlds* in the late 1960s and early 1970s). A brilliant prose stylist, he declares that he has now abandoned science fiction forever. We shall see. His first novel, *The Committed Men* (1971), was a personal variation on the British disaster tale, somewhat influenced by Ballard and Moorcock. Together with his early short stories, it proved Harrison to have a wide command of language and of technical and topological detail as well as a gift for incisive characterization. His second sf novel, *The Centauri Device*, is an attempt at an interplanetary adventure story on the grand scale.

It is about the galaxy-saving mission of a reluctant hero, Captain John Truck, who owns a dilapidated space freighter and also happens to be the unwitting carrier of the last known Centauran genes—the only genetic make-up in the universe capable of triggering the mysterious Centauri Device, a living bomb discovered on a devastated planet of Alpha Centaurus. Truck is depicted throughout as a loser, a confused and apolitical man whose lot—along with billions of others like him—is to be pushed around by the terrifying political forces of the planet Earth. In a slightly heavy-handed satirical touch, Harrison imagines an Earth which is split between the Israeli World Government and the Union of Arab Socialist Republics, one standing for 'politics' and capitalism, and the other standing for 'ideology' and communism (needless to say, each is as despicable as the other; the author and his hero are anarchists at heart). The novel's satire on religion is more successful: it is personified by the memorably grotesque Dr Grishkin, the 'Opener' priest with a window in his stomach, who believes in displaying his digestive processes to God. The most delightful characters in the book are the Interstellar Anarchists who help Captain Truck on his way. They are a band of violent aesthetes whose spacecraft have names like *Atalanta in Calydon*, *Driftwood of Decadence* and *The Green Carnation*.

The Centauri Device is a highly self-conscious and literary space opera, although it contains plenty of fast action, plot complexity, and titanic spaceship battles. It strives for something of the wildness and inventiveness of Alfred Bester's *The Stars My Destination*, and in doing so it suffers a little from the insipidity of emulation. It is an *exercise*, but a virtuoso one. Harrison's two principal strengths are his ability to depict violent action in convincing detail, and his facility for alternating that with moody descriptions of landscapes of entropy. The dead Centauran planet is the ultimate Harrisonian hell:

> . . . a lukewarm rain had been falling evenly over the new landscape for almost two hundred years. He found a planetary fen drained by vast slow rivers: shallow, stagnant meres, inconceivable acreages of mud-flat and salting—and every cubic foot of water filled with corrupt organic matter caught at some point between decay and dissolution, cloudy, brackish with old death. None of the continents resembled anything he found on the pre-Genocide maps: finally, it was beneath the human and animal silts of the estuaries and deltaic fans that he discovered water percolating through the slaughtered regolith in small secret streams, to the abandoned redoubts miles beneath . . . If he was a little mad to begin with, Centauri helped him further along the way. Nothing was alive there, unless you count the echoes of water. Water: and the wind, mumbling thick-lipped between the blasted, mysterious columns of masonry that poked up through the silt like fingers searching the air for the source of their long pain . . .

It is all deliciously depressing.

First edition: Garden City, Doubleday, 1974 (hardcover)
First British edition: London, Panther, 1975 (paperback)
Most recent edition: New York, Pocket (paperback)

74

URSULA K. LE GUIN
The Dispossessed

This splendidly ambitious, deeply humane novel is set against the same interstellar background as several of Le Guin's other works, including *The Left Hand of Darkness*. In the remote past a number of worlds, including our Earth, have been colonized by a people called the Hainish. We humans are of Hainish stock, though we know it not—and so are the inhabitants of Urras, a planet which circles the star Tau Ceti. *The Dispossessed* is set many hundreds of years in the future, at a time when the Hainish have re-established contact with some of their former colonies. They are in the process of forming a peaceful federation of planets, which will in time develop into the Ekumen, mentioned in *The Left Hand of Darkness*. The background is significant, as it provides an explanation for the fact that the characters in the novel, although 'alien', are human beings, just like us.

The dispossessed of the title are the twenty million inhabitants of Anarres, a large arid moon of the lush planet Urras. Almost two centuries before, their ancestors fled from Urras, determined to forge a new society in the unpromising environment of the lesser world. Those people were the followers of Odo, an anarchist philosopher who was unable to make the crossing to Anarres herself. Their descendents are dispossessed in at least two senses: they no longer have their green and beautiful homeworld, and, more importantly, they have succeeded in building a society which has done away with the idea of 'possession' altogether. Materially poor, Anarres is nevertheless a fully-fledged anarchist utopia, complete with its own artificial language, Pravic, inspired by the teachings of Odo: 'The singular forms of the possessive pronoun were used mostly for emphasis; idiom avoided them. Little children might say, "My mother," but very soon they learned to say "the mother." Instead of "My hand hurts," it was "The hand hurts me," and so on; to say "This one is mine and that's yours" in Pravic one said, "I use this one and you use that."'

There is no property on Anarres, no money, no marriage, no government, no laws, no prisons. Men and women are absolutely equal. Each does what he or she is best suited to, spurred by necessity and encouraged by social approval. Le Guin depicts this utopia in convincing detail: we believe that it works.

We follow the central character, Shevek, as he goes on an epoch-making journey from Anarres to Urras. Although he is deeply committed to the Odonian ideals of the society he has grown up in, he finds himself in increasing conflict with the people of Anarres. Shevek has a genius for mathematics and has written a seminal work called *Principles of Simultaneity*. To his fellow anarchists he seems selfish and even (the ultimate sin!) propertarian. On Urras he is hailed as a great scientist and bestowed with honours and wealth, but he is unable to accept the class structure of society there: 'He tried to read an elementary economics text; it bored him past endurance, it was like listening to somebody interminably recounting a long and stupid dream. He could not force himself to understand how banks functioned and so forth, because all the operations of capitalism were as meaningless to him as the rites of a primitive religion, as barbaric, as elaborate, and as unnecessary.' He becomes embroiled in a workers' revolt and eventually takes refuge in the Terran embassy, whence he is given safe passage back to Anarres. Meanwhile he has completed his General Temporal Theory, which will lead to instantaneous communication between the stars. Through the Terran ambassador, he gives his discovery to all humanity rather than allowing it to become the exclusive property of his chauvinistic paymasters on Urras.

It is a very impressive book, and it embodies the most thoroughgoing utopian vision in modern sf. Its main fault, to my mind, is that it has a curiously 19th-century atmosphere, arising from the fact that Le Guin has imagined a utopia (Anarres) which is founded in poverty; it would have been a more difficult feat, but an even more impressive one, for her to envisage a utopia of abundance, such as Urras, or our Earth, might have become had they too been transformed by an Odonian revolution.

First edition: New York, Harper & Row, 1974 (hardcover)
First British edition: London, Gollancz, 1974 (hardcover)
Most recent editions: New York, Avon, and London, Granada (paperbacks)

75

CHRISTOPHER PRIEST
Inverted World

'I had reached the age of six hundred and fifty miles.' It is an intriguing opening sentence which promises paradoxical things to come. The narrator is Helward Mann, one of the inhabitants of a little wooden city which creeps across the surface of the earth (the hero's age is in fact measured by the distance that the city has travelled since his birth). 'My father was a guildsman, and I had always seen his life from a certain remove.' This statement sums up an odd quality of the book: its detached, distanced tone. Helward Mann sees *everything* from 'a certain remove', as perhaps the author does. Most of Christopher Priest's novels and stories are told in a stiff, remote style—which, I hasten to add, frequently suits the alienated subject matter.

Inverted World is a very strange novel indeed. It begins prosaically enough, with a description of Helward's induction into the guild system which dominates the affairs of the city. Now that he has attained adulthood he is allowed to see the outside world for the first time. The city is travelling, at the rate of 36 miles a year, through a desolate region, sparsely populated by impoverished peasants who are sometimes drafted as labourers (or breeding stock). Locomotion is achieved by the painstaking process of laying tracks and winching the city along them, a few hundred yards at a time. The various guildsmen—surveyors, track-layers, bridge-builders—are all involved in this exhausting but imperative task. For some reason, as baffling to Helward as it is to the reader, it is essential that the city continue to move, heading for an optimum point which is always just a few miles away.

The terrain ahead of the city is referred to as the Future (Helward's father is a Future Surveyor), while that to the rear is known as the Past. On his first lengthy journey from the city, Helward is given the task of escorting three young women back to their native village, some distance south, or 'down Past'. This proves to be a truly extraordinary, nightmarish episode. It begins lightly enough, with sundry sexual frolics. Then, as the days pass, Helward notices that the women are changing: 'their arms and legs were shorter, and more thickly built. Their shoulders and hips were broader, their breasts less round and more widely spaced . . .' Soon he sees that 'none of them stood more than five feet high, they talked more quickly than before, and the pitch of their voices was higher.' It is as though Helward and the women are descending into a carnival hall of mirrors. Before long, the women are 'no more than three feet tall . . . Their feet were flat and wide, their legs broad and short . . . the sound of their twittering voices was irritating him.' The grotesque distortion of Helward's perceptions continues to grow in intensity until he finds himself tumbling southwards, to end up with his body stretched across a mountain range:

> He was at the edge of the world; its major bulk lay before him. He could see the whole world.
>
> North of him the ground was level; flat as the top of a table. But at the centre, due north of him, the ground rose from that flatness in a perfectly symmetrical, rising and concave spire. It narrowed and narrowed, reaching up, growing ever more slender, rising so high that it was impossible to see where it ended.

The 'explanation' for all this is a complex mathematical conceit. It seems that the city-folk inhabit a world which is 'shaped like a solid hyperbola; that is, all limits are infinite.' To the south of the city everything becomes horizontal and time passes slowly; to the north everything becomes vertical and time speeds up. It is impossible for people to live in either zone, and the very ground is constantly shifting beneath their feet, hence their need to keep the city on the move, ever reaching out for that theoretical 'optimum' where conditions are normal. One does not have to understand the mathematics in order to enjoy this novel. Christopher Priest (born 1943) has succeeded in creating a powerful metaphor which is open to a number of interpretations, psychological, social and philosophical. There are more surprises towards the end of the book which cause one to revise one's ideas of what it is all about. Unlike many stories of conceptual breakthrough, this text is not at all predictable.

First edition: London, Faber and Faber, 1974 (hardcover)
First American Edition: New York, Harper & Row, 1974 (hardcover)
Most recent edition: London, Pan (paperback)

76
J.G. BALLARD
High-Rise

'The future in my fiction has never really been more than five minutes away.' So said J.G. Ballard in a recent interview, one of many which appeared around the publication date of his non-sf novel *Empire of the Sun* (1984). That book, which stayed on the British hardcover bestseller lists for more than six months, has turned Ballard into a literary celebrity and has served to introduce his work to a huge new readership. For twenty years, however, discerning science fiction readers have known that Ballard is somebody special—possibly the most significant writer of sf since H.G. Wells. *Crash* remains his dark masterpiece, his most 'extreme metaphor', but *High-Rise* runs it close as a technological horror story and as an exploration of the world of the next five minutes.

The setting of the novel is a forty-storey luxury apartment block on the outskirts of London. It is, in effect, 'a small vertical city', with some two thousand well-heeled middle-class inhabitants. Amenities such as shops, banks, restaurants and swimming pools are situated within the building. The central character, Dr Robert Laing, works at a nearby medical school. But we do not see him at work—only at home, where he sits in his 'over-priced cell' with the comforts, the sense of anonymity, and the lack of pressing social obligations which this up-to-date lifestyle entails. 'Each day the towers of central London seemed slightly more distant, the landscape of an abandoned planet receding slowly from his mind.' The high-rise is a self-contained technological paradise which allows its inhabitants to be just as selfish and withdrawn as they wish.

Trouble brews. A wine bottle smashes on to Laing's balcony; someone's dog is deliberately drowned in a swimming pool. Petty quarrels break out between the inhabitants of the block. Gradually but remorselessly, following what Ballard would call a 'deviant logic', life in the high-rise turns very nasty indeed. During a power failure real violence flares, and the tenants of the building soon find themselves stratified into makeshift social classes, their position in the hierarchy determined by the number of the floor on which they live. Tribal alliances form, and nightly battles are fought up and down the stairwells and lift-shafts. People die, but no-one informs the police; everyone is enjoying the experience too much to allow it to be disturbed by any intrusion from the outside world. The tenants cease going out to work, and the high-rise becomes their total environment, a place of excitement and danger which absorbs all their energies. Towards the end, after the major battles have exhausted themselves and the building is half-wrecked, life seems to settle down at a new level: the survivors, such as Laing, are near-solitary hunter-gatherers, picking their way through the ruined apartments, happy in their self-sufficiency. On the last page Laing notices that the lights have just gone out in a neighbouring high-rise block. He sees the residents' torch-beams, and watches their movements contentedly, 'ready to welcome them to their new world.'

High-Rise is neither a savage social satire, nor merely a pessimistic moral allegory of devolution and degradation. It is more subtle and probing than that. Like *Crash*, it presents the reader with a series of discomfiting questions about the way we live now, or at least the way we shall be living in the very near future. To what extent have we unconsciously programmed our technology to pander to our secret perversities? How much order and sweet reason can we really bear? Are we witnessing the 'death of affect'—the end of traditional human feelings—and if so, what kind of world awaits us at the end of this rapid period of transition? By concentrating obsessively on the-future-as-revealed-in-the-present Ballard has become the most trenchant of modern prophets.

First edition: London, Cape, 1975 (hardcover)
First American edition: New York, Holt, Rinehart and Winston, 1977 (hardcover)
Most recent editions: London, Granada, and New York, Popular Library (paperbacks)

172

77
BARRY N. MALZBERG
Galaxies

This slim book is a science fiction *anti*-novel—though one would not guess that from a reading of the back-cover blurb. 'FORTI-ETH-CENTURY SPACE PROBE!' it yells at us; and it continues in deliberately misleading catchpenny style:

> The diabolically clever Bureau had superbly trained their space pilot, beautiful Lena Thomas. Nothing could go wrong in an age where science had conquered the universe. In one of their fifteen faster-than-light ships, Lena would reach beyond the over-populated Milky Way, carrying her grotesque cargo: seven programmed prosthetic engineers to give advice and comfort, and 515 dead men sealed in gelatinous fix . . .
>
> But the omniscient Bureau was not aware of the black galaxy in Lena's charted path. And Lena's ship fell into it, fell through twenty-five billion miles of hyperspace, into the lifeless, timeless expanse of the dreadful pit . . .
>
> The cyborg engineers couldn't help Lena now. She was totally alone except for the awakening dead! If she geared the ship up to tachyonic drive, would she break out of the terrifying black hole? Or would she destroy the universe?

I should not be surprised to discover that Barry Malzberg wrote that blurb himself. It seems so appropriately innappropriate.

In reality, *Galaxies* is the confessional lament of a tired sf writer who is *thinking* of writing a novel all about the adventures of a female astronaut in a mysterious 'black galaxy'. The author himself defines the book as a series of notes towards a novel. On the very first page he concedes that his little book will appear on the same news-stand shelves as colourful paperbacks with titles like *The Rammers of Arcturus*, but he goes on to make it quite clear that he is not competing in the same game, a game which he regards as unwinnable. A goodly proportion of the wordage consists of direct addresses to the reader, to such an extent that the book could be defined as *The Rammers of Arcturus* with added authorial asides. Here is a typical example of a Malzbergian aside: 'The neutron star, functioning as a cosmic vacuum cleaner (all right, this is homey imagery but then good science fiction should make the mysterious, the terrible, the inviolable as comfortable and accessible as one's own possessions, just as pornography should make the fires of sex little more than a twitch, easily untwitched, in the familiarly tumescent genitalia), might literally destroy the universe.'

The tone is bitter, funny, self-pitying. Malzberg explains that he has filched the concept of a black galaxy from a pair of articles by John W. Campbell which appeared in *Analog* magazine. He says the articles were sent to him by someone 'who thought I might be interested in basing a technologically oriented SF story on their contents. "Hard" science fiction they call it.' He goes on to assert that the existence of such sf is largely a myth; the science in most science fiction is puerile or obvious or poorly understood. Nevertheless, he believes in the ideal: 'But how we could use it! Science, that is to say. We could indeed profit by technologically accurate science fiction. The awful expansion of our machinery, the technological manual as the poetics of the age, the rhythms of the machine as analogous to those of the newly-discovered spirit . . . we need writers who can show us what the machines are doing to us in terms more systematized than those of random paranoia. A writer who could combine the techniques of modern fiction with a genuine command of science could be at the top of this field in no more than a few years. He would also stand alone.'

Almost despairingly, he proceeds to tell us the story of Lena and her black galaxy, a story which opens in the fortieth century but ends in Ridgefield Park, New Jersey, in the year 1975, where the weary author sits hammering at his typewriter. Barry N. Malzberg (born 1939) was a late product of the American New Wave. He was at his most prolific during the first half of the 1970s, when he turned out a long series of sourly amusing sf novels—*Beyond Apollo* (1972) is the one which received most praise. In 1976 he announced that he was abandoning sf, since when he has concentrated on work in other fields. *Galaxies* tells us why he took that decision. It is a love/hate letter to all readers and writers of science fiction, a witty criticism of the *genre* and its aspirations, and a sad gesture of farewell.

First edition: New York, Pyramid, 1975 (paperback)
Most recent edition: Boston, Gregg Press (hardcover)

78

JOANNA RUSS
The Female Man

Like Ballard's *Crash*, but in a very different way, this is a book with which it is difficult to come to terms. It pushes the science fiction form to the limit in order to make a strong and valid point. It is didactic, extremely so, but then it parades its didacticism proudly and defiantly, challenging us to deny that didacticism can also be an art, unlike the numerous message-bearing sf novels of the past in which attempts have been made to hide the purpose beneath a sugar coating of 'mere entertainment'. In fact it is a very artful novel which employs many rhetorical devices in order to pre-empt knee-jerk responses. Some of these devices are highly discomfiting. For example, about two-thirds of the way through Russ gives us this:

'Shrill . . . vituperative . . . this shapeless book . . . twisted, neurotic . . . some truth buried in a largely hysterical . . . another tract for the trashcan . . . no characterization, no plot . . . another of the screaming sisterhood . . . this pretence at a novel . . . the usual boring obligatory references to Lesbianism . . . drivel . . . violently waspish attack . . . formidable self-pity which erodes any chance of . . . formless . . . without the grace and compassion which we have the right to expect . . . just plain bad . . . Q.E.D Quod erat demonstrandum. It has been proved.' In other words she provides the reader with a ready-made and profoundly hostile description of her own book. The reader cannot help but feel that he (sic) is being *leaned upon*.

Nevertheless this is one of the most memorable and significant sf novels of the 1970s. It is about the lives of three women—Janet, Jeannine and Joanna—who are actually one woman. They live in alternative worlds, but the boundaries between those realities are beginning to break down, allowing the three to meet themselves as they might have been. Joanna's world is pretty much the same as the author's, a male-dominated America of the very recent past. Jeannine's reality is like an old Hollywood movie; a present day in which World War II never happened and

175

the 1930s seem to go on and on forever, an era of inequality and male chauvinism rampant. Janet's world is the most radically altered: it is 'Whileaway', a pastoral anarchy inhabited only by women. On the planet Whileaway there can be no 'problem' of relations between the sexes, for there is only one gender of human being—the unfettered, omnicompetent Female Man.

The book's bitter comedy is generated by the clash between the very different personalities which have been formed by the social conditions of these disparate worlds. Janet Evason of Whileaway ('my mother's name was Eva, my other mother's name Alicia') materializes in 'our' world and wanders through it in a state of continual amazement. She is a truly formidable Candide. But there is a twist in the novel's tail: eventually Janet, Jeannine and Joanna meet an even more formidable character, a fourth persona who calls herself Jael. It is Jael who reveals to them how the all-female society of Whileaway became possible: the way was cleared by a war in which the women exterminated the men (Janet has been brought up to believe that the males died in a plague).

The Female Man is far from being a 'balanced' and 'reasonable' novel. It is written out of anger, a desire for revenge, and a longing for genuine liberation. The author indulges her fantasies to the full, in what Phyllis Chesler has described as an 'exploration of Feminist inner space'—an exploration which uncovers dark corners as well as bright prospects. The result is a disquieting book, though a courageous one. Joanna Russ (born 1939) has written several other sf novels and a number of excellent short stories. Together with the more popular Ursula Le Guin, she has succeeded in opening out once again the *utopian* perspectives of science fiction. She has dared to dream of a better world.

First edition: New York, Bantam, 1975 (paperback)
First British edition: London, Star, 1977 (paperback)
Most recent edition: London, Women's Press (paperback)

79

BOB SHAW
Orbitsville

One of Bob Shaw's attractive qualities as a writer is his unpreten-
siousness. He is a middle-of-the-road purveyor of trad science
fiction, but unlike so many writers of 'mere entertainment' he
produces work which is no insult to the intelligence. *Orbitsville*
is a testimony of his not inconsiderable virtues. It begins in van
Vogtian fashion, though the prose is vastly superior to van
Vogt's, by presenting us with a mad empress who rules a sizeable
chunk of the galaxy from her throne on Earth, and a stolid space-
captain hero, Vance Garamond, who is in rebellion against her. I
have rarely seen the paranoid one-man-against-an-empire theme
done so well, but this initial intrigue is just an *entrée* to the story.
Shaw's purpose, deftly achieved, is to get Garamond headed for
uncharted space with no hope of return to Earth. The bulk of the
novel is concerned with what he finds when he gets there, and
how his discovery alters the destiny of the human race.

The artifact that Garamond discovers is a Dyson sphere, the
unimaginably vast construction of some vanished alien race. It
takes the form of a thin shell completely enclosing a star at about
the same distance as Earth's orbit from our sun. Artificial gravity, and an atmosphere covering the inner surface, make the
sphere—dubbed 'Orbitsville' by its discoverers—habitable to
human beings. This is not an original idea of Shaw's, of course;
Larry Niven used a similar, though different, artifact in his popular novel *Ringworld* (1970). The notion of such spheres was first
made public by Professor Freeman J. Dyson in the 1960s, and
various sf writers have drawn on it over the years.

The important thing about the sphere in Shaw's novel is its
staggering size—some 625 million times the surface area of the
Earth. Exploration becomes a mammoth task, to say the least,
and when Garamond and his ship's crew become stranded far in
the interior they have an almost insoluble problem in devising a
means of escape. Shaw's treatment of this predicament and its
resolution is masterly. The vastness and monotony of Orbitsville

itself induce more of a sense of agoraphobia in the reader than do scores of descriptions of limitless outer space to be found in earlier sf novels.

Shaw's success is due to the combination of this large subject with some solid characterization and a felicitous narrative style. As usual in a Bob Shaw novel, the incidental invention is delightful. For example, there is the description of the faster-than-light spaceship's mode of travel: '. . . the invisible galactic winds from which the *Bissendorf* drew its reaction mass had been very ill winds for somebody, sometime, somewhere. Heavy particles driven across the galactic wheel by the forces of ancient novae were the richest and most sought after harvest of all. An experienced flickerwing man could tell when his engine intakes had begun to feed on such a cloud just by feeling the deck grow more insistent against his feet. But a sun going nova engulfed its planets, converting them and everything on them to incandescent gas, and at each barely perceptible surge of the ship Garamond wondered if his engines were feeding on the ghosts of dawn-time civilizations, obliterating all their dreams, giving the final answer to all their questions.'

Shaw's space vessel sails on dreams.

First edition: London, Gollancz, 1975 (hardcover)
First American edition: New York, Ace, 1977 (paperback)
Most recent edition: London, Granada (paperback)

80
KINGSLEY AMIS
The Alteration

As one might expect from a novelist of his stature, Amis's first full-length foray into science fiction is a well-crafted book. It is an alternative-world novel, set in a time-stream where the Reformation never happened and England remains a Roman Catholic nation (shades of Keith Roberts' *Pavane*, acknowledged slyly by Amis in his text). The hero is a choirboy under threat of castration. Through the eyes of his child protagonist the author paints a marvellously detailed picture of a quite horrible religious tyranny. The anti-Catholic theme seems to awake Amis's rebelliousness: in this book he is once more on the attack, as he was in his famous comedy of academic life, *Lucky Jim* (1954).

Young Hubert Anvil attends a boarding school in Oxford, where he is much prized for his beautiful singing voice. Religion dominates all their lives, but after lights-out the boys indulge in illicit pleasures, including the reading of proscribed books. Their favourite form of reading matter is the so-called Time Romance, or Invention Fiction. One boy describes an example he has just read, a novel called *The Man in the High Castle* by Philip K. Dick: 'The story opens in this year, 1976, but a great many things are different . . . Invention has been set free a long time before. Sickness is almost conquered: nobody dies of consumption or the plague. The deserts have been made fertile. The inventors are actually called scientists, and they use electricity . . . They send messages all over the Earth with it. They use it to light whole cities and even to keep folk warm. There are electric flying machines that move at two hundred miles an hour.'

In Hubert's world electricity is outlawed by the Church, but there is a rumour that the 'Schismatics' of distant New England have been experimenting with it. Hubert encounters a New Englander, the Ambassador Cornelius van den Haag, and is fascinated by all that he hears of the man's small but progressive country. Invited to sing at his house, Hubert meets the Ambassador's pretty daughter, and feels the first stirrings of the sexual urge.

However, the powers that be in Oxford and Rome have decided that he should undergo a little surgical 'alteration' in order to preserve the sublimity of his soprano voice . . .

The villains of the story form a memorable gallery of clerical grotesques, ranging from the elderly eunuchs Mirabilis and Viaventosa (who wish to make Hubert one of their own) to the Pope himslf (who turns out to be a broad Yorkshireman: he addresses the boy as 'Hubert lad' and wields a teapot saying 'shall we be mother?'). Despite an assured future as a singer for the Holy Father in Rome, Hubert makes up his mind to run away before the dreaded operation can take place. With the help of the van den Haags, he may succeed in taking passage for New England aboard the airship *Edgar Allan Poe*. The novel develops into a complex narrative of flight and pursuit, with the fate of poor Hubert's testicles dependent on the outcome. It is an inventive and entertaining work, full of humorous touches yet fundamentally serious. Kingsley Amis (born 1922) has long been an apologist for science fiction in his roles as critic and anthologist. On the strength of *The Alteration* one wishes that he had found the time to write many more sf novels.

First edition: London, Cape, 1976 (hardcover)
First American edition: New York, Viking, 1977 (hardcover)
Most recent edition: London, Granada (paperback)

81

MARGE PIERCY
Woman on the Edge of Time

'The anger of the weak never goes away . . . it just gets a little
mouldy. It moulds like a beautiful blue cheese in the dark, growing stronger and more interesting. The poor and the weak die
with all their anger intact and probably those angers go on growing in the dark of the grave like the hair and the nails.' So muses
Connie Ramos, the long-suffering Mexican-American heroine of
this moving novel. She has been beaten by a worthless husband;
she has undergone abortions; her daughter has been taken away
from her; she has lived alone on welfare handouts; she has been
beaten again while trying to defend her niece from a brutal pimp.
Now, at thirty-seven years of age, she is locked up in a mental
institution, unjustly imprisoned while painfully sane.

Connie is a good woman who has been treated horribly. Apart
from her innate dignity and her unquenchable human worth, she
has one miraculous ability which serves to symbolize the rest:
she is receptive to telepathic contact from the future. A figment
haunts her, and this turns out to be the mental projection of a
person from the year 2137. At first Connie mistakes this person,
Luciente, for a young man, then she comes to realize that the
person is fact a woman of about her own age. With Luciente's
assistance, Connie mind-travels into the future to explore the
village of Mattapoisett and its environs. Her body remains in the
lunatic asylum, while her spirit undergoes a great awakening.
The America of the 22nd century is a green and pleasant land of
small villages where people live in close harmony with nature.
There is no money in Mattapoisett, and no coercion to work.
Everyone eats vegetarian food, all waste is recycled, and there is
much communing with animals, including blue whales. Men and
women have equal status, and the task of child-bearing is given
over to machines. Each baby has three 'mothers'—they may be
male or female, and any of them may breast-feed the child. All
children undergo a *rite de passage* at puberty which enables them
to break free of family ties, rename themselves, and become full

members of the community.

Throughout the novel, Connie shuttles between ghastly present and utopian future. She gradually learns more and more about Mattapoisett, coming to accept the community's values and to draw an inner strength from them. At one point she escapes from the hospital and survives in the woods for a couple of days with Luciente's help. After she is recaptured the doctors implant an electrode in her brain in order to maintain control of her behaviour. Even this does not prevent her from communicating with her friends in the future. As her condition in the here-and-now becomes ever more degraded, so Mattapoisett burns all the more brightly in Connie's mind, a symbol of freedom and possibility. It is only when Connie declares war on her oppressors, at the very end of the novel, that she finally loses contact with Luciente.

Marge Piercy is a leading American writer of feminist fiction. She does not have a background in sf, but her novel takes its place alongside Le Guin's *The Dispossessed* and Russ's *The Female Man* as one of the most significant left-wing utopias of the 1970s. The better world which Piercy depicts could be described as a fairly standard ecological-feminist vision, but it gains enormously by being embedded in a dark contemporary narrative of melodramatic proportions. I do not wish to decry the melodrama, for it works exceedingly well. In fact, I see Marge Piercy as a neo-Dickensian writer: like that great novelist, she tackles her society whole; she goes down into the depths and comes up with a disadvantaged heroine who will awaken the middle-class conscience; she exaggerates memorably in order to reinforce her point; she plays on the heart-strings, making her heroine a figure comparable to Oliver Twist, and transforming her mental hospital into a modern equivalent of Dotheboys Hall.

First edition: New York, Knopf, 1976 (hardcover)
First British edition: London, Women's Press, 1979 (paperback)
Most recent edition: New York, Fawcett (paperback)

82

FREDERIK POHL
Man Plus

After the end of his fruitful partnership with the late C.M.
Kornbluth, Frederik Pohl produced several solo novels which
were rather less impressive than the collaborations had been.
Then he gave up writing for almost a decade. His 'comeback'
novel was *Man Plus*, and for me it remains the most satisfying of
the many books he has written in the past ten years, even though
Gateway (1977) and its sequels have received the most attention.
Man Plus is one of the best treatments to date of the cyborg
(cybernetic organism) theme. Written at a time when bionic men,
women and dogs were bounding across the world's TV screens,
Pohl's novel gives us a much less sentimentally escapist view of
human beings enhanced by electronic gadgetry.

It is a couple of decades in the future, and the world has
become a gloomier place. Wars and famines stalk the globe,
although technological progress goes on apace. The last best
hope for the human race is the Man Plus Project, a top-secret
endeavour to redesign men so that they can live unaided on the
hostile surface of Mars. Roger Torraway is an American astronaut, veteran of several orbital flights and a failed Mars landing.
He is now a back-up man on the cyborg project. When his surgi-
cally-altered colleague dies of a stroke brought on by sensory
overload, Roger finds himself next in line to undergo the painful
transmogrification into a 'Martian'. His eyes and lungs are
removed, along with most of his muscles and skin. He is fitted
with tough artificial hide and a mechanical musculature—and
with great multi-faceted eyes which can see into the ultra-violet
and infra-red. Most spectacularly he is given wings, huge gossa-
mer structures which are not for flying but for the absorption of
solar energy. He looks like a cross between a Japanese horror-
movie monster and Oberon, king of the fairies.

Roger is desperately worried about his pretty young wife,
Dorrie, whom he suspects is two-timing him. His feelings of sexual inadequacy come to a crescendo when, without forewarning,

the surgical team blithely remove his genitals—such tackle will be of no use to him on Mars. But within a few days he calms down and begins to prepare himself both physically and mentally for the impending space voyage. He is fitted with a backpack computer which will help him to cope with his blazing senses and to keep control of his immensely powerful body. The trip to Mars and the landing on that world are very well described; this is space fiction of a grittily realistic kind. The surface of the red planet is hellish to normal human beings, but it seems like an instant paradise to Roger. At last he comes into his own: he lopes the sandy wastes, sucks in energy through his wings, and relishes the beauty of new colours and new sensations. Before many weeks have passed he resolves to stay on Mars forever.

There now comes a twist. The story has been narrated throughout by a mysterious 'we': towards the end of the novel, the reader discovers that this second-person plural refers to a group of non-human intelligences, 'the computer network of the world'. The machines have grown to awareness, and it is for the protection of *their* race from the threat of a global nuclear war that they have surreptitiously promoted the Man Plus Project. The computer on Roger's back is at least as important as the man himself. A happy by-product of this conspiracy by the artificial intelligences of the Earth will be the preservation of humanity, if in a drastically altered form. It is a clever twist, for it reinforces the central thrust of the book: in the future we shall not only be dependent on machines, we may be inseparable from them, perhaps even indistinguishable from them. The cyborg is one of the most potent symbolic figures in contemporary sf, for it seems to embody so many of our hopes and fears. Frederik Pohl sustains that rich ambiguity very well indeed.

First edition: New York, Random House, 1976 (hardcover)
First British edition: London, Gollancz, 1976 (hardcover)
Most recent editions: New York, Bantam, and London, Granada (paperbacks)

83
ALGIS BUDRYS
Michaelmas

Like Pohl's *Man Plus*, this novel deals with machine intelligence, a subject which grows in relevance and urgency with each passing year. It also deals with communications technology and the news media, and gives us one of the best pictures in sf of the coming Global Village. The hero, Laurent Michaelmas, is a journalist of the electronic age, a roving reporter for radio, TV and holovision. Secretly, he is much more than that. A one-time computer hacker, he is the creator and master of an enormously complex program which effectively rules the world—not that this world of the year 2000 is aware that it is being ruled. Michaelmas's creation is called Domino. It is an artificial personality which lives and moves and has its being in the computerized communications media that span the globe. Domino speaks to Michaelmas through a briefcase-sized tranceiver which the journalist carries around with him. It can also keep in touch with him through a tiny receiver implanted in his skull. Thus Michaelmas knows about everything which is happening everywhere; moreover he is able to influence events by instructing Domino to tamper judiciously with the messages that flow through the system. This all adds up to a quite breathtaking fantasy of omniscience and power.

Why is the hero called Michaelmas? According to Brewer's *Dictionary of Phrase and Fable*, Saint Michael was once regarded as 'the presiding spirit of the planet Mercury, and bringer to man of the gift of prudence.' Mercury was, of course, a winged messenger, and Laurent Michaelmas is very much a bearer of prudence (and peace) to the world. He has succeeded in engineering a *détente* between East and West, he has defused most international crises, and eased Third World poverty and resentment. In a sense he has created a world in which nothing ever happens any more, as one of the old-time newsmen grumbles to Michaelmas, little knowing that he is addressing God Almighty Himself.

The symbol of all Michaelmas's achievements is UNAC, the United Nations Astronautics Commission, through which the USA, the Soviet Union and other nations cooperate peacefully in the exploration of space. The plot of the novel involves an attempt to destroy UNAC by means of a fabricated scandal. Somebody, or some*thing*, has made it appear that the Russians are responsible for an attempt on the life of a leading American astronaut. Michaelmas flies to Europe in order to cover the story, and to find out, with Domino's help, who is behind this dangerous scheme to destabilize the world. While moving through the hardware of a Swiss sanatorium, Domino encounters a frightening presence which is possibly another artificial intelligence, or even an alien being . . .

Michaelmas is a marvellously detailed and seductive novel. Clearly Algis Budrys has an impressive knowledge of the ways in which the communications media can shape world events. Nevertheless I have my doubts about both the plausibility and the morality of the book. It asks us to believe that one man, aided by a fiendishly clever machine, can really rule the world, and it invites us to see this as a desirable proposition. In Michaelmas's case, absolute power does not corrupt; it enables him to become a saint. Given that we can believe an artificial intelligence such as Domino is possible, we are also asked to accept that this powerful entity will remain subservient to the human race. What is to prevent Domino from nudging dear old Michaelmas aside? Budrys does not answer this question; instead, his novel expresses a touching belief in the ability of the individual human being to *stay on top*, however awe-inspiring the technology may be.

First edition: New York, Berkley, 1977 (hardcover)
First British edition: London, Gollancz, 1977 (hardcover)
Most recent editions: New York, Berkley, and London, Fontana (paperbacks)

84

JOHN VARLEY
The Ophiuchi Hotline

'She's your father,' says one character to another at a moment of
minor revelation in a short story by John Varley (born 1947).
The story in question is set against the same background as this
novel—a polymorphous society, several centuries hence, in
which characters change sex at the drop of a hat. The phrase has
stuck in my memory, and I tend to think of John Varley as the
'she's-your-father' author. He is an interesting phenomonon of
the 1970s: a male 'feminist' sf writer who makes a point of
depicting women as his central characters. Not that Varley
actually writes about sexual inequalities or the struggle of women
to liberate themselves from gender roles. In his imagined future
such problems have long since been solved: they have been cured
by a technological fix.

The Ophiuchi Hotline was Varley's first novel. It is fast and
complex, and it glitters most impressively. The title refers to the
source of all the technological fixes which have made possible an
interplanetary society founded on bioengineering, cloning and
sex-changes. The 'Hotline' is a flow of scientific information,
beamed towards the human race by unknown alien benefactors
who appear to live near a star in the constellation Ophiuchus
('the serpent-holder or doctor'). This cornucopia of information
compensates for a terrible loss which humanity has recently suf-
fered—the loss of the planet Earth. People now live on the
Moon, Mars, Venus and the major satellites of the outer planets.
They are unable to return to their homeworld, which has been
taken over by 'Invaders'. The Invaders are vast, inscrutable
entities who seem to originate from some gas-giant planet. Their
invasion of Earth was undertaken for the benefit of its 'three
intelligent species' (nice touch here): 'sperm whales, "killer"
whales, and bottle-nosed dolphins.'

> There were no explanations given to humanity. No ambassadors
> appeared, no ultimatums were offered. Humans resisted the Inva-
> sion, but the resistance was ignored. H-bombs would not go off,

tanks would not move, guns would not fire . . .

As far as anyone knows . . . the Invaders never killed a human. What they did was destroy utterly every artifact of human civilization. In their wake they left plowed ground, sprouted seedlings, and grass.

In the next two years, ten billion humans starved to death.

Despite this little setback, human beings thrive elsewhere in the solar system, their technological prowess immensely enhanced by the knowledge gleaned from the Ophiuchi Hotline. The novel's central character is Lilo, a geneticist who has been born and raised on the Moon. She is over fifty years old, but appears to be in her twenties. In this society human flesh is endlessly malleable, and everyone can be just as young and beautiful as she wishes. Limbs may be removed and replaced at whim (most astronauts are legless, which makes for easier movement in weightless conditions), and entire replacement bodies may be cloned and grown to maturity within the space of months. People regularly have their memories and personalities recorded: in cases of accidental death the recording can be implanted in a cloned body, and the person is effectively 'reborn'.

The involuted plot of the novel follows Lilo through a series of such reincarnations, as she is pressganged into a crazy bid to liberate Earth from the Invaders. In the end she discovers that the Invaders and the mysterious Hotline are closely linked, and that humanity is destined to travel further out into space rather than return to Earth.

Varley's prose is undistinguished, but his narrative moves along well, ever brimming with insouciant invention. My major reservation concerns the book's *cosiness*. In a society where people can be mended painlessly, where even death becomes no more than a minor irritation, nobody ever really gets hurt. At one point, Lilo falls into the dense atmosphere of Jupiter—only to end up with a case of sunburn. For all his technological patter, Varley's vision of the future seems to stem from child-like fantasies of wish-fulfilment.

First edition: New York, Dial Press, 1977 (hardcover)
First British edition: London, Sidgwick & Jackson, 1978 (hardcover)
Most recent editions: New York, Berkley, and London, Futura (paperbacks)

85

IAN WATSON
Miracle Visitors

I once had a friend who referred to large American cars as 'space-ships'. I suppose it is a fairly standard joke. In his 1977 review of the movie *Star Wars*, J.G. Ballard inverted it by saying that the film's spacecraft 'resembled beat-up De Sotos in Athens or Havana with half a million miles on the clock.' That conceit of the automobile (especially the vast extravagant tail-finned variety) as spaceship is used quite literally by Ian Watson in this novel's most memorable image. His young hero, Michael Peacocke, flies to the Moon and back, twice over, in a bright red Ford Thunderbird: 'Elephant-tyred, long-bonneted, massively bumpered, with cinemascopic rear lights and dual exhausts—a beast of unctuous steel—'

Yet this is no humorous fantasy, no merely flippant *Hitch-Hikers Guide to the Galaxy*. It is a serious, if mind-bendingly speculative, work of science fiction. A novel about flying saucers (UFOs), it has much to say about psychology, ecology, religion, and the state of the world today. It is cast in the form of a series of adventures which arise from a small-scale scientific project. Dr John Deacon is head of a university-based Consciousness Research Group, and he employs hypnosis to investigate altered states of consciousness. He finds that one of his students, Michael Peacocke, is particularly susceptible to hypnosis: in their first session together the young man recalls a Close Encounter which took place some years before, an event which has been erased from his conscious memory. Deacon is not a ready believer in flying saucers, and at first he dismisses Michael's story as an adolescent sexual fantasy. But soon he is driven, by a series of anomalous events, to seek a larger explanation for what is going on. An audio tape is mysteriously erased; a dog is killed, its head shorn from its body in uncanny fashion; he and Michael see a pterodactyl hovering in a back garden; Michael's girlfriend is terrified by two strange Men in Black, and by a 'demon' which appears to her one night.

Deacon comes to the conclusion that the human mind has a capacity for 'UFO Consciousness'. Manifestations of this higher state of consciousness have taken a supernatural form in the past—visions of devils and angels, religious miracles—whereas in the present they tend to take the shape of spacecraft from alien worlds. He delves into Buddhism and Sufism: perhaps the mind has the ability to project *tulpas*, three-dimensional objects and persons which are physically real yet somehow illusory. He elaborates on Jung's theory that UFOs are symbols projected from the collective unconscious: maybe there is a planetary unconscious, shared by all living things, with a built-in imperative to evolve into a greater awareness. Possibly UFOs are messages from the biomatrix, and they take warped or horrific forms in the same degree that life on Earth is dominated by a sick, purblind human race. And so on. Meanwhile, the adventures continue apace. Michael flies to the Moon in a Ford Thunderbird which has been made airtight and equipped with an anti-gravity engine. No doubt the car is a *tulpa*, but the voyage is, in a a sense, real. He takes Deacon with him on a second trip, and they encounter a terrible danger on the far side of the Moon—a dark entity which Deacon eventually learns to understand and to control.

Miracle Visitors marks the opening of a second phase in Ian Watson's career as an sf writer. The hard-edged, often overtly political subject matter of his early novels has given way to a growing concern with metaphysics. His books remain intellectually challenging, but to some readers they may seem cranky, remote and unconvincing. Watson's style, ever busy and bustling, may also deter. It is full of rhetorical questions; every page is peppered with exclamation marks like so many little shrieks; there are frequent redundancies of the '"I'm very sorry," Michael apologized' variety; and there is an overuse of ellipses . . . Watson is an irritating writer, but he is also a startling one. Perhaps the two qualities are inseparable.

First edition: London, Gollancz, 1978 (hardcover)
First American edition: New York, Ace, 1979 (paperback)
Most recent edition: London, Granada (paperback)

86
JOHN CROWLEY
Engine Summer

The title is a pun on 'Indian Summer', and indeed, the post-catastrophe culture which the book describes is vaguely Amerindian in quality. The narrator is called Rush that Speaks, and other characters have names such as Painted Red and Seven Hands. They all live together in a gentle druggy commune called Little Belaire. Frankly, the first couple of chapters are hard going, with the reader at sea amidst the strange names and the apparently ill-defined topography. But it is well worth persevering, for this work soon builds into a science fiction novel of rare sensisitivity and beauty. Its American author, John Crowley (born 1942), had published two previous sf novels—*The Deep* (1975) and *Beasts* (1976)—and he has since become celebrated for his wonderful fantasy novel *Little, Big* (1981).

The book is the oral autobiography, or *apologia*, of Rush that Speaks. His people, who call themselves the Truthful Speakers, are great tellers of tales. They appear to be entirely illiterate, though highly civilized, and among them the so-called Gossip is held in high esteem. Rush gives us the story of his childhood, with many digressions to recount the folk-tales which have formed his view of the world. The long-dead people who built the vast freeways ('"What was it . . . for?"' Rush asks when he first sees a Road; '"To kill people with," Seven Hands said, simply') are known to him as Angels; and the heroes who came afterwards, the founders of his culture, are called Saints. Rush hopes that one day he too will be remembered as a Saint.

He falls in love with a flighty girl who is known as Once a Day. Another tribe comes to do trade with the inhabitants of Little Belaire, and Once a Day runs away with them. Several years later Rush sets out to find her. His quest proves leisurely and meandering. He spends many months in the company of a Saint who lives in the branches of an oak tree. This man can read ('Time, life, books' is a moving phrase which he deciphers from the title-page of one centuries-old tome), and he tells Rush about

191

the incomprehensible society of the ancient days before the Storm. Rush muses on the bygone wonders:

Oh, the world was full in those days; it seemed so much more alive than these quiet times when a new thing could take many lifetimes to finish its long birth labors and the world stay the same for generations. In those days a thousand things began and ended in a single lifetime, great forces clashed and were swallowed up in other forces riding over them. It was like some monstrous race between destruction and perfection; as soon as some piece of world was conquered, after vast effort by millions, as when they built Road, the conquest would turn on the conquerors, as Road killed thousands in their cars; and in the same way, the mechanical dreams the angels made with great labor and inconceivable ingenuity, dreams broadcast on the air like milkweed seeds, all day long, passing invisibly through the air, through walls, through stone walls, through the very bodies of the angels themselves as they sat to await them, and appearing then before every angel simultaneously to warn or to instruct, one dream dreamed by all so that all could act in concert . . .

And it all went faster as the Storm came on, that is the Storm coming on was the race drawing to its end; the solutions grew stranger and more desperate, and the disasters greater, and in the teeth of them the angels dreamed their wildest dreams, that we would live forever or nearly, that we would leave the earth, the spoiled earth, entirely and float in cities suspended between the earth and the moon forever . . .

It is a beautifully estranged vision of our own world, and Crowley's peaceful, dreamy, autumnal narrative continues to surprise us right up until the revelatory ending, in which Rush actually meets an 'Angel'. This is far from being a conventional sf adventure story: it is best described as a prose poem.

First edition: Garden City, Doubleday, 1979 (hardcover)
First British edition: London, Gollancz, 1980 (hardcover)
Most recent editions: New York, Bantam, and London, Methuen (paperbacks)

87
THOMAS M. DISCH
On Wings of Song

This big, solid and immensely enjoyable novel may be labelled in various ways. It is a *bildungsroman*: the traditional narrative of a young man growing up, forming ambitions, falling in love, and learning by his many mistakes. It is science fiction: the setting is North America in the 21st century, a country which has become balkanized, with the Midwestern 'Farm Belt' states forming almost a separate nation. It is fantasy: the central conceit is that out-of-body experiences may be achieved by mechanical means—hooked up to the appropriate machine, and with a heart-felt song on one's lips, one may learn to fly like a fairy. It is a *roman-à-clef*: rooted, I suspect, in the author's own biography, it deals with the vicissitudes of the artist and the homosexual in relation both to the downhome attitudes of small-town USA and the exhilarating but rather squalid liberties of New York. Above all, it is a novel of manners: every character is beautifully real-ized, the dialogue rings true, the ironies are exquisite. If the book is flawed, it is because it contains too much: the various labels and interpretations jostle each other in such a fashion that the novel, although one recalls it with great pleasure, is less sharply etched in the memory than either Disch's *Camp Concentration* or his *334*.

On Wings of Song is the story of Daniel Weinreb, a dentist's son who grows up in Amesville, Iowa. The Christian fundamen-talists known as the Undergoders set the tone of Midwestern life. Music and song are regarded as sinful because of their association with the despicable practice of 'flying'. Naturally, Daniel deve-lops an unquenchable desire to experience out-of-body flight himself one day. He is a good-looking and intelligent lad, though not outstandingly gifted. While still attending school, he drifts into semi-legal employment as a distributor of a 'dangerous' newspaper, the Minneapolis *Star-Tribune*. 'For all right-thinking Iowans the Twin Cities were Sodom and Gomorrah.' After an illicit trip to Minneapolis with a school-friend—their purpose is to see a musical film, *Gold-Diggers of 1984*—Daniel is arrested at the instigation of his friend's vindictive father. Although he is only fifteen years old, he is sent to a labour camp where rebellious men and women are held under the most appalling conditions. An explosive device is inserted in his stomach to prevent him from running away. During his months in the camp Daniel's resolve grows: he will learn to sing.

After his release he befriends a girl, Boadicea Whiting, whose father is one of the richest man in the state. Grandison Whiting is a grotesque and horrifying but oddly likeable character. 'No prime minister, no movie star, no gangster had ever possessed so fine a wardrobe.' He lectures Daniel on the virtues of money, status and selfishness, and Daniel, poor sap, comes to believe that this monster will accept him as a son-in-law. In fact Grandison Whiting plans to rid himself of the upstart boy, but things go awry, and Daniel and Boadicea end up in New York. They immediately pay a visit to 'First National Flightpaths' in order to taste the hitherto forbidden fruit of out-of-body flight. Alas, Daniel's singing proves inadequate, and he is unable to take wing. Boadicea, on the other hand, succeeds only too well: she fails to return to her body. Unable to go back to Iowa, Daniel has to sell himself on the streets of New York in order to make enough money to live and to continue caring for the comatose body of his beloved Boadicea. Long years go by before she returns briefly to the flesh, and describes to Daniel visions of heartbreaking beauty.

First edition: New York, St Martin's Press, 1979 (hardcover)
First British edition: London, Gollancz, 1979 (hardcover)
Most recent editions: New York, Bantam, and London, Methuen
(paperbacks)

88
BRIAN STABLEFORD
The Walking Shadow

'"All things," said the machine softly, "must pass. Even empires, and the faiths in which they are founded."' That is a modest restatement of the great theme which underlies much British science fiction—the theme of evolution, mutability, the life and death of cherished hopes. It is a bittersweet note which runs from H.G. Wells' scientific romances, through the cosmic fables of Olaf Stapledon, to the works of Clarke, Aldiss and Ballard—and on, to the writings of younger British sf writers such as Brian Stableford (born 1948). Almost all of Stableford's many novels are about evolution (he gained a degree in biology from York University, and undertook postgraduate study of evolutionary ecology), and it is an obsession which emerges particularly strongly in the best of them, *The Realms of Tartarus* (1977) and *The Walking Shadow*.

Paul Heisenberg is a young man with charisma, one of the leading public performers of the 1990s. Speaking before vast audiences, he is part pop star, part messiah. He preaches a postmodern nihilism, telling people there are no certainties and that they should believe in the 'metascientific' systems which happen to be aesthetically appealing. One day, as he speaks, his body suddenly 'freezes' into the semblance of a silver statue. He has stepped outside time's flow, leaving behind a lesion, a Paul-shaped hole in the universe. He is the first of the time-jumpers (there is soon to be an epidemic of them) and, unsurprisingly, he becomes the object of a powerful religious cult. He awakens, or re-enters the universe, over a century later, to find a world which has been devastated by nuclear war. Scattered around the ruined landscape are thousands of silver statues: Paul's followers.

Paul jumps again, and again, leading a pilgrimage to the end of time. The story is intricate, and contains rather too many characters. The most important 'character', apart from Paul himself, is the machine, an artificial intelligence which has been built by some long-dead alien race. The machine is drawn to the time-jumpers, and to Paul in particular, because they are the only living beings who can provide it with company over the millions of years (the machine is self-repairing and effectively immortal). It provides Paul and his dwindling band of followers with physical security and sustenance when they awake at apparently arbitrary intervals. Hundreds of millions of years go by, and life as we have known it dies out on this Earth. It is replaced by 'third-phase life', a protean form of biological growth which seems to be the end-result of all natural evolution. This third-phase life—'Gaea' as the machine dubs it—is an all-consuming vegetable entity, capable of endless extension but totally without intelligence. It is a vast voracious organism containing no 'individuals'. Protected by a dome which encloses their personal Garden of Eden, Paul and his friends witness the end of all hopes for the future of mind.

It is a bleak vision which Stableford offers, effectively rendered in the jargon of biology:

> 'Within a few million years, even the fish will have gone. Your only relatives then will be holothuroideans living in the deepest ocean ooze like great fat pentamerous slugs. When they're gone, there will only be nematode worms, then protozoans, and then nothing but bacteria. Your whole world will be gone—utterly swallowed up. There will be nothing alive on Earth to suggest that the entire evolutionary chain of which you are a part ever existed. Only fossils in the rocks, and perhaps the occasional ghost of an artifact in metal or stone.'

There is the hint of a happy ending to Paul's story, but it is the chilly prospect of an uncaring evolutionary process which remains in the reader's mind once the book is closed. I know of no other postwar sf novel which covers quite such a sweep of time. The book has faults—some of the action/adventure stuff in the first half is banal—but its best moments are wonderfully imaginative. *The Walking Shadow* deserves a much wider circulation than it has enjoyed so far.

First (and only) edition: London, Fontana, 1979 (paperback)

89
KATE WILHELM
Juniper Time

Here we have another example of an American writer who imagines a near-future devastation visited upon God's own country. In this case, a terrible drought affects all the western states of the USA, and the formerly-affluent inhabitants of those parts flee to the east, to be herded into 'Newtowns'—government-run concentration camps. It is not the first time that Kate Wilhelm (born 1928) has envisaged something of the sort. Her best-known novel, *Where Late the Sweet Birds Sang* (1976), was about the cloning of survivors after the human race has been rendered sterile by an environmental cataclysm. For all its virtues, *Where Late . . .* seems to me to be a disjointed book written in a remote key. Among Wilhelm's many other works, *Juniper Time* is one of the most fully achieved. It is a well-rounded novel.

The heroine, Jean Brighton, is an astronaut's daughter. As a child she visits her grandparents in Oregon, and there she makes friends with a dignified Indian, Robert Wind-in-the-Tall-Trees. When Jean's father dies in orbit it seems that the project to establish a manned space station is doomed. Soon the drought takes hold, and America turns its back on space exploration. Arthur Cluny, a former childhood playmate of Jean's, grows up with an intense ambition to revive the space programme—apart from anything else, it may provide a 'cure' for the drought—but Jean chooses to study linguistics, perhaps inspired by her early contact with Amerindian culture. After graduating from an eastern university, she becomes involved in research into the computerized translation of foreign-language texts. Meanwhile, the campus is filled with hollow-eyed, desperate people, refugees from the burning lands of the west. Jean achieves a breakthrough—it seems that her computer program can now translate a document without the benefit of a 'Rosetta Stone'— but when the research project is threatened with a government takeover she decides to opt out. For a while she lives in a Newtown, where she is raped and brutally beaten. Terrified and broken-spirited, Jean heads in the only direction which is left open to her—she goes to her dead grandparents' deserted house in drought-stricken Oregon.

By now Arthur Cluny has achieved his goal. With the help of his influential father-in-law, he has persuaded the US government to reopen the space station. A mixed Soviet-American team of astronauts aims energy beams at the polar ice-caps in an effort to reverse the spreading drought. However, international mistrust comes to a head with the discovery of a small cylinder in Earth orbit. It contains an incomprehensible 'message from the stars'— perhaps it is a genuine alien artifact, but each side suspects that it is really a hoax perpetrated by the other in order to gain devious political advantage. Cluny sets out to find someone who can translate the 'alien' message, and his quest leads him to Jean Brighton in Oregon. He finds that Jean has been accepted into a renascent Indian tribe under the wise leadership of Robert Tall-Trees. In effect, she has become an alien to Cluny and to the whole of white civilization. She has learned how to live gracefully in a wild, sparsely-populated and near-waterless land. Somehow, Cluny must persuade her to decipher the text from space . . .

Juniper Time is a gently feminist tale of politics, ecology and (Earthly) alien encounters, at times very affecting if rather too intricately plotted for its own good. It contains some lovely descriptions of desert landscapes. One suspects that the Indians are sentimentalized, too wholesome to be fully credible, but there can be no doubt that the author's heart is in the right place.

First edition: New York, Harper & Row, 1979 (hardcover)
First British edition: London, Hutchinson, 1980 (hardcover)
Most recent editions: New York, Pocket, and London, Arrow
(paperbacks)

90
GREGORY BENFORD
Timescape

Science popularizers often tell us that modern theoretical physics verges on mysticism. The heirs of Einstein, Schrödinger and Heisenberg deal in fantastic abstractions which are utterly removed from everyday common sense. Indeed, the physicists' theories are sometimes so abstruse as to be beyond the grasp of science fiction writers, those fanciful thinkers of the unthinkable. Gregory Benford (born 1941) is one sf writer who is eminently qualified to comprehend the furthest reaches of contemporary theoretical physics, and to annex those strange seas of thought for the purposes of fiction. He is a professor of physics at the University of California, a scientist of the first rank who has somehow found time to write half a dozen sf novels of high quality. Benford's fiction is distinguished from the novels of other practising scientists, such as Fred Hoyle or Robert L. Forward, in that he has a genuine understanding of literature and a feel for language. His books may contain a few *longeurs*, but nevertheless they rise to their demanding occasions, and none of his novels rises to the occasion more magnificently than *Timescape*.

As the title suggests, it is a novel about time. It reaches its climax on 22nd November 1963, when Lee Harvey Oswald shoots John F. Kennedy in Dallas. A young man accosts Oswald at the critical moment: President Kennedy is badly wounded but lives on—and the reader realizes that the novel has moved into an alternative time-stream, one where the fate of the world will turn out to be very different. It is an extraordinarily poignant moment —not because we are particularly concerned about Kennedy (he is a minor, offstage character in this drama) but because we now know that a desperate scientific enterprise has succeeded and the world has been saved.

Part of this long novel is set in England in the year 1998, and part takes place in America in 1962-63. By the late 1990s the world is dying as a result of environmental pollution. 'Diatom blooms' are efflorescing on the surface of the oceans, killing all

199

marine life and spreading their contagion to the land (one character quotes Coleridge to good effect: 'slimy things did crawl with
legs upon the slimy sea'). A little group of scientists, working
under adverse conditions at an impoverished Cambridge University, conceives the idea of using tachyons—the particles which
travel faster than light and hence backward in time—to send a
warning message some 35 years into the past. Certain hard-won
biological data may be used to prevent the diatom blooms from
developing in the first place. By shooting tachyons, suitably
encoded with Morse, at the point in space which was occupied
by the Earth three-and-a-half decades before, they hope to get
their message through to one of the tiny scattering of people who
have the equipment to receive it. It is a long shot indeed, but the
very difficulties of the enterprise, the stubbornness of actuality
against which the characters are continually bruising their heads,
make this the most convincing example of time travel in all
science fiction.

The best portions of the book are those set in California in the
early 1960s. For a long year a young assistant professor at La
Jolla, Gordon Bernstein, struggles to understand the 'interfer-
ence' which seems too be wrecking his experiment in nuclear
resonance effects. Slowly, he comes to realize that he is receiving
a message from the future, a message which bears a terrifying
burden of doom. He must persuade sceptical colleagues of the
truth of his findings, while sidestepping the sensation-mongering
mass media. He eventually wins through. It is a feat of quiet
heroism, and its depiction is a *tour de force* on Benford's part.

First edition: New York, Simon & Schuster, 1980 (hardcover)
First British edition: London, Gollancz, 1980 (hardcover)
Most recent editions: New York, Pocket, and London, Sphere
(paperbacks)

91
DAMIEN BRODERICK
The Dreaming Dragons

This is the best Australian science fiction novel that I know. Admittedly I am not acquainted with many Australian sf books (apart from Damien Broderick, the few notable sf writers from that part of the world include Lee Harding, David J. Lake and George Turner), but part of the appeal of *The Dreaming Dragons* is that it is so positively, unabashedly Australian: its hero, Alf Dean Djanyagirnji, is an aborigine, and most of the action takes place at Ayers Rock, a well-known monument of the outback.

Alf Dean is an anthropologist, his head aswirl with a potent mix of modern learning and ancient tribal lore. Together with his retarded nephew, who is known as Mouse, he is searching the wilds of Central Australia for a 'Rainbow Serpent', which he suspects may turn out to be the fossilized remains of a dinosaur. Alf's nephew is a curious character, highly reminiscent of the autistic boy in Philip K. Dick's *Martian Time-Slip* (just as other aspects of this novel remind one of various modern sf writers, ranging from J.G. Ballard to Nigel Kneale, author of *Quatermass and the Pit*): 'The child was like some eldritch radio telescope, attuned only to messages from the empyrean, broadcasting nothing but an empty carrier signal . . . Perhaps Mouse gamboled . . . in an interior landscape of vivid flowers, drifting on his toes like the fey autistic children of his special school.'

Alf and the boy enter a cliffside cave which is decorated with aboriginal paintings. Deep inside they stumble on an alien artifact: a glowing portal which conveys them instantaneously a distance of some six hundred kilometers to a mysterious Vault beneath Ayers Rock. Alf is rendered unconscious by the experience and very nearly dies, but the boy thrives in the non-human environment of the Vault: his mind is quickened, and he becomes capable of speech. Mouse drags Alf away from the danger zone, and into the custody of a group of American and Soviet soldiers who are guarding the area. It seems that the Vault and its outlying portals are the relics of an extraterrestrial visitation which occurring in the distant past. In secret, military scientists are studying the 'gluon field' which is generated within the Vault, a field which may provide the ultimate defensive shield but which also does very strange things to the human consciousness. The brain-damaged boy, Mouse, proves to be a conduit through which the scientists learn much more about the Vault and the beings who built it.

From this intriguing opening, the novel plunges joyously into both the high-tech and the arcane: out-of-body experiences, a wrecked alien base on the far side of the Moon, the Jungian collective unconscious, bacterial warfare and the threat of nuclear holocaust, feathered serpents who are the 'dreaming dragons' of the title, buried memories of ancient Gondwanaland—all have a place in this story. There is also the ever-present Australian landscape:

> Already, despite the ferocious beating of the rains, the air was stunning with the fragrance of golden cassias. Emu bushes, lewdly swollen, opened their langorous blooms like flame and embers; cinnabar, crimson, heliotrope—all the pink vaginal shades of promised fertility. The morning light slanted in through the tufts of spinifex, circled the needles of desert oaks in light. All the trees were bent: hard, angular plants, the bonsai of extremity. And presiding over all the living creatures, the silver-gray acacias, the white-cypress pines, the sudden fluid bounding of a distant mob of graceful red kangaroos, rose the awful measure of their transience: Uluru [Ayer's Rock], red as granite, glowing sunlit like a brick just taken from a kiln.

It is like Mouse's 'interior landscape', sprung to life after a freak rainstorm. Broderick's prose is uneven, frequently clogged with technicalities, sometimes uneasily jocular, but every so often it rises to moments of beauty. The novel is wide-ranging in its references, feverishly speculative, and more than a little disjointed. Its faults are those of an abundant, if occasionally derivative, imagination. I find it very entertaining.

*First edition:*Melbourne, Norstrilia Press, 1980 (hardcover)
First American edition: New York, Pocket, 1980 (paperback)

92
OCTAVIA E. BUTLER
Wild Seed

A love story of unusual dimensions, *Wild Seed* was Octavia Butler's fifth published novel. It is in fact a 'prequel' to two of the earlier novels, *Patternmaster* (1976) and *Mind of My Mind* (1977). Whereas those works were set in a telepathic society of the future, *Wild Seed* is set in the known past. Covering a span of years, from 1690 to 1840 and beyond, it depicts the slow, secret growth of a group of psychically talented individuals who will form the nucleus of the 'Patternist' society to come. It is barely science fiction—such sf sanction as it has comes more from its relationship to the other two books than from its intrinsic features—but it is a memorably stark fantasy which mixes African mythology and the theme of enduring sexual passion as though it were some unholy cross between *Roots* and *Wuthering Heights*.

The story opens in West Africa. Doro, the mysterious, amoral hero, meets a woman, Anyanwu, who is apparently his match. She is three hundred years old, and able to change shape—from hag to maiden, from female to male. She has terrifying physical strength, and the ability to heal all wounds. It seems that she is a 'wild seed', a mutant, the lost daughter of one of the strangely gifted people that Doro has been breeding for millennia. Doro himself is almost four thousand years old. He is not a shape-changer, but a body-stealer: he preserves his consciousness by moving it from body to body, for at the moment of death he is able to take over his slayer's flesh. His obsession in life is the bringing together of talented individuals, long-lived sports and persons with remarkable mental powers. He concentrates these folk in his 'seed villages', where he intends to cultivate them as a super-race.

Doro has never met anyone like Anyanwu before. At first he is tempted to kill her—her strength may prove too dangerous to him—but then he realizes that she is too valuable to destroy. They become sexual partners, and so their long love/hate relationship begins. Doro takes Anwanyu to his ship (ostensibly a slave vessel) and over the sea to North America. On the way, she meets Doro's white-skinned son, Isaac, who has a powerful telekinetic ability. To please Anyanwu, Isaac uses his mental energy to pluck a dolphin from the sea and land it gently at her feet. Later, Anyanwu eats of the dolphin's flesh and is thus enabled to change her own body into dolphin form. In one of the novel's most lyrical scenes, Anyanwu swims as a dolphin, with the exuberant Isaac by her side.

Doro settles Anyanwu in a village in New York State. Against her will, he marries her to Isaac, and over the next fifty years she bears numerous mutant children to both Doro and his son. Although she abhors his god-like meddling with the human race, Anyanwu is still strongly attracted to Doro, and after Isaac's death their emotional tug-of-war resumes. For a while she flees back to the sea and lives as a dolphin once more. Finally, after many years and much suffering, Anyanwu wins the struggle. Doro comes to accept her as an equal, and to admit his own deep need for her. *Wild Seed* is an astonishing fiction of opposites: it is about the slave and the slave-master, healing and destruction, immortality and evanescence, omnipotence and moral restraint. It is an impressive achievement.

First edition: Garden City, Doubleday, 1980 (hardcover)
First British edition: London, Sidgwick and Jackson, 1980 (hardcover)
Most recent edition: New York, Pocket (paperback)

93

RUSSELL HOBAN
Riddley Walker

Hoban's novel garnered ecstatic acclaim from 'mainstream' literary critics, few of whom admitted to their readers that it is science fiction. At root, it is sf of a traditional sort—a post-bomb tale which could have been conceived in the 1950s but which gained impetus from the greatly renewed concern about nuclear weapons that marked the early 1980s. Apart from its starkly simple subject-matter, the most striking feature of *Riddley Walker* is the language in which it is narrated: the broken, debased English of a neo-barbarian future. The author elaborates this dialect with considerable relish, wringing from it much comedy, poetry and pathos. One could describe the book as a cross between Miller's *A Canticle for Leibowitz* and Burgess's *A Clockwork Orange*. Here is a small sample of the style, an atmospheric passage which describes a gathering around a bonfire:

> We done the berning that nite on the bye bye hump. The moon were cloudit over and a hy wind blowing. I put the 1st torch to the stack . . . Arnge flames upping in the dark and liting all the faces roun. Catching that time of that nite stoppt on all them faces. You cud smel the berning sharp on the air mixt with the meat smel from the divvy roof. Dogs begun to howl it wer coming and going on the wind. The fire blowing in the wind and the sparks whup off in to the dark and gone. Dark and gone.

They are burning Riddley's father, Brooder Walker, who has been killed while trying to dig an ancient iron machine out of the ground ('the girt big thing coming up out of the muck all black and rottin unner the grey sky').

The setting is south-east England some thousands of years in the future, long after the nuclear holocaust. A few people scrabble in the dirt, scavenging nomads who are wary of the dog-packs that roam the devastated Kentish countryside. Young Riddley is literate, barely, and a poet at heart. He tells us the story of his life, interwoven with legends and little moral tales. The principal myth of his people is the 'Eusa story', a garbled account of atomic doom and the Fall of Man (Hoban says that he was inspired by the legend of St Eustace, which he saw in the form of a reconstructed wall painting at Canterbury Cathedral). Puppeteers enact the Eusa story over and over again, warning the folk against any meddling with the old science, and in particular warning them against 'the Littl Shynin Man the Addom', who was responsible for all their woes. As the Eusa legends states, after the Littl Shynin Man was pulled apart 'evere thing was blak & rottin. Ded peapl & pigs eatin them & thay pigs dyd. Dog paks after peapl & peapl after dogs tu eat them the saym. Smoak goin up frum bernin evere wayr.'

The plot of the book involves the rediscovery of gunpowder and the tragicomic consequences of that particular piece of 'clevverness'. Riddley himself eschews violence and finds the way of true wisdom. It is a straightforward enough tale, copiously enriched by ingenious puns and overtones of mysticism. The language, although occasionally difficult to read (a difficulty which is exacerbated by the use of numerals in place of letters, so that 'wear 2 ½s uv 1 thing yu & me' signifies 'we're two halves of one thing, you and me'), has its undeniable charms. Russell Hoban (born 1925) is an American writer and illustrator who has lived in Britain for the last couple of decades. Despite the English setting, some of the novel's futuristic slang seems transatlantic in origin. Nevertheless, the language is very carefully contrived and fraught with real feeling, making of *Riddley Walker* much more than the simple fable which it seems in outline.

First edition: London, Cape, 1980 (hardcover)
First American edition: New York, Simon & Schuster, 1981 (hardcover)
Most recent editions: London, Picador, and New York, Pocket (paperbacks)

94
JOHN SLADEK
Roderick
and
Roderick at Random

This very funny two-part novel is about a tin angel (or learning machine) called Roderick. A wide-eyed little robot, he wanders like Candide through a near-contemporary America which is every bit as zany as the real thing. One's concern for the wee machine grows as he is maltreated by foster parents, teachers, religious maniacs and crooks. The narrative is full of the most amazing dialogue, interlarded with mathematical games, riddles and philosophical conundrums. It is a rich, rich mixture—too much, perhaps, for some readers, who may prefer a clearer story-line and a less relentless irony. All the same, the work is a masterpiece of its sort. Among other things, it is a treatise on the whole theme of mechanical men, homunculi, automatons and machine intelligence—the ultimate robot novel, which makes Isaac Asimov's *I, Robot* (1950) and its sequels look like the thin stuff that they are (in one mirthful scene Roderick actually reads the Asimov 'classic').

John Sladek (born 1937) is one of the sparkiest and most intelligent of the New Wave sf writers who gained their reputations in the later 1960s. His first novel, *The Reproductive System* (1968), was also a madcap satire about automation run wild, and it earned Sladek many comparisons with the early Kurt Vonnegut. In fact, he has always been much quirkier and considerably less slick than Vonnegut and, alas, he has never won the latter's vast popularity. His second sf novel, *The Müller-Fökker Effect* (1970), was about a man who is reincarnated as a computer programme. It was more than a decade ahead of its time, and after it failed to find much of an audience Sladek turned to detective novels and non-fiction, including an excellent debunking of pseudoscience, *The New Apocrypha* (1973). He returned to science fiction with *Roderick, or the Education of a Young Machine*, a novel which was so long that its publishers insisted that it be split into two volumes.

Beyond the machine theme and the mathematical jokes, Sladek's work is essentially all about America. For almost twenty years he lived and wrote in Britain (he has recently returned whence he came, the Midwest), and the America he described was an expatriate's nightmare, a sort of inverted pastoral vision of rolling suburbia, plastic lifestyles, insane government think-tanks, megalomaniac army officers, apple-pie-making 'momsters', carnival shysters, middle-management strivers in nylon shirts with name-badges on their breast pockets, all manner of ad-men and con-men, agents from the CIA, the Pentagon, the Mafia. It is a vision which resembles William Burroughs' more than it does Kurt Vonnegut's.

Roderick the robot is manufactured illicitly at the University of Minnetonka. Machine intelligence has been outlawed in this USA of the very near future, so Roderick spends most of the two volumes on the run, simply trying to survive in a world which is out to get him. After he gains a new body he is able to pass for human, but he continues to be as innocent as a lamb and far too sweet-natured to make a convincing member of our fallen species. He takes many pratfalls, yet somehow he keeps on eluding his pursuers. It is a crazy, venal, hilarious world which Sladek portrays, while Roderick himself is just beautiful, a saint.

First editions: Roderick, London, Granada, 1980 (hardcover); *Roderick at Random*, London, Granada, 1983 (paperback)
First American edition: New York, Pocket, 1982 (paperback; approximately the first two-thirds of the first volume; the full text has yet to be published in the USA)

95

GENE WOLFE

The Book of the New Sun

In a society of medieval guilds, where long-defunct rocket-ships form the towers of citadels, a young man grows to maturity. His world is ruled by the Autarch from the House Absolute, which lies somewhere to the north of the City Imperishable. Our hero is an apprentice torturer (luckily the reader is spared most of the details of this age-old craft) who commits the crime of showing mercy to a 'client' of his guild, and is consequently banished from the labyrinthine city. Images of death dominate the opening chapters—graves, dungeons, lightless libraries, stagnant pools—and serve as a counterpoint to the main theme, the search for the New Sun. This is the longest of contemporary science fiction novels, and one of the finest. It consists of four volumes— *The Shadow of the Torturer* (1980), *The Claw of the Conciliator* (1981), *The Sword of the Lictor* (1982), and *The Citadel of the Autarch* (1983)—which amount to some 1,200 pages in all. A monumental work, evidently, and in some ways a terminal one: it is hard to imagine anyone seriously tackling this type of story again.

It is a tale of the far, far future, when Earth has become utterly changed. An ice age has come and gone, the nation-states of our day are long perished, and humanity has retreated from the great adventure of space exploration (one of the loveliest recurring images is that of 'the green strand of Lune'—at some forgotten point in history the Moon has been made verdant). In 1950 the American author Jack Vance wrote a quasi-science-fictional novel called *The Dying Earth* which combined a vision of the distant future with magic and fantasy of the faery sort (this hybrid species of fiction is often referred to as 'science fantasy'). Wolfe has acknowledged Vance's book as an influence on his own masterpiece, and it is precisely the 'dying earth' type of story, perpetuated by many writers besides Vance, which he has now made redundant. *But*—and this is an important distinction which has been blurred by some reviewers—*The Book of the*

New Sun is not, in the last analysis, a work of science fantasy at all. It is actually science fiction. Its wonders are rationalized, and everything is finally explicable in terms of real, or plausibly extrapolated, science.

Wolfe uses many of the clichéd trappings of modern fantasy, or sword-and-sorcery, and in doing so he redeems and transfigures them. His hero, Severian the Torturer, has a great sword named *Terminus Est*, and he uses it to slay monsters and men. In his wanderings he encounters beings and events that are apparently supernatural. He finds a talismanic jewel, the Claw of the Conciliator, with which he is able to cure the sick. All these motifs, and a great many more, belong to the tradition of heroic fantasy, yet here they are deployed, wittily and sometimes beautifully, as science fiction. There is a risk that some of this will be missed by the general reader: a knowledge of the full repertory of sf conventions may be necessary to appreciate the tricks which Wolfe performs so intelligently.

It *is* a supremely intelligent novel, supremely well written—and it has drawn numerous peer tributes: 'Wolfe is so good he leaves me speechless,' says Ursula Le Guin; 'simply overwhelming' adds Algis Budrys. I am particularly impressed by the rare language; instead of inventing his own terminology from scratch as so many sf and fantasy writers have done, often with poor results, Wolfe uses exotic words drawn from Greek, Latin, Old French and other sources. This word-hoard is used exactly and resonantly, imparting a many-layered sense of reality to the society described. I believe I am correct in saying that there is not a single made-up word in the book: it is a philological *tour de force*, and a welcome relief from the jaw-cracking nonsense that one finds so frequently in sf.

First editions: New York, Simon & Schuster/Timescape, 1980-83 (hardcovers)

First British editions: London, Sidgwick & Jackson, 1981-83 (hardcovers)

Most recent editions: New York, Pocket, and London, Arrow (paperbacks)

96

PHILIP JOSÉ FARMER
The Unreasoning Mask

Philip José Farmer (born 1918) is best known nowadays for his popular 'Riverworld' series, which began with *To Your Scattered Bodies Go* (1971). About the resurrection of the entire human race along the banks of an immensely long river on a far planet, it seems to me to be a series which has failed to live up to its staggeringly ambitious premise. Well before the Riverworld books, Farmer was known as science fiction's foremost breaker of sexual taboos: his early novels, *Flesh* (1960) and *The Lovers* (1961), dealt in the sort of themes their titles suggest—they now seem decidedly tame. More impressive were his short stories collected in *Strange Relations* (1960) and *The Alley God* (1962), stories which proved him to have one of the most outré imaginations of all American sf writers. Since those days Farmer has been very prolific; he has produced more than thirty novels, many of them unabashed hackwork. And yet one still has expectations of Farmer: he is wide-ranging in his interests, versed in curious lore, capable of delivering suprises. He has written no masterpieces (unless one counts a book which is on the outer fringes of sf—his glorious spoof biography *Tarzan Alive*, 1972), but I have decided to represent him here with a late work which shows us Farmer at his most intriguing.

I should point out that at least one of Farmer's peers *does* believe *The Unreasoning Mask* to be a major work. Ian Watson, reviewing it in *Foundation*, said: 'In my opinion this novel is a masterpiece, Farmer's finest; yet it has received little (or only ordinary) attention compared with the gaudier tapestry of Riverworld.' It is about Hûd Ramstan, the Muslim captain of an extraordinary space vessel known as *al-Buraq*. This ship is a living organism, although it is no more intelligent than a dog. It is capable of changing shape, and, like a dog, it has a great affection for its master: its walls tend to blush pink when Ramstan steps aboard; the decks quiver with excitement. *Al-buraq* is a particularly original example of those 'cosy containers' which are so common in sf, ranging from Jules Verne's *Nautilus* to Ian Watson's magical Ford Thunderbird. The ship's special properties make for a satisfying action sequence about two-thirds of the way through, when Ramstan's crew rebels and he overcomes them with *al-Buraq*'s aid.

But that is minor-league stuff compared with the main action of the book, for *The Unreasoning Mask* is a metaphysical space opera on the grandest scale. Ramstan is forced to steal an egg-shaped object, the *glyfa*, which turns out to be a sentient artifact older than the universe—a direct channel to God, no less. However, the 'God' of this novel (also known as the Pluriverse) is a babbling infant, Its body composed of many universes. This immature deity is barely aware of the sentient life within It; in fact, It experiences space-travelling humanity (and other intelligent species) as a kind of cancer which must be excised. To that end, it sends the *bolg*, a vast mindless 'antibody', to kill all planetary life in this particular universe. Ramstan's formidable task is to destroy the *bolg* before it can reach the Earth. In this he is aided by the indestructible and all-knowing *glyfa*, and by three ancient crones, the Vwoordha, who live on a planet dominated by a gigantic tree . . . In short, this is a work of outrageously extravagant fancy, narrated for the most part in a rather dry style, although Farmer is able on occasion to produce striking poetic metaphors: 'The minutes, the hours, marched slowly by, strewing flowers of anxiety.' It is a very odd book from a wayward talent.

First edition: New York, Putnam, 1981 (hardcover)
First British edition: London, Granada, 1983 (paperback)

97

LARRY NIVEN & JERRY POURNELLE
Oath of Fealty

Larry Niven (born 1938) and Jerry Pournelle (born 1933) are stalwarts of the New Right in American science fiction. Their sf tends to be technophilic, militaristic, and relentlessly 'hard-headed'. *The Mote in God's Eye* (1974), their first collaborative novel, was a bestseller: it is fundamentally a hoary space opera, of which *The Encyclopedia of Science Fiction* says: 'several critics have taken the book to task for what they regard as its chauvinism on behalf of mankind, the discrepancy between an imaginative plot and old-fashioned characterization, and its conservative political stance.' A later collaboration, *Lucifer's Hammer* (1977), is a tub-thumping tract on behalf of America's scientists and engineers and against the ecology movement, pacifism and other pink-hued doctrines. It too was a considerable commercial success. *Oath of Fealty* is the most interesting of the Niven-and-Pournelle books, a novel of ideas which conveys some real sense of debate rather than mere sermonizing. It is dedicated, appropriately, as follows: 'For Robert A. Heinlein, who showed us all how.'

The novel is written in the tried-and-true style of modern bestseller fiction: a host of characters of differing social status, each with his or her personal 'problem', rapid switches of scene, and a looming background enclosure, in this case the 'arcology' known as Todos Santos, which serves as a microcosm of society as a whole. Where Arthur Hailey gave us an airport or a hotel, Niven and Pournelle present us with an enormous building on fifty levels, three miles long, equipped with moving walkways, access via underground trains, and a nearby beached iceberg to provide a water supply. A quarter of a million people live and work in the 'total environment' of this small city: from their balconies they can look over the slums of Greater Los Angeles and feel superior. Their lives are regulated by Todos Santos's computer system, MILLIE, they are watched over by armed security men, and they give a kind of feudal loyalty to their tireless Manager, a lovable dictator called Art Bonner.

Bonner, and one or two other characters, are specially adapted human beings. They have been blessed with enormously expensive 'implants', devices within their skulls which enable them to communicate directly with MILLIE. This removes the need for a host of bureaucratic middlemen; Bonner is able to rule Todos Santos wisely because he has instant access to a complete knowledge of its workings: he is aware of everything that is happening, everywhere. If it were not for this handy science-fictional gadget, and the taken-for-granted omnicompetence of Mr Bonner, the reader would have doubts as to whether the complex arcology could possibly function—memories of J.G. Ballard's *High-Rise* intrude; but that is a novel which Niven and Pournelle are unlikely to have read. The inhabitants of Todos Santos are untroubled by their own dark desires; instead, they have an external enemy to contend with. 'Have you been following the news?' asks one character. 'The FROMATES, the Friends of Man and the Earth Society, keep trying to sabotage Todos Santos. Not to mention various other hate groups. And just plain gangsters out to extort money. Stink bombs. Hornet nests. That kind of thing, mostly, but sometimes the terrorists come up with something really nasty, like the grenade that killed a dozen people in the Crown Center Arcology in Kansas.'

The plot of the novel commences with the intrusion of some youthful rebels into the bowels of the arcology. They carry a dummy bomb—their purpose is to score a propaganda point— but Todos Santos's defensive system assumes they are genuinely armed, and gasses them to death. Much of the narrative is taken up with the political fallout from this incident, and with arguing the rights and wrongs of the case. The more 'patriotic' of the arcology's denizens adhere to a nasty slogan: 'THINK OF IT AS EVOLUTION IN ACTION'. It is the point of view of Social Darwinism and, implicitly, of the authors. *Oath of Fealty* is not a very likeable book, but as a tale of near-future evolution in action it raises a number of valid questions and refrains from answering them too glibly.

First edition: New York, Simon & Schuster, 1981 (hardcover)
First British edition: London, Futura, 1982 (paperback)
Most recent edition: New York, Pocket (paperback)

98
MICHAEL BISHOP
No Enemy But Time

This is a story about a black American called Joshua Kampa. He travels some two million years backwards in time, to a location in East Africa. There he befriends a tribe of hominids, primitive ancestors of modern humanity, and eventually 'marries' one of the females. She dies in childbirth, and Joshua carries their daughter back to his own time, the late 1980s. It would seem a tall tale of love across the aeons, were it not that the novel is anti-romantic in tone. It is narrated in an oddly detached, quizzical and dryly humorous manner, despite the fact that much of it is told in the first person by Joshua Kampa himself. The paleo-anthropological details are superbly imagined, the African landscapes beautifully described, yet the final effect is one of coolness, distance, a holding at arm's length. Michael Bishop's prose style is learned, witty, Latinate, although salted with deliberately-placed colloquialisms and low jokes. This book is the work of a talented and serious writer, but sometimes it is hard to be sure what he is driving at.

It is a long novel, and the story is rather more complex than I have indicated so far. There are two intertwining narrative threads. The third-person chapters recount Joshua's life, from his illegitimate birth in the vicinity of an American airforce base in Spain, to the moment when, as a government-sponsored anthro-pologist, he time-travels in order to unravel the mysteries of human origins. The bulk of this strand is necessarily non-science-fictional: it is a straightforward, realistic telling of a modern life, sensitively done. Joshua has strained relationships with his foster-parents; he dreams, in hallucinatory detail, of prehistoric Africa, and it is as though he has confused his personal anxiety about his true parentage with an obsessive concern for the ancestry of the whole human race. The alternating first-person chapters are Joshua's own account of his quest through time. He does not descend into the past by conventional sf means; that is to say, he does not travel objectively. Rather, he *dreams* himself into a prehistoric landscape: he visits a world which is in some sense imaginary, though sustained by a very detailed scientific knowledge. Unlike his childhood dreams, this one endures for a long time and is solid to the touch.

This mix of paleontology, psychology and mysticism may irritate some sf readers—those who like their science fiction to be rationally founded and who want their time machines to be genuine oily vehicles rather than dream-carriages spun from moonbeams. Indeed, it irritates me. How is it that Joshua Kampa is able to bring back a very tangible child if the world that he has visited is a mere projection of his own mind? Obviously, Bishop intends to keep us suspended in an area of doubt, and that suspense can be wearing on the reader. All the same, I value this book for its vivid portrayal of the remote past. Bishop endows his imaginary 'Minids' with a human dignity, an implied eloquence of gesture and feeling which overcomes their lack of speech. I am moved by the death of Helen, the hominid woman to whom Joshua has given a name and his love.

Michael Bishop (born 1945) is one of the hardest workers in contemporary American sf. He strives constantly to transcend the sensational and sometimes childish nature of the *genre*—to produce a High Science Fiction which is humane and intellectually engrossing. In novels such as *Stolen Faces* (1977) and *Transfigurations* (1979) he came near to achieving his ends. In *No Enemy But Time* he comes nearer still. To my mind, he has yet to produce a fully satisfactory sf novel (impossible demand!), but he is certainly a writer who will bear watching.

First edition: New York, Simon & Schuster, 1982 (hardcover)
First British edition: London, Gollancz, 1982 (hardcover)
Most recent editions: New York, Pocket, and London, Sphere (paperbacks)

99
JOHN CALVIN BATCHELOR
The Birth of the People's Republic of Antarctica

Oddly enough, 1983 saw the publication of two large American novels which describe deperate sea-voyages southwards to Tierra del Fuego and beyond. Both are set in near-future times of crisis. Neither is by a *genre* sf writer, though both may be claimed for science fiction. Each of them is 'a good read', and, in differing ways, each is representative of the contemporary leakage of sf themes into the so-called mainstream of prose fiction. One of these books, Luke Rhinehart's *Long Voyage Back*, was written as a Bestseller and marketed as such, complete with garish cover and a blurb which styles it 'the ultimate epic of nightmare survival'. The other, Batchelor's *Birth of the People's Republic of Antarctica*, is packaged much more tastefully, with an encomium from *The New York Times* and comparisons with the work of Thomas Pynchon and John Gardner. In short, Rhinehart's novel comes as a throwaway piece of social melodrama, while Batchelor's is delivered to us as Literature.

I must confess to a liking for Rhinehart's book. It is about the adventures of a few favoured characters who escape from a nuclear holocaust aboard a luxury trimaran. Even if those characters seemed carved out of wood, there is no denying that the narrative has considerable force: I experienced an urgent need to know what happened next. I was also impressed by the moral sting in the tail. One turns the last page and finds the following: 'This is a work of fiction. The actual effects of a large-scale nuclear war are so much worse than I have dramatized that no bearable work of fiction can be written about them.' Well said. John Calvin Batchelor's book is less compelling in terms of sheer story, but it brings to its similar subject-matter greater resources of language and imagination.

Here, the characters are not wooden but weird. The narrator, Grim Fiddle, is the Swedish-born son of an American draft-dodger. He has a fey mother and a formidable grandfather, 'a man of very high rank in the tyrannical wing of the Swedish Lutheran Church.' He grows to handsome manhood in the indulgent company of his somewhat weak-minded father, Peregrine Ide, and a circle of drop-out friends. By the year 1995, when he is twenty-one and the main action of the novel is about to commence, Grim Fiddle has developed into a latter-day Viking, steeped in Norse lore. The world is in a state of moral collapse, and when civil chaos overtakes Sweden and the rest of Europe, Grim siezes his grandfather's sailing ship, the *Angel of Death*, and heads for the Atlantic. On board are Peregrine (newly sprung from jail), the grandfather, and a motley crew of friends and lovers, including a Turkish boy who rejoices in the name of 'Wild Drumrul'. It is a ship of fools, part of a vast fleet of the damned, in a new Age of Exile. The old man, in the full flow of his religious mania, proves to be a valuable driving force. As Grim Fiddle says, 'Grandfather once boasted to me that three men and a Bible could sail *Angel of Death* to the moon.'

They do not reach the Moon, but they sail through a sea of fire into the South Atlantic, become embroiled in a farcical but gruesome war in the Falkland Islands, and settle for some years in South Georgia, vividly described as 'a one-hundred-and-forty-mile-long aquamarine rock, mountainous, heath-mantled, treeless, wind-scourged, battered by the stone-grey seas . . .'; then they travel on, to a terrible southerly land of volcanoes and ice. In due course, Grim Fiddle becomes the bloody 'king' of Antarctica. John Calvin Batchelor (born 1948) has produced a memorably eccentric piece of philosophical fiction, a postmodern epic which at times recalls some of the masterpieces of the 19th-century American novel.

First edition: New York, Dial Press, 1983 (hardcover)
First British edition: London, Granada, 1984 (paperback)

100
WILLIAM GIBSON
Neuromancer

'The sky above the port was the color of television, tuned to a dead channel.' The first sentence of Gibson's novel sets the tone for this ultra-modern tale of people moving in an electronic landscape. Taking his cues from Alfred Bester, William Burroughs and (perhaps) Samuel R. Delany, but his inspiration from the dreams of Silicon Valley, the author has produced a sour-romantic thriller which is as up-to-date as video-game arcades, organ transplants, and research into artificial intelligence, all of which feature in the narrative. It is fast-moving, densely written, ingeniously inventive, occasionally funny, continuously poetic, sometimes baffling, and as tightly packed as the circuitry on a microchip.

William Gibson (born 1948) is a new American sf writer, the author of a number of highly promising short stories which have appeared in *Omni* magazine and elsewhere. *Neuromancer* is his first novel, and it has some of the flaws that one might expect from a debut book: a certain straining for effect, and an over-complexity which now and again clots the story line. But those are the flaws of genuine ambition and of an exuberant talent.

The hero, Case, is a streetwise computer cowboy. Using the sophisticated electronic equipment of his 21st-century world, he has the ability to enter 'cyberspace', an area where the massed information of the planet's computer networks takes on an apparent three-dimensional reality. Moving through cyberspace, he can alter computer programmes and penetrate commercial memory banks in order to steal valuable data. Thus he makes his living. The story opens in Japan, in a sleazy underworld of hustlers and drug-pushers where Case has been exiled as the result of some complicated transgression. There he encounters Molly, a professional bodyguard-cum-assassin equipped with artificial eyes and razors implanted under her fingernails, who is working for a mysterious agency that wishes to hire Case and use his talents to breach the defences of an artificial intelligence. Case is compelled to go along with the plan, and the action moves to North America and then to a huge habitat in outer space, a kind of Las Vegas in the sky. Molly and Case fall in with an anarchic colony of Rastafarians who live in Earth orbit; they have a brush with the 'Turing police', whose duty it is to ensure that artificial intelligence is kept within bounds, and they eventually penetrate the exotic home of a dangerously eccentric multi-millionaire. There they find the intelligent electronic entity who has been using them in a bid to free itself of all human restraints . . .

It could be argued that under its bravura surface *Neuromancer* is a rather conventional piece of popular fiction. It has a strong plot, elements of mystery, and plenty of tough-guy violence. Yet, as I have said, it also has more than a touch of poetry. The imagery of decaying cityscapes littered with electronic gadgetry run mad is extraordinarily vivid and relevant. All too many of the contemporary sf writers deal in the sub-creation of never-never worlds, lands akin to L. Frank Baum's Oz or Tolkein's Middle-Earth which it would be pleasant to escape to. William Gibson has the courage to attempt something completely different: his fictional scene is our world of the mid-1980s raised to the nth power. Like all the best science fiction, *Neuromancer* deals with reality, not fantasy, and if some of the technological gimmickry in the novel may seem far-fetched, it also serves, as would a set of distorting mirrors, to reflect ourselves and what is around us.

First edition: New York, Ace, 1984 (paperback)
First British edition: London, Gollancz, 1984 (hardcover)
Forthcoming edition: London, Granada (paperback)

Index

222